Young Americans *for* Freedom

Igniting a Movement

Wayne Thorburn

Contents

Introduction and Acknowledgements

In September 1960, a new organization came into being. It would be the first national grass-roots conservative political group that would subsequently launch many other components of what became the conservative movement in the United States. Organized by college students and young adults, Young Americans for Freedom would play an important role in the politics of the last forty years of the 20th century. After a period of decline around the turn of the new century, Young Americans for Freedom is once again a vibrant and active force on many high school and college campuses.

The following pages provide a brief history of Young Americans for Freedom and its contributions to the development of conservatism in America. Much of this work includes material previously presented in more detail in *A Generation Awakes: Young Americans for Freedom and the Creation of the Conservative Movement.* Those wishing more detail on YAF's history are directed to that earlier work. However, since its publication Young Americans for Freedom has become associated with Young America's Foundation and had a rebirth of activity not apparent when the previous work was published in 2010. Thus, an updated history of the organization that reflects its activities over the past fifty-five years is appropriate.

This work would not have been possible without the contributions of literally hundreds of former members of Young Americans for Freedom who shared their recollections and experiences from their time of involvement in the organization. Their comments and observations have aided greatly in telling the story of Young Americans for Freedom and its contributions to the development of the conservative movement.

Patrick Coyle, Vice President of Young America's Foundation, is due immense thanks for his efforts to collect material on Young Americans for Freedom over the past fifteen years, including his efforts to rebuild the organization after its acquisition by the Foundation in 2011. Likewise, this work would not have been possible, nor would the earlier history, *A Generation Awakes*, without the encouragement and support of Ron Robinson and the financial assistance of Young America's Foundation.

Young Americans for Freedom: Igniting a Movement is not simply a recitation of past times in American political history. While it does discuss much that occurred in the latter half of the 20th century, it is also a call to continued commitment, growth, learning, and involvement in the current century. Generations come and go, but Young Americans for Freedom continues as a force for preserving and extending conservative principles as new generations become leaders in American society.

— 1 —

Before There Was a Conservative Movement

W ITH THE END OF WORLD WAR II, American society was entering a period of significant change and reorientation. The transition to a peacetime economy, the return of hundreds of thousands of veterans, and the development of a more substantial threat to Western values from a wartime ally – all confronted Americans as the decade of the 1940s approached its closing. While there was no longer a President Roosevelt in the White House, his economic policies had become institutionalized and accepted by the majority of Americans. As Lionel Trilling observed, liberalism had become the dominant, if not the only, ideological viewpoint accepted by those Americans who considered broader philosophical questions.[1]

Prior to the 1950s, the opposition to liberalism centered mainly around a defense of free enterprise, with economists Ludwig Von Mises and Frederick Hayek the leading defenders.[2] Hayek's book, *The Road to Serfdom*, not only provided a comprehensive rejection of socialism but also clearly tied together all forms of collectivism – socialism, communism, and fascism – and challenged the view that Nazism and fascism were "right-wing" movements.[3] Hayek represented the European classical liberal tradition whose emphasis on economics and individualism contributed much to late 20th century American conservatism. [4] To a large extent, however, von Mises and Hayek were perceived as crying in the wilderness while majority opinion was dominated by those who accepted the

New Deal and a progressively growing involvement of the state in the economy.[5] George Nash, pre-eminent historian of the modern conservative movement, observed that as World War Two ended, "There were, at most, scattered voices of protest, profoundly pessimistic about the future of their country. Gradually during the first postwar decade these voices multiplied, acquired an audience, and began to generate an intellectual movement."[6] Change would slowly begin to appear as conservative publications and publishing houses were established in the late 1940s.

As the war was approaching a conclusion, a new periodical appeared to challenge both the economic as well as the foreign policy of the Truman Administration. Begun as a weekly newsletter distributed to daily newspapers, *Human Events* would subsequently change its format and distribution method in the early 1950s, becoming a fixture in what would develop into a conservative movement.[7] In 1947 there appeared a new publishing house that would make an important contribution to the distribution of conservative ideas and the popular acceptance of conservative writers. The Henry Regnery Company provided a vehicle for the exposition of many mid-century conservative writers and continues publishing important conservative works.[8]

Nevertheless, in the late 1940s those opposed to New Deal economic policies and a foreign policy only slowly perceiving the challenge of Soviet Communism remained a rather small minority. Politically, the Republican party was still dominated by the forces that would nominate Wendell Willkie, Thomas Dewey and eventually Dwight D. Eisenhower as presidential candidates while the Democrats confronted a challenge from the left in former Vice President Henry Wallace's Progressive party and from the segregationists in Governor J. Strom Thurmond's Dixiecrat movement. While change was on the horizon, it was a time when, "*conservatism* was not a popular word in America, and its spokesmen were without much influence in their native land."[9]

There remained a conformity to the prevailing liberal outlook such that those who challenged it were viewed as outside the mainstream. As John Andrew commented: "whatever seemed to deviate from the 'consensus' position on any issue became susceptible to charges that it represented an 'extremist' view and should therefore be dismissed as dangerous and perhaps even un-American."[10] While the conservative presence grew in the 1950s and early 1960s, it would continue to be confronted by this charge of being outside the mainstream of liberal orthodoxy.

As the decade of the 1950s began, several new developments were to challenge this prevailing orthodoxy. Despite the common perception of this decade as one of conformity and social conservatism, it was a time of significant challenge to the accepted American way of life. In 1951, J. D. Salinger's *Catcher in the Rye* was released. Salinger's use of profanity, sexual references and teenage angst both created controversy and became a regular feature of American Literature classes.[11] Six years later, Jack Kerouac would produce what would become a classic of the "beat generation" with his *On The Road*.[12] Through the characters of Dean Moriarty and Sal Paradise, mid-century youth traveled around underground America and experienced drugs, sex and jazz.

In general terms, however, Kerouac's heroes were expressing, and his readers were cherishing, a new emphasis on individualism. As Stan Evans observed, "(t)he world against which the beatnik reacts is not the world of conservatism, with its emphasis on volition and variety, but of Liberalism, with its insistence upon external uniformity."[13] Kerouac's fictional hero tells his readers that his "chief hate was Washington bureaucracy; second to that, Liberals, then cops." Rebecca Klatch sees this emphasis on independence and autonomy as producing a similar trend among young activists of the left and right in the 1960s that she calls "...an affinity for values such as individual freedom, the impulse against bureaucracy and big government, the questioning of centralized authority, and the embrace of decentralization and local control."[14]

Indeed, a new student left also was emerging in the late 1950s, often led by "Red diaper babies," children of radical and Communist professionals. In 1957, a left-wing campus party opposed to capital punishment, nuclear testing, and anti-communism became active at the University of California at Berkeley, followed by similar efforts at the University of Wisconsin and the University of Michigan where its impetus came from Tom Hayden, then editor of the *Michigan Daily*.[15]

By the 1950s new cinematic heroes had appeared also in the form of Marlon Brando in "The Wild Ones," released in 1953 and resulting in increased interest in motorcycles and leather jackets. Two years later James Dean starred in "Rebel Without a Cause," a film whose popularity among young viewers was not lessened by the tragic death of its star at age 24. In the music world the merging of aspects of gospel, blues, and pop into a new genre called rock and roll created a specifically youth-oriented music. Perhaps best typifying this radical departure from the past was Elvis Presley whose first record appeared in 1954. Two years later Presley appeared on the highly popular entertainment program, "The Ed Sullivan Show," where his gyrations while viewed by some adults as too sexually suggestive were appreciated by many of the younger female viewers. By the end of the decade, another music format became popular with college students. Folk music brought with it an emphasis on political messages, almost all oriented to the left and critical of the prevailing establishment.[16]

Even more dramatic changes to the social milieu developed out of the Supreme Court's historic 1954 decision in *Brown* v. *Board of Education*. Sweeping away years of *de jure* segregation based on a policy of supposed "separate but equal" facilities for Black children in public schools, the Court's decision would begin a long, painful and never ending path towards equal protection of the laws for all American citizens. The reaction of many conservatives who stressed states' rights in a Federal system of government would produce a lasting political impact on American society as more and more Black Americans shifted from their previous support of the Republican Party to an overwhelming commitment to the Democratic Party.

To a large degree these social changes, far different from a bland conformity too often placed on the decade, contributed to the rising interest among young people in creating their own alternative to what they perceived as a prevailing liberal establishment. This assertion of a role to play in the creation of America's future was present among what would be called conservative youth as well as those who challenged the establishment from the left. As one future leader of conservative youth observed in looking back at the 1950s and the rising involvement of right-wing youth, "(I)t was not strict obedience to political elders then but the rebellion of youth and the idealism of young people which while today is credited to the Left is seldom appreciated as also a vital ingredient of the young Right."[17] By the end of the decade, many American young people were ready to express their opposition to the establishment.

Separate and apart from the social changes and trends occurring in mid-century America, political developments were also challenging the prevailing orthodoxy. For many Americans there was developing a growing realization that international Communism posed a serious threat to the West. America and its allies became embroiled in a defense of South Korea from the efforts of its Northern compatriots and the Chinese Communists to overrun it, a conflict that would end only with an uncomfortable stalemate. The internal threat of Communist subversion became known to more Americans with the trial of Ethel and Julius Rosenberg in 1951 and their execution two years later. It was also a time of House Committee on Un-American Activities hearings, the so-called "Hollywood Ten," the Whittaker Chambers testimony implicating Alger Hiss in espionage activities, and the efforts of Senator Joseph McCarthy to remove security risks from the Federal government. [18] The impact of Chambers disclosures about Soviet penetration of the Federal government and his subsequent book cannot be overemphasized. As J'Aime Ryskind, one of the early conservative youth leaders of the 1960s observed, "My mother really felt that there were two books in Western Civilization. One was the Bible and the other was Whittaker Chambers' *Witness.*" [19] Likewise, it was admiration for Senator McCarthy's efforts that provided the first overt political act by a young high school sophomore in New Orleans. Setting up a table in Jackson Square, Doug Caddy collected signatures on a petition supporting McCarthy and forwarded them to Washington, DC.

Caddy would later serve as a prime organizer of the new conservative youth organization.[20]

While the United States followed a policy described as containment, the government also sent mixed messages to the captive nations of Eastern Europe and the Baltic, including messages on Radio Free Europe. Then came 1956 – and the tragic efforts of the Hungarian people to become independent of the Soviet bloc, only to be crushed by the Russian army tanks while the United States and Western Europe stood by.[21] The events surrounding this tragic event made a lasting impact on several individuals who were to become leaders of a new conservative youth organization. Many early young conservative activists mention specific events associated with communism as motivating their political interest and involvement, especially the Hungarian uprising.[22] Carl Thormeyer, who was to organize a Young Americans for Freedom chapter at Penn State some five years later, cited the Soviet suppression of the Hungarian freedom-fighters as an event that radicalized him for conservative political action.[23]

The latter part of the 1950s also saw the launching of the first Soviet satellite, Sputnik, in 1957. The building of private bomb shelters became the latest home improvement project and elementary school students were instructed to cover their heads and duck under their desks during civil defense drills, supposedly protecting themselves from possible Soviet attacks. In 1959, Fidel Castro and his forces succeeded in defeating the government of Fulgencio Battista and installed a Communist regime in Cuba just miles off the Florida coast. In response to Sputnik and the need for more scientific and technical expertise, the Eisenhower Administration obtained congressional support for passage of the National Defense Education Act in 1958. As a measure passed on the basis of its contribution to national defense, the Act required recipients to swear loyalty to the United States and indicate whether they had belonged to any organizations deemed subversive. As will be seen later, the passage of a Federal program of aid to higher education tied to national security had a major impact on the development of a national conservative youth organization in 1960.

While the nation was undergoing dramatic social changes and confronting a growing challenge from the Soviet Union, the decade also saw the beginnings of a substantial conservative intellectual and political presence.[24] Although some may claim that modern conservatism became evident with the end of World War Two and the start of the Cold War, it did not begin to present a noticeable challenge to the dominant liberal ideology until the early 1950s.[25] It was then that the writings of William F. Buckley, Jr., Whittaker Chambers, Russell Kirk, and a few others introduced the intellectual world to a renewed challenge from the right and provided modern conservatism with a firm intellectual and historical foundation.

Building on the free-market opposition to socialism, the Foundation for Economic Freedom (FEE) was created in 1946 by Leonard Read and a group of distinguished scholars and business leaders. The Foundation published a number of studies on economic issues during its early years. In 1954 the Foundation took over publication of *The Freeman,* a journal that had been edited by Henry Hazlitt and John Chamberlain since 1950, and made it into a monthly vehicle for the promulgation of free market economics.[26] Over the subsequent years, FEE would sponsor numerous seminars on economic issues and have a significant impact on the development of young conservatives and libertarians.

It was a precocious college student recently returned from World War II and enrolled at Yale University who would impact American society for more than a half-century and in the process help build a conservative movement. In 1946, William F. Buckley, Jr. entered what was widely perceived to be a conservative, if not staid, institution of classical learning. He was part of the largest class in Yale's history, two-thirds of its members being veterans of World War II. As one of his classmates observed, "Bill was someone to be reckoned with immediately. He was taking initiatives as soon as he got to Yale. He arrived in full stride."[27] Active in the Yale Political Union, a member of the debating team and selected for "Skull and Bones," by his senior year he had become chairman of the *Yale Daily News.* What Buckley found was an institution living off its past heritage of orthodoxy while promoting collectivist economic and social theories and heterodox religious beliefs, if any at all. [28] Buckley made his commitment to economic individualism and Christian theology known throughout his years at Yale, often in somewhat confrontational situations. But it was once he had graduated that a major critique of his alma mater – and American higher education by extension – would be produced to major applause and condemnation.

One year after graduating from Yale, William F. Buckley, Jr., at the age of 25, had his first book published. *God and Man at Yale* became a best seller with the first printing of 5,000 copies selling out in a week.[29] He maintained that Yale "has produced one of the most extraordinary incongruities of our time: the institution that derives its moral and financial support from Christian individualists and then addresses itself to the task of persuading the sons of these supporters to be atheistic socialists."[30] Perhaps the most quoted passage occurs where Buckley describes his overall perspective on the conflict confronting the West: "I myself believe that the duel between Christianity and atheism is the most important in the world. I further believe that the struggle between individualism and collectivism is the same struggle reproduced on another level."[31] This summation of the philosophical and ideological conflict would continue to provide a foundation for the remainder of Buckley's career.

Then in 1953, a new work appeared that argued for a traditional conservatism based on Anglo-American sources and especially Edmund Burke. The author was Russell Kirk, then a young history instructor at Michigan State University, and the book was titled *The Conservative Mind*. [32]   As his publisher observed about the relevance of the work, coming as it did in the early 1950s, "What was lacking was a general concept that would bring the movement together and give it coherence and identity. It was the great achievement of Russell Kirk's *The Conservative Mind*, published in 1953, to provide such a unifying concept. Kirk offered convincing evidence not only that conservatism was an honorable and intellectually respectable position, but also that it was an integral part of the American tradition." [33]   The book received a considerable number of reviews, both positive and critical, in widely circulated newspapers and magazines as well as more academic journals. Kirk had brought respectability and relevance to a tradition too often thought only continental and irrelevant to the contemporary American scene.[34]

The *Conservative Mind* was more than merely a recitation of the essential elements of a traditionalist conservatism, nor solely a compilation of the contributions of important writers of the past. It was a critique of the dominant liberal orthodoxy but it was even more than this. The work was also a call to action. Clearly Kirk believed that there was an important tradition, an American tradition, which had been usurped but could be brought back to the fore of society. Kirk's message would be heard by young conservatives of the 1950s and beyond. As one future young conservative leader observed, "…his was the first rallying cry for a restoration of principles under a *new* conservative banner, one not inextricably tied with the interests of the Republican Party…" [35] There were others who contributed to this intellectual renaissance of conservative thought throughout the 1950s, and other works by Kirk as well, but the publication of *The Conservative Mind* had a profound impact on what was not yet a conservative movement.

What was missing more than anything else was a serious, broad-based journal in which to present, explain, and expound upon conservative thought and its relevance to contemporary America. As Lee Edwards observed, "In 1955, liberals had eight magazines of opinion they could read and write for, including *The New Republic, The New Leader, the Reporter,* and *The Nation*; conservatives really had none." [36] Once more it was William F. Buckley, Jr. who was to provide the answer.

With a cover date of November 19, 1955, the initial issue of *National Review* appeared and American political journalism has never been the same. In a publisher's note, Buckley stated that the magazine's purpose was to stand "athwart history, yelling 'Stop" at a time when no one is inclined to do so." [37] Buckley had recruited a broad coalition of anti-liberal writers comprising those who could be best described as traditional conservatives, libertarian and individualistic free market advocates, as well as those whose main focus was anti-communism. As E. J. Dionne observed, "The intellectual coalition represented by Buckley's editors and contributors was to lay the basis for the conservative political coalition of the future." [38] Together they represented the three main components of the developing conservative movement: traditional values, free market economics, and anti-communism.

The significance of the founding of *National Review* cannot be overemphasized. George Nash concluded that, "if National Review (or something like it) had not been founded, there would probably have been no cohesive intellectual force on the Right in the 1960s and 1970s." [39] Another historian of the conservative movement in America, Jonathan Schoenwald, calls the founding of *National Review* perhaps the most important occurrence of the 1950s in terms of influencing the growth of conservatism in America. [40] In creating his magazine, Buckley had taken one more step towards the development of a conservative movement.

Some four years after founding his magazine, William F. Buckley, Jr. appeared again as the author of another book, *Up From Liberalism*. The introduction was provided by the junior senator from Arizona, Barry Goldwater, and had a forward by well-known novelist John Dos Passos. Perhaps the most representative section is the concluding two paragraphs of the book where Buckley provides his perspective on the relationship of man and government.

> *I will not cede more power to the state. I will not willingly cede more power to anyone, not to the state, not to General Motors, not to the CIO. I will hoard my power like a miser, resisting every effort to drain it away from me. I will then use my power, as I see fit. I mean to live my life an obedient man, but obedient to God, subservient to the wisdom of my ancestors; never to the authority of political truths arrived at yesterday at the voting booth. That is a program of sorts, is it not? It is certainly program enough to keep conservatives busy, and liberals at bay. And the nation free.* [41]

Buckley's book became a best seller, especially on college campuses, setting forth an aggressive and forward-looking conservatism that was beginning to appeal to many youth. In this respect *Up From Liberalism* served as a precursor to another forthcoming work by that same junior senator from Arizona that appeared on bookshelves one year later.

Buckley has been rightly described as "America's all-purpose conservative thinker." [42] But he was more than simply a thinker, writer or debater. Buckley's goal in all that he undertook was to see conservatism become a mass movement.

In this sense he was, as Tom Reiss described him, "a reconciler and an institution builder."[43] Lee Edwards observed, "in the 1950s and 1960s Buckley by his words and his actions forced the reigning Liberal Establishment to acknowledge that a major new political force had emerged in America." Edwards, who knew him well and worked with him in the vineyards for more than fifty years, went one step further by calling him the founder of the modern conservative movement. [44] As we shall see, the fingerprints of Bill Buckley appear throughout the history of not only the young conservative organization but also nearly all significant responsible conservative groups over the last half of the Twentieth Century.[45]

Whether it was the journals and other publications distributed by the Intercollegiate Society of Individualists, the impact of books by Buckley, Kirk and several others, or the periodic information obtained from *National Review* and *Human Events*, conservatives now had a growing source of information and education. In her interviews with former conservative youth activists, Rebecca Klatch noted that this intellectual base was critical to their political development: "What is clear is that books and ideas played a key role in helping these youth think through issues, in confirming the direction of their beliefs, in instigating their commitment to politics." [46] Supplementing this written material were the various campus speakers sponsored by ISI as well as the numerous seminars and institutes for students provided by ISI and the Foundation for Economic Education. There now existed the beginnings of a consistent philosophical opposition to the prevailing liberal sentiment in American society. What remained was the ability to convert these beliefs into political action.

That political expression of a new conservatism was to be found in a middle-aged United States Senator from Arizona named Barry Goldwater. By the end of the 1950s, the junior senator from Arizona was gaining recognition as the political spokesman for the nascent conservative movement. Barry Goldwater differed from Mr. Republican, Robert A. Taft. He was from a small Western state, not from a politically renowned family, not a powerful member of the Senate Establishment; yet, in these differences, Goldwater manifested the dominant characteristics of much of the developing movement.

Barry Goldwater was beginning to establish himself as a national political figure. Dean Clarence Manion of the Notre Dame Law School, a well-known conservative leader of the time, convinced the Senator to author a book reflecting his political philosophy and stands on a number of contemporary issues. To this proposition Goldwater agreed and began to work with L. Brent Bozell, brother-in-law of William F. Buckley, Jr., on what would become one of the best-known political books of the last fifty years.[47]

The Conscience of a Conservative first appeared in March 1960 in a printing of 10,000 copies from the Victor Publishing Company of Shepherdsville, Kentucky, anything but a major publishing house and not even a known conservative imprint.[48] There was no question but that *Conscience of a Conservative* was a radical attack on the existing liberal orthodoxy and a call for greater emphasis on individual freedom and limited government. As Goldwater put it, "...for the American Conservative there is no difficulty in identifying the day's overriding political challenge: it is to preserve and extend freedom." [49] To this end, a true statesman has a commitment to divest himself of the power entrusted to him. In so doing, he proclaimed:

> *I have little interest in streamlining government or in making it more efficient, for I mean to reduce its size. I do not undertake to promote welfare, for I propose to extend freedom. My aim is not to pass laws, but to repeal them. It is not to inaugurate new programs, but to cancel old ones that do violence to the Constitution, or that have failed in their purpose, or that impose on the people an unwarranted financial burden. I will not attempt to discover whether legislation is 'needed' before I have first determined whether it is constitutionally permissible. And if I should later be attacked for neglecting my constituents' 'interests,' I shall reply that I was informed their main interest is liberty and that in that cause I am doing the very best I can.[50]*

This new book was clearly a call to arms that would be received not only by political activists of the day but also by a new audience of younger readers just reaching political maturity.

Historian John Andrew maintains that much of its appeal to college students was its directness and independence: "Goldwater attacked not only liberals and Democrats, but Republicans as well. This gave his message an aura of principled purity that sharply contrasted with other rhetoric of that political year."[51] As one of those future young conservative leaders viewed it, *Conscience of a Conservative* became a political calling card, "...written in the same rebellious, provocative spirit of Bill Buckley and the other Knights errant of the pioneer 50s."[52] Goldwater himself took pride in the impact he perceived his book having on thousands of young people.

> *I think it had a tremendous impact. It was an inexpensive book, and young people bought that book as fast as they could buy it. I think the young people were influenced by it. The most delightful thing I hear when I travel around the country is, "You got me interested in politics, you and your book."[53]*

Now the conservatives had not only a political leader in Goldwater but also a political tome that summarized their key philosophical and political positions.

Lee Edwards maintains that Goldwater, Russell Kirk, and William F. Buckley, Jr. were the three critical pillars of the developing movement: "First came the man of ideas, the intellectual, the philosopher; then the man of interpretation, the journalist, the popularizer; and finally the man of action, the politician, the presidential candidate."[54] With the contributions of these men and others, the stage was set for the creation of a national political movement.

Freedom, Tradition, and Anti-Communism

As the decade of the 1950s came to a close, three essential pillars could be seen as contributing to the foundation of a new conservative movement. First in time and in emphasis for some of those who would lead this emerging movement was free-market economics and a steadfast opposition to collectivism. Whether called individualists, classical liberals, or libertarians, these individuals put primary emphasis on individual freedom and a government limited in its scope.[55] A second and quite different approach stressed the importance of traditional values, the relationship of society to the individual, and the need for preserving order. The primary exponent of this position is Russell Kirk as outlined in his many published works. An emphasis on opposition to communism served as the third ingredient of modern conservatism. Anti-communism was a clean break from the isolationism that had been dominant among conservatives from the 1930s forward. With the involvement of several former Marxists, "the issue was not the old fight over interventionism or isolationism; it was whether or not the United States would be willing to wage war against the evils of Communism."[56]

Bringing these three somewhat disparate trends together into a single movement would be a major challenge, and one which periodically rose up to create dissention and division in the movement. Leading this effort to create a synthesis of tradition and freedom was Frank Meyer, one of the editors recruited by William F. Buckley, Jr. when he started his magazine in 1955. Meyer maintained that both traditionalists and individualists should recognize that Western Civilization was based on reason operating within tradition, that freedom could not be exercised in any meaningful way outside a framework of order. This attempted marriage of the two outlooks came to be known as fusionism.[57] As Lee Edwards observed, "Frank Meyer, the intellectual father of fusionism, and Barry Goldwater, the first political apostle of fusionism, sought to unite, not divide, all conservatives. Their goal was a national movement guided by constitutional principles of ordered liberty." [58] It was, according to one of those soon-to-be conservative youth leaders Donald Devine, an emphasis on using libertarian means in a conservative society for traditionalist ends.[59]

By molding together anti-communism, a concern for individual liberty, and a respect for order and tradition, a new conservative movement was being created. In this manner the decade ended with a working philosophy and a public following for conservatism. Across America, stirrings of conservative sentiment were present among intellectuals and writers, political leaders and aspiring young politicians, journalists and commentators. This new purely American conservatism that molded together individual liberty and societal order with a firm opposition to communism was beginning to attract the attention of college undergraduates and graduate students. The effort that would eventually result in the establishment of a young conservative movement would begin, however, in the late 1950s in response to what was perceived as an unwillingness to express loyalty to the United States.

Creating An Organizational Framework

The organization that in September 1960 became Young Americans for Freedom can be traced back to the efforts of two college students in December 1959. At that time, student opposition to repeal of the "loyalty oath" provisions of a new Federal education program first crystallized young conservative political action throughout the nation. The National Defense Education Act (NDEA) of 1958 [60] was one of the efforts undertaken in reaction to the Soviet Union's launching of Sputnik. Initially, it provided funds to colleges and universities for science, mathematics, and foreign language studies and to finance low-interest loans to students. As the Act's title implies, the justification for this Federal involvement in education was to assist in the provision of defense of the nation.

One of the provisions of the Act required that college students who received loan money as part of the NDEA program must swear loyalty to the Constitution and affirm that they are not members of any organization that believes in or teaches the overthrow of government by force or violence.[61] In the Fall of 1959, several university presidents announced that they would no longer participate in the NDEA student loan program because they believed the requirement of a loyalty oath pledge abridged academic freedom. Senator John F. Kennedy introduced a bill to remove the requirement for a loyalty oath and most observers anticipated that it would pass in 1960.[62] However, two college students, Douglas Caddy and David Franke, had a different perspective.

Douglas Caddy grew up in Louisiana and Texas at a time when conservatism was only beginning to develop as an alternative to the prevailing orthodoxy.[63] As a sophomore in high school he became active in conservative politics in New Orleans and volunteered to collect signatures supporting Senator Joseph McCarthy. David Franke was raised in Texas and started expressing conservative political opinions even earlier than Caddy. He became interested in politics after reading a copy of John T. Flynn's attack on socialism, *The Road Ahead*, while still in junior high school.[64]

Caddy and Franke first met in the summer of 1957 when they, along with William Schulz, were chosen in the first college journalism internship program sponsored by *Human Events*.[65] Here they worked with M. Stanton Evans who was then managing editor of the conservative weekly and would subsequently, at age 27, become editor of the *Indianapolis News*. They also met Carol Dawson, who was involved with the College Young Republicans at Dunbarton College.

By the Fall of 1959, Caddy and Franke saw that most college students were being portrayed as opposed to the "loyalty oath" provision of NDEA student loans and began organizing campus opposition to repeal as a means of coalescing conservative students around the country. [66] Caddy and Franke prepared articles and announcements that were published in *Human Events, National Review*, and *The Individualist*. Using contacts from ISI and YRs, they found representatives at campuses across the nation, including Harvard, Yale, Antioch, and University of Michigan. This helped them to compile the names of supportive college students on index cards, creating the initial basis for a national conservative youth organization. [67]

In January 1960, the "Student Committee for the Loyalty Oath" announced a governing board of students from thirty colleges and universities. Kennedy's repeal bill passed the Senate on an unrecorded vote but the proposal then died in the House Education and Labor Committee. Historian Rick Perlstein rightly describes the Student Loyalty Oath effort as the beginnings of a youth conservative movement in America.[68] As Doug Caddy summed it all up, "Out of this cauldron came the beginnings of the modern conservative mass movement. Franke and I were put in touch with hundreds of like-thinking students around the country."[69] With this under their belts, the young conservative activists could move on to greater tasks.

It was the person and political beliefs of Senator Barry M. Goldwater that provided the impetus for the next effort at organizing young conservatives. Northwestern University student Robert Croll took the lead in establishing a "Youth for Goldwater for Vice President" committee in the Spring of 1960. At the Midwest Conference of College Young Republicans that April the first sentiment for Goldwater became evident as the delegates passed a resolution endorsing the Arizona Senator for Vice President. A fellow Northwestern student, John

Kolbe, who would play an important role in the development of a permanent conservative youth organization, had sponsored the resolution.

On May 12, 1960, Croll announced the formation of "Youth for Goldwater for Vice President." The Steering Committee comprised Doug Caddy and David Franke, along with Robert Harley of Georgetown University, John Weicher of the University of Chicago, and Richard Noble, treasurer of the California Young Republicans.[70] Croll was convinced that Goldwater would be the perfect candidate and that he would accept such a request from Richard Nixon, the presumed 1960 Republican presidential candidate. By early July, he could announce the existence of active Youth for Goldwater groups in thirty-two states and on sixty-four college campuses.[71]   As one of the activists noted, "In Goldwater, we had a candidate who inspired the young as well as the old." [72]   Croll's committee placed advertisements in *The Wall Street Journal* and *National Review* seeking both members and financial supporters.

Later that same month these young conservatives would gather in Chicago for the 1960 Republican National Convention. As historian John Andrew noted, "Youth for Goldwater for Vice President…gave these activists a focal point for their activism and led them to battle Republican moderates at the GOP national convention in Chicago that July."[73]   Indeed, it was this effort to influence the direction of the GOP that would produce the nucleus for a national conservative youth organization that came into being only months later.

The 1960 Republican National Convention provided an important and rather unique political experience for the young conservatives who had been active in the "Youth for Goldwater for Vice President" organization. It was an opportunity for them to meet and become familiar with others of similar disposition who were toiling in the vineyards of the "Youth for Nixon" organization but shared their conservative outlook on issues and saw the need for a permanent conservative youth organization.   But it also brought them in contact with Marvin Liebman, former Communist, and then impresario of numerous right-leaning organizations. Liebman worked closely with Charles Edison, Chairman of the Board of the McGraw-Edison Electric Company and former Democratic Governor of New Jersey. While a former Democratic officeholder and briefly Secretary of the Navy under Franklin D. Roosevelt, Edison was a conservative who supported a number of Republicans, including Congressman Walter Judd of Minnesota.

Judd had been selected to serve as keynote speaker at the convention. A former medical missionary to China, he had made a name for himself as a stirring orator and an advocate of a strong policy of opposition to communism.[74] Liebman and Edison decided that they would form an organization to promote Judd for the vice-presidential nomination and four weeks before the convention they announced "Americans for Judd for Vice President" with former Governor Edison serving as Chairman. However, Liebman had also been working closely with Doug Caddy and David Franke from the "Youth for Goldwater for Vice President" effort. This resulted in one of the strangest semi-coordinated efforts at any political convention. When Liebman put up the funds for both operations, " This was probably the only time two national vice presidential campaigns were charged to the same American Express account."[75] Neither Judd nor Goldwater were to receive the vice presidential nomination but the young conservatives were, nevertheless, to set in place the plans to form a permanent organization.

On nominating night at the convention, Arizona Governor Paul Fannin placed in nomination the name of his state's favorite son, Barry M. Goldwater. The Youth for Goldwater forces had organized a major demonstration of support for their favorite candidate and a resounding demonstration took place on the floor of the convention. But Goldwater realized that he was not to be the nominee for President or for Vice President in 1960 and so he went to the podium and asked that his name be removed from consideration. Among his comments to the delegates was a call for future action: "Let's grow up conservatives. If we want to take this party back – and I think we can someday – let's get to work." [76] The excitement was over, but the real work of organizing conservatives remained before them.

At the end of the convention, Senator Goldwater met briefly with the leadership of the Youth for Goldwater for Vice President group to thank them for their efforts. According to Doug Caddy, Goldwater told them they should "turn your group into a permanent organization of young conservatives. The man is not important. The principles you espouse are. Do this and I shall support you in any way I can."[77] And that is exactly what these young conservatives did shortly thereafter. True to his word, Goldwater remained a strong supporter of the organization created only a few weeks after the Chicago convention, even many years later when some members of the organization became critical of the Senator's stands on social issues.

Liebman and Edison were impressed with the effort put forth by the young conservatives. They decided to host a luncheon for those who had worked on the two projects of promoting Goldwater and Judd. As Edison stated, "let's see if we can get these kids to continue to work together in some way, some how. Let's see if we can keep this thing going." [78] So the day after the convention, the young conservatives gathered for lunch in the Columbia Room of the Pick-Congress Hotel. Just as Goldwater had previously, Edison exhorted them to continue their efforts by forming a permanent organization. Doug Caddy, who was to assume a position with McGraw-Edison, was designated to develop a plan for a subsequent meeting. A suggestion was made to hold the next meeting at the family home of William F. Buckley, Jr. and the Buckley family agreed.[79] As Buckley noted, "The word went out, and a month and a half after the convention, as summer lingered in New England, a hundred young people gathered at Great Elm, where, over three days, they would lay the foundation of Young Americans for Freedom."[80] Once more, William F. Buckley, Jr. was present at the creation of another important component of the burgeoning conservative movement.

— 2 —

The Movement Begins

B<small>ARRY</small> G<small>OLDWATER</small>'s <small>ADMONITION</small> that conservatives should "grow up" and work was not lost on the young activists who had worked so hard in Chicago at the 1960 Republican National Convention. Once settled in New York City, Doug Caddy prepared an organizational meeting to discuss the formation of a permanent youth group. In early August, Caddy and Annette Courtemanche, a student at Molloy College, drove to Sharon, Connecticut to familiarize themselves with the facilities at the Buckley family home and make arrangements for hotel accommodations for those who would attend. Known as "Great Elm" for the tree that shaded the side lawn, the Buckley home would provide a suitable setting for the gathering.

By mid-August, plans were in place for the meeting. Using contacts developed through the Student Committee for the Loyalty Oath, the Youth for Goldwater for Vice President campaign, Youth for Nixon, and the interaction with other students in Chicago, Caddy created an Interim Committee to provide credence to the letter of invitation. Serving on the Interim Committee were James Abstine (then Chairman of the Indiana Young Republicans), Robert Croll (organizer of the Youth for Goldwater for Vice President effort), David Franke (co-chair of the Loyalty Oath committee), Robert Harley (Chairman of the DC College Young Republicans), Richard Noble (Treasurer of the California Young Republicans), James Kolbe (the Northwestern student who had sponsored the first resolution to endorse Goldwater for Vice President), as well as George Gaines of Tulane, Clendenin Ryan of Georgetown, Scott Stanley of the University of Kansas, John

Weicher of the University of Chicago, Brian Whelan of Loyola University, and Suzanne Regnery (daughter of the publisher).

Over the heading "Interim Committee for a National Conservative Youth Organization" a letter, signed by Doug Caddy, went out to various students and other young adults who were perceived as likely to be interested in the goal of starting a permanent group. According to the letter, it was sent to 120 youth leaders who were invited to meet, at their own expense, in Sharon, Connecticut on September 10 and 11, 1960. Clearly stressed was the fact that this would be at the family home of William F. Buckley, Jr., already well known as a leader of American conservatives. As the letter concluded, "The Sharon Conference can be of historic importance… You can be an integral part in setting the initial stages of this great movement." To enforce the connection with the effort in Chicago, printed at the bottom of the letterhead was a quote from Senator Barry Goldwater: "the preponderant judgment of the American people, especially of the young people, is that the radical, or Liberal, approach has not worked and is not working. They yearn for a return to Conservative principles."

Two weeks later a memorandum was sent to the expected attendees along with a tentative agenda. In the preliminary materials, the gathering was labeled "Great Elm Conference" but it would soon become known as the Sharon Conference after the name of the Connecticut town where it was held. Events began with remarks by former New Jersey Governor Charles Edison. On Saturday morning temporary committees were appointed and Brent Bozell spoke on "Why a Conservative Political Youth Organization is Needed." Panel discussions were held throughout the day and at lunch the speaker was Victor Milione, President of the Intercollegiate Society of Individualists (ISI). As the initial letter of invitation made clear, this new venture was to be distinct yet in harmony with the purposes of ISI. Historian Niels Bjerre-Poulsen stresses this very point in outlining the founding of Young Americans for Freedom, "While ISI's stated goal was a conservative intellectual awakening on the campus, YAF was almost solely designated for political action by implementing and coordinating the activities of conservative youth groups."[81] In this way YAF was crucial in the "…transformation of the conservative movement from one of intellectuals to a politically active movement. In the 1960s, YAF became the foot soldiers for Bill Buckley and Barry Goldwater's politically active philosophies."[82] No longer would conservatives view themselves as solely "the Remnant" standing outside and decrying the trends and tendencies in society and government. Now they would be taking direct action to influence and redirect American society.

And so it was that on September 9, 1960, nearly one hundred young conservatives from forty-four colleges met at the Buckley home for what would be an historic development in the creation of a conservative movement.[83] While the opening remarks on Friday night came from Charles Edison, the remainder of the weekend was under the direction of the young conservatives, with more senior conservatives present but mainly as observers. As Matthew Dallek noted, "it was the young who made the decisions and shaped the group...Although Buckley, Liebman, and several other prominent conservatives over the age of thirty attended the conference at Buckley's estate, the ninety young conservative leaders from forty-four colleges in twenty-four states wrote the mission statement, took care of the logistics, and decided on a name for their organization."[84]

Just who were these people making the decisions on the creation of a new conservative youth organization? Not counting those "senior" conservatives in their thirties such as Buckley, Marvin Liebman, and Bill Rusher, seventy-eight were college students and an additional eighteen listed no affiliation with an academic institution, nearly all having previously graduated from college. At a time when the vast majority of high school graduates were not yet enrolling in America's colleges, this was a relatively elite group. Nearly twenty-five percent (18) of those affiliated with a college were from the Ivy League, with Yale producing eight attendees. Twenty-two students attended what could be best labeled as private, selective enrollment institutions, with Northwestern University represented by five students. Twelve participants came from major state universities, led by a contingent of four from the University of Minnesota. Twenty-two students attended religiously affiliated colleges or universities, predominantly Roman Catholic, with Fordham University providing four students. Finally, four students, including two from Hunter College, attended other government colleges.

As in most political gatherings of the time, males predominated among the ninety-six young participants. However, the ratio was not quite as overwhelming as one might expect, with sixteen females and eighty males among the attendees. Of the eighteen without a college affiliation, some were recent graduates like Carol Dawson and Doug Caddy, while others, such as Lee Edwards and Stan Evans, had recently begun successful careers. The oldest of the ninety-six was only twenty-seven at the time.

While there was not unanimity on all points, there was agreement among the vast majority present on the need for creating a new organization. Yet, what it would be called, who would be eligible to join, and what would be its guiding principles remained to be decided. A lively discussion took place as to a name for the new organization. Some present wanted to continue use of the conservative label by clearly calling it "Young Conservatives of America." Still others wanted a more inclusive name that would allow the participation of libertarians and anti-communists who did not associate themselves with the conservative label. Douglas Caddy believed that the group should try to be inclusive and bring people in while some of the others in attendance wanted to exclude those who held somewhat differing perspectives. In the end, in a close vote of 44 to 40, the name "Young Americans for Freedom" was chosen.[85]

The second dispute that required a vote of those present concerned the maximum age for membership. Some argued that no one over twenty-seven should be eligible to join, a limit that would have soon excluded a few of those participating. But the prevailing sentiment was that the organization should be more inclusive and, in another close vote the limit was set at thirty-five.[86] What remained for the founders of the new organization was to adopt a statement of principles, a brief and concise document that would summarize the philosophical and ideological position of Young Americans for Freedom. Recently appointed as editor of *The Indianapolis News* yet still only twenty-six years of age, M. Stanton Evans had been given the assignment to draft a possible statement. He did so on his way to the conference and then at Sharon was assisted by Carol Dawson and David Franke in finalizing a document to be presented to those in attendance. The statement began by speaking of the current challenge facing society and the need for young people to take action: "In this time of moral and political crisis, it is the responsibility of the youth of America to affirm certain eternal truths." [87]

There was general agreement on most points in the draft statement, including that political freedom cannot long exist without economic freedom; that government's purpose is to preserve internal order, provide for defense of the nation, and administer justice; that the Constitution is the best document designed to ensure a balance between empowering and limiting government; that the market economy both maximizes individual freedom and most effectively produces goods. Those present agreed also on a strong assertion of national interest in foreign policy and recognition of the fundamental threat to freedom from communism:

> *That we will be free only so long as the national sovereignty of the United States is secure; that history shows periods of freedom are rare, and can exist only when free citizens concertedly defend their rights against all enemies;*

> *That the forces of international Communism are, at present, the greatest single threat to these liberties;*

> *That the United States should stress victory over, rather than coexistence with, this menace; and*

> *That American foreign policy must be judged by this criterion: does it serve the just interests of the United States*

Three points in the statement occasioned debate and discussion. Some objected to language strongly supporting states' rights. Still others believed the statement too effusive in its support of the free market. But the more significant division occurred over the reference to the Creator when the statement referred to "the individual's use of his God-given free will." As Bill Buckley noted later, "Would the Young Americans acknowledge God, so to speak, by name? That required a vote, and orthodoxy won out."[88] It was a close vote according to some of those who attended, testifying to the broad range of individuals participating in the conference. Religious questions or what are now referred to as "social issues" were not of major concern to the organization and Young Americans for Freedom remained through its first twenty-five years as basically a secular organization.[89]

Writing about the document some ten years later, its main author Stan Evans explained the reason behind the inclusiveness of the Sharon Statement: "In broad terms, the statement was meant to embrace both the 'traditionalist' and 'libertarian' schools within the conservative community…The statement assumes these emphases are inter-dependent and that it is impossible to have one without the other."[90] Clearly, the third element in the composition of modern conservatism, a strong anti-communism, was also present in the statement. As Matthew Dallek noted, "anti-statism, economic laissez-faire, and militant anti-communism – three of the ideological pillars that would support a resurgence of conservatism in American life – had been articulated by YAF on September 11, 1960."[91] Years later, William A. Rusher reflected back on the document adopted by these young conservatives and concluded that: "nowhere else, for many years, did anyone attempt so succinctly and comprehensively, let alone so successfully, to describe what modern American conservatism was all about."[92]

Robert Schuchman of Yale Law School was selected to be the first National Chairman of the organization. Tragically, in 1966 at the age of 27, Schuchman died of a cerebral hemorrhage. He had graduated from Queens College with honors, received his law degree from Yale and, at the time of his death, held a research fellowship in law and economics at the University of Chicago Law School. Schuchman was a member of Phi Beta Kappa, the Mont Pelerin Society (an international association of libertarian and conservative intellectuals founded by F. A. Hayek) and The Philadelphia Society (an American society of conservative intellectuals). Schuchman's death was a tremendous loss to the conservative movement and was certainly felt by the organization.[93]

Douglas Caddy was appointed National Director with responsibility for the day-to-day operations of the new entity. Six regional chairmen were named, five of whom had backgrounds in the College Young Republicans. Thirteen others were selected for the National Board representing various areas of the country, eleven of whom were undergraduate or graduate students. These twenty-one individuals were charged with the responsibility of bringing into reality the aspirations of the group that had assembled at Great Elm.

As the weekend came to an end, the young people in attendance had put in place an organization to accomplish a number of objectives. Clearly they had formed an organization by and for young conservatives. After some discussion and disagreements, they had articulated their own positions in the Sharon Statement. By this statement and by their organizational efforts they were prepared to take a radical stand and challenge what they perceived as the liberal establishment in control of America. They were committed to training a new cadre of conservative leaders, leaders who were not content to view themselves as permanent outsiders in American society. To this end, they were dedicated to political action designed to bring about conservative victories. It was not enough to discuss and debate philosophical and ideological principles. They would put their beliefs into concrete action to produce change in America. Historian John Andrew summed it up: "Theirs was an ideological and philosophical radicalism. Whatever their opposition to the prevailing political system, they retained a firm conviction that the system would respond if only they could seize power."[94] Seeking and seizing political power would be one of the major objectives of the new organization.

Bill Buckley gave the closing speech on Sunday afternoon, commending the participants on what they had accomplished and the path that they had set for themselves. He was impressed with their desire to turn their beliefs into action. As he commented in the next issue of *National Review,*

> *A new organization was born last week and just possibly it will influence the political future of this country, as why should it not, considering that its membership is young, intelligent, articulate and determined, its principles enduring, its aim to translate these principles into political action in a world which has lost its moorings and is looking about for them desperately? ... Ten years ago the struggle seemed so long, so endless, even, that we did not dream of victory... the difference in psychological attitude is tremendous. They talk about* affecting *history; we have talked about* educating *people to want to affect history.* [95]

Leaving Sharon, the young conservatives were excited to take on the new challenge and build a national organization of college students and young adults. Carol Dawson recalled, "We felt like pioneers. It was challenging...it was...a thrill to travel up there and be among those people."[96]

Years later, writer Rick Perlstein attempted to describe the feelings of many who attended the founding meeting.

> *For young conservatives who had discovered their idiosyncratic political faith from National Review, from ISI and Foundation for Economic Education pamphlets, from Human Events, who were ridiculed whenever they spoke up in class about the spiritual crisis for the West and against "peaceful coexistence" with a slave empire – for many of them, for the very first time they felt like they were not alone.*[97]

They had formed a permanent structure; now the real work began to build YAF into an organization. Going back to New York City, Doug Caddy vowed to make Young Americans for Freedom into a force for conservatism on campuses across the nation. The framework had been established and the leadership selected. Now the organization needed to gain acceptance both in the media and from other conservatives. It would have to attract members and establish local chapters.

While the media might be slow to recognize the significance of the events in Sharon, other conservatives were encouraged. According to historian Matthew Dallek, YAF "gave the conservative movement a psychological boost not felt since the founding of National Review in 1955. The very appearance of YAF–the first conservative youth group devoted to political action – invigorated the larger movement.[98] Writing in 1980 on the significance of Young Americans for Freedom, James Roberts commented, "the founding of YAF was, in retrospect, probably the most important organizational initiative undertaken by conservatives in the last thirty years."[99] For the first time, an activist group of young conservatives could organize across the country in a permanent framework. Furthermore, Young Americans for Freedom could provide a training ground in political action, public relations, and educational methods. From that initial conference in 1960, Young Americans for Freedom would play an important role in the development of a leadership cadre and become an essential part of the conservative movement.

Young Americans for Freedom was coming into being as a national conservative youth organization at a time when there was no "conservative movement" as it is known today. As David Franke was about to leave George Washington University and move to New York City to start work at *National Review* in the summer of 1960, Doug Caddy organized a tribute dinner in his honor. The speakers at the event were Bill Buckley and Bill Rusher from the magazine, Reed Larson of the National Right-to-Work Committee, and James L. Wick, publisher of *Human Events* while telegrams were read from Senator

Goldwater and Governor Edison. As Caddy noted, "About twenty-five persons were present. In 1960, this was the size of the Conservative Movement's leadership – 25 persons who could easily fit into a small hotel dining room."[100]

Where conservative groups did exist on campus, there was a tendency to be both exclusive and to view themselves as part of a remnant holding forth against the tides of history. Charles Mills recalls the situation he found at Yale, "YAF brought a breath of fresh air with its open recruiting of everyone it could get."[101] It was not just Yale that had such traditions of exclusivity. At other East Coast colleges, Young Republican clubs were often seen as exclusive representatives of upper class society.[102]

Realizing the significant differences between the early and late 1960s is important when understanding the development of Young Americans for Freedom. To some degree, YAF was an early indicator of what would occur later in the decade. Those who joined the new organization were dedicated to bringing about change in society. Their enemy was what they perceived as the Establishment – and it was a liberal establishment that they saw in power on campus and in the Nation's Capitol. National Chairman Robert Schuchman contrasted his views with those of an earlier generation when he said, "My parents thought Franklin D. Roosevelt was one of the greatest heroes who ever lived. I'm rebelling from that concept" while Roger Claus, a University of Wisconsin student, proudly noted that, "You walk around with your Goldwater button, and you feel the thrill of treason."[103]

What brought these young conservatives together was a general suspicion of big government and, indeed, any kind of concentration of power. This led to an opposition to the welfare state and the continued policies of the New Deal, programs that they viewed as challenging the work ethic and the sanctity of the individual. Yet they were not anti-government for it was seen as having legitimate functions to perform, first and foremost the preservation of national defense. As the Sharon Statement declared, this meant a commitment to victory over, rather than co-existence with, Communism.[104]   Of the three pillars of modern American conservatism – tradition and order, free market economics, and vigorous opposition to Communism – Young Americans for Freedom would concentrate on the last two primarily in its early years.

Doug Caddy returned to New York City after the conference in Sharon, Connecticut and began the process of establishing a permanent organization. As Caddy observed, "From virtually the beginning we were besieged by students from around the country interested in joining. Clearly the time was ripe for such an organization to ignite a grassroots conservative revolt."[105]

Throughout the Fall of 1960 it remained difficult for Young Americans for Freedom to gain media coverage in most areas of the country. To break through this barrier, the organization determined that they would need to take some dramatic actions. When the Board met again after the November elections two such events would be planned for early 1961. Of greatest significance, a decision was made to sponsor what was then described as a fundraising dinner in New York City in March 1961 with Senator Goldwater to be invited to serve as the major speaker. This event subsequently was modified to become the first major political rally sponsored by YAF.

A second topic of discussion concerned the efforts to abolish or severely de-fund the House Committee on Un-American Activities (HUAC). Leaders in Young Americans for Freedom became aware of the plans of left-wing groups opposed to HUAC to stage a major demonstration in Washington, DC on the opening day of the 87th Congress in January. The objective of these left-wing groups was to convince the House of Representatives to abolish the committee and, thus, cease any investigation into Communist activities in the United States. YAF leaders determined that this would be their first counter-demonstration and the word went out to be in Washington in January to confront those who would abolish HUAC.

Over the years, Young Americans for Freedom would conduct many demonstrations, both in favor of conservative policies as well as in opposition to left-wing efforts. According to Jonathan Schoenwald these activities were "only means, not ends…YAF leaders understood that through these relatively insignificant activities they were building the basis of a long-lasting political movement."[106] Such demonstrations as the one planned for January 1961 would be a means of obtaining media coverage, of building a sense of camaraderie among its membership, of recruiting new supporters and members, and of advancing their policy objectives. As David Franke, organizer of the Greater New York Council of YAF noted, "If our political enemies on the left were holding a rally, demonstration, march, etc., it was sure to be covered in the liberal media. A counter-protest thus gave us a better chance of getting coverage ourselves."[107]

Young Americans for Freedom saw its mission as developing conservative groups on college campuses as well as in communities. One of the major topics of discussion concerned YAF's attitude towards the National Student Association. Formed in 1947 as a federation of student body leaders, it had expanded over the years to include approximately 300 student governments on college campuses. If YAF was to become an effective young conservative organization, then it needed to take stands on, and play a role in, student campus issues. Involvement to some extent in NSA would be a logical undertaking.

YAF's Board Members were provided with a confidential report on the 13th Annual Congress of NSA held at the University of Minnesota from August 17 to September 1, 1960. While different organizations were represented at the Congress, ranging from Young Republicans to the Young Socialist Alliance, "literature on aid-to-education, disarmament, pacifism, and international relations was of one viewpoint only." Among the resolutions passed at the Congress were those urging the United States to adopt a policy of unilateral nuclear disarmament and calling for the abolition of the loyalty oath and disclaimer provisions of the National Defense Education Act student loan program. Another resolution stated that radical changes should be made in the operations of the House Un-American Activities Committee or it should be abolished. These positions on foreign policy and anti-communist topics were totally at odds with the stands of YAF.

After much discussion, the Board unanimously agreed, "that for the present time YAF will encourage participation in NSA but only for the purpose of reformulation from within. After next year's convention of NSA, YAF will reevaluate its policy towards NSA to see whether total withdrawal should be advocated." [108] For the next few years YAF did involve itself in efforts to reform NSA but by the mid-1960s it concluded that such involvement was futile and it formed an ad hoc group called STOP-NSA, acronym for Students to Oppose Participation in the National Student Association. Several YAF members participated in the establishment of a rival organization of college student groups, Associated Student Governments (ASG) that was founded in 1964 and recruited members from several colleges that had withdrawn from NSA.

A decision was made to begin publishing a YAF magazine in 1961. It would be a vehicle for young conservatives to present their views on current issues as well as report on the various events taking place in the organization. Lee Edwards agreed to serve as the first editor with an editorial board consisting of Carol Bauman, Kenneth E. Thompson, William M. Schulz, and C. Robert Ritchie.

Launching out on a new endeavor gave a sense of belonging to many young conservatives who had previously felt isolated and as merely part of a remnant, at odds with the prevailing culture. Now slightly more than three months old, the organization had to turn its attention to gaining recognition, building its membership, and forming local chapters to provide an avenue for activity by these new recruits.

The year 1961 arrived with a major challenge for Young Americans for Freedom. It had committed itself to rallying support for the House Committee on Un-American Activities. Would it be able to produce a respectable number of individuals for a demonstration in Washington? How would the left-wing demonstrators react? Would the media give any coverage to the YAF counter-demonstration? Was there sufficient support among young conservatives to pull off such an event? January 2nd would provide an answer to these questions.

As those opposed to the House Un-American Activities Committee assembled at Washington's All Souls Unitarian Church, several busloads of young conservatives, organized by the newly-formed Greater New York Council of YAF, were on their way from New York City to the Nation's Capital. Joined by DC area YAF members and other anti-communists, that afternoon more than four hundred YAF members gathered in Lafayette Square across from the White House to counteract a smaller group of anti-HUAC pickets. They had organized a conservative picket line and demonstration calling for continued support of HUAC and increased surveillance of the Communist Party.[109] While it took them some time to acknowledge it, the significance of this event was not missed by the Left as these young conservatives had beaten them with their own methods. Both *The Nation* and *The Progressive* commented on this audacious display by this upstart new group.[110] As Stan Evans concluded, "Conservatives had finally grasped the key importance of such displays – their impact on the public mind."[111] From that point on, as Gregory Schneider observed, "YAF members served as shock troops for the conservative movement, seizing on tactics such as picket lines and marches that had been employed by leftist and Communist groups in the past."[112]

By February, the Greater New York Council of YAF led by David Franke had succeeded in forming community-based chapters throughout the city. The clubs were formed to sponsor educational programs and social affairs, to engage in political action, and to participate in rallies and demonstrations such as the pro-HUAC effort in Washington, DC. To Don Devine, who was Kings County (Brooklyn) YAF Chairman at the time, "New York was the center of YAF at the beginning and everything we did was new and exciting."

One of the first places where a chapter was organized was in the Greenwich Village neighborhood of Manhattan, "to let the Liberals and those to their left know that no bastion is safe for them anymore," according to Franke.[113] Going into the lion's den of New York liberalism, the young conservatives proudly displayed their anti-communism. As writer Marvin Kitman reported about a showing of "Operation Abolition" by the chapter, "Recently the Greenwich Village chapter of YAF rented an off-Broadway theater to bring the film to the attention of its community. The event was klieg-lighted by the press and picketed by the Young People's Socialist League."[114] Karl Ziebarth was a recent Yale graduate working in New York City. Having been chairman of the "Party of the Right" at Yale, he joined Young Americans for Freedom and soon was President of the Eastside YAF chapter. As he recalled, it was "lots of fun and we enjoyed being the rebels in the left-wing world of New York City." If ever there were a question as to who was being bold, audacious and even radical, the young conservatives could provide the answer.

A decision had been made to convert the planned March fundraising dinner into an awards rally at the Manhattan Center in New York City. This would require attracting a much larger attendance for the center had a capacity of slightly over 3,000. With a commitment from Senator Goldwater to serve as keynote speaker, the young conservatives went ahead with their bold plans. The Board also decided to incorporate Young Americans for Freedom, testifying to the permanence of the organization they had created.

While much discussion centered on forming new college chapters, David Franke emphasized the need to dispel the idea that YAF was limited to students. He believed that, as was occurring in New York City, YAF needed to establish a base among young professionals in the neighborhoods of major cities. Following Franke's lead, effective metropolitan councils were organized in Boston, Philadelphia, Washington, Indianapolis and other cities by the end of 1961. YAF was able to create many of these community-based young adult chapters because, to a very large extent, YAF was the only successful responsible conservative organization at that time.

March 1961 was a very active month for the new organization. The first issue of its new magazine, *New Guard*, appeared under the editorship of Lee Edwards. Starting out as a sixteen page publication it would grow in size and continue as a monthly or ten times a year magazine until 1978 when it was converted to a quarterly magazine with interim newsletters, and would be published sporadically thereafter. As the initial editorial noted,

> *Ten years ago this magazine would not have been possible. Twenty years ago it would not have been dreamed of. Thirty-five years ago it would not have been necessary. Today,* The New Guard *is possible, it is a reality, and it is needed by the youth of America to proclaim loudly and clearly:*
> *We are sick unto death of collectivism, socialism, statism and the other utopian isms which have poisoned the minds, weakened the wills and smothered the spirits of Americans for three decades and more.*[115]

For the first time, young conservatives had a vehicle for publishing their own writings and developing their own journalistic and research skills. *New Guard* would serve an important role in building a conservative movement, communicating ideas, events, and activities of relevance to YAF members as they constructed a "grass roots" base on campuses and in communities.

Initial distribution of this first issue took place on March 3rd at a rather auspicious occasion when Young Americans for Freedom sponsored its First National Awards Rally. Awards would be given to a number of nationally known conservatives and the keynote speech would be by Senator Barry Goldwater.

The question remained, however, just as it had been in the early morning hours of January 2nd in Washington, DC, could YAF pull off such an audacious undertaking?

On the evening of March 3, 1961 more than 3,300 shouting and cheering conservatives filled every inch of sitting and standing room in the Manhattan Center while an estimated 6,000 others were turned away. Meanwhile, some 150 left-wing pickets paraded across the street.[116] As the *New York Times* reported the next day, "The audience spilled into the aisles on the main floor and the two balconies. Some pressed close to the stage. Others crouched on the balcony stairs… The line of persons trying to get into the rally stretched five abreast to Ninth Avenue …The police ordered the doors closed at 8:15 P.M. when the hall filled, and told the waiting line that no more tickets were available."[117] Young conservatives had flown in from Denver, bused in from Washington, Philadelphia and Boston, driven from Yale and Princeton, and taken the subway from Queens and Brooklyn. YAF had more than filled the hall in the middle of Manhattan.

As Senator Goldwater was introduced and approached the podium, the crowd went wild. Balloons filled the air and the chant went up over and over, "We Want Barry" as students held forth signs indicating the name of their colleges or neighborhoods: Bay Ridge YAF, Newton College, Yale, Queens, and on and on. Goldwater's speech was billed as "The Conservative Sweep on the American Campus" and focused directly on the occasion and the presence of thousands of young people in the audience.

> *We are being caught up in a wave of conservatism that could easily become the political phenomena of our time….This wave of conservatism is beginning to take on the appearance of a unique American phenomena and, as such, can reach into every nook and cranny of human life with recognizable significance to all of our people.*
>
> *Now where is the impetus for this sudden, vigorous revival of interest in the fundamental principles upon which our nation was founded coming from? I believe it is coming from the youth of the nation. It has all the earmarks of youth. It is fresh. It is intelligent. It is inquisitive. And it is energetic. And, I'm not guessing when I say these things. I've been out there where it is going on and I've had many opportunities to observe it at first hand.*
>
> *Now I have been aware for some time of this ferment of conservatism on our college campuses. I'm not just discovering it for the first time as are many of the newspaper and magazine people who come to my office for an explanation.*

> *But, even so, I want you to know that what I am finding
> as I visit college after college and high school after high school is
> downright amazing. I have been literally dumbfounded at the
> numbers of students who turn out for the meetings, not by any
> means because I am the speaker, but because it is a conservative
> movement. And because they are searching for new answers. They
> know that this thing that has gone along for thirty years and
> has cost four hundred billion dollars under the phony name of
> liberalism has not worked.*[118]

The Senator went on to urge his audience to think beyond the White House, to propose alternate policies consistent with the principles of limited government and individual responsibility, and to take a longer view of the challenge confronting them. He concluded by reminding his young listeners that the task involves reinforcing the spirit of freedom in Americans while emphasizing responsibility in their own lives. At the conclusion of Goldwater's speech, the cheers began again, the signs went aloft and the audience left knowing that they had participated in an historic occasion. As Stan Evans later commented, "…it was the sheer audacity of the enterprise which made it so enjoyable."[119]

With the culmination of the 1960-61 academic year YAF helped sponsor three summer schools at Princeton, Yale, and C. W. Post College. The schools were organized to support a greater understanding of the conservative philosophy. Among the featured faculty at these short sessions were Henry Hazlitt, well-known columnist for *Newsweek* magazine and author of *Economics in One Lesson*; Frank Meyer and William F. Buckley, Jr., of *National Review*; and Professors Gerhart Niemeyer, Sylvester Petro, Stefan Possony, Robert Strausz-Hupe, and Frederick Williamson.[120] Over the next decade, YAF would continue to sponsor weekend conferences, summer schools, and other educational opportunities either in conjunction with other organizations or by itself.

Perhaps the most significant and lasting action in July 1961 was the decision of Robert Schuchman, David Franke, and William Cotter to form a New York corporation under the name "The Freedom Party, Inc." While the Freedom Party did not play a role in the 1961 city elections, its incorporation would have a meaningful impact on the intended actions of other conservatives. Later in 1961, a group of senior conservatives determined that there was a need for a new party that would challenge the long-established Liberal Party. By creating a conservative minor party that could grant or withhold its nomination to major party candidates, the founders hoped to move both parties, but especially the Republicans, more to the Right. Specifically, they wished to counteract the influence of Nelson Rockefeller on the New York Republican Party and hamper his efforts to obtain the Republican presidential nomination. At its founding, the new party was perceived as being a strategic lever to impact the two major parties rather than a force created to win elections on its own.[121]

Schuchman and the other YAF leaders had created their party mainly to protect the name "Freedom" and to deny its use by the Labor Council. With no continuing plans for their party, the YAF leaders were willing to turn the corporation over to those interested in forming an on-going conservative party. Gaining control of an existing corporation allowed them to file a name change with the Secretary of State. As one of the founders explained, "By changing the name of an existing corporation, rather than organizing a new one, we avoided the need for approval by the Attorney General and a Supreme Court judge, which might have meant delay and complications."[122] Thanks to the YAF leaders action in July 1961, the Conservative Party of New York was on its way to fielding candidates in the 1962 state elections. In fact, its candidate for Governor, David Jacquith, received sufficient votes to secure a permanent ballot line for the party and it continues to play an important role in New York State.

From its inception, Young Americans for Freedom was committed to involvement in purely student and campus affairs, an area where it would continue to play a role. Building on Carol Dawson's report on the 1960 NSA Congress, YAF determined to continue its involvement with NSA but encourage reforms of the organization. By May, Doug Caddy let it be known that YAF was going to participate in the 1961 NSA Congress. As he told one reporter, "We will attend in force. NSA has never before been challenged. They have a bureaucracy committed to an extremist liberal viewpoint. They are completely out of line with what the average American student thinks." [123]

While YAF was planning its strategy to influence the direction of NSA, the left took note of the challenge. On June 8, 1961, a mimeographed letter was sent to a small group of NSA activists by Al Haber, leader of Students for a Democratic Society (the newly adopted name for what had been the Student League for Industrial Democracy). Haber noted that conservatives had made inroads at the 1960 NSA Congress and called for efforts to restrict further conservative expressions at the 1961 Congress.[124] A report on "The Young Americans for Freedom and the New Conservatives" was prepared by SDS member Usher Ward and distributed in preparation for the Congress. The paper tried to link YAF with the John Birch Society and therefore outside the mainstream of American politics. [125]

Arriving in Madison, Wisconsin, the YAF members attempted to reform the structure of NSA and redirect the NSA Congress to a more conservative position.

According to one rather critical writer the YAF members in Madison came to all the NSA sessions armed with tape recorders and prepared texts duplicated in advance. They were able to promote their positions effectively and by "never getting too far from a microphone, speaking up on all occasions, and holding press conferences, YAF was able to create the impression of strength beyond its numbers." [126] For the first time the leaders of NSA confronted an organized conservative opposition.

When the delegates in Madison refused to suspend the rules and allow William F. Buckley, Jr. to address the Congress, YAF and ISI sponsored a rally in the parking lot of their headquarters hotel. Buckley then spoke to about 400 people at the rally. While YAF failed to make any significant and lasting impact on the left's domination of NSA, YAF National Chairman Bob Schuchman maintained that a beachhead had been established. [127] Moreover, the NSA leadership now had to devote considerable effort to retaining members as more campuses became aware of the left-wing orientation of the organization.

YAF continued to present a conservative alternative at future NSA Congresses but its strategy changed to one of encouraging student governments to withdraw from membership in NSA. Within a year, more than one hundred colleges and universities had withdrawn from the organization. [128] Three years later, YAF allied with others to help form a new organization, Associated Student Governments of the United States (ASG). This new group clearly stated in its title that it represented student councils and not all students. Moreover, its policy emphasis was geared to student and campus issues and not national politics. ASG quickly grew to become a major force for representation of student governments on campuses throughout the late 1960s and on. [129] As Greg Schneider has noted, "In some small way, YAF's opposition to the leadership of NSA represented the first shot fired in the 1960s campus wars between Left and Right." [130]

Throughout 1961 YAF began to expand its presence on campuses and in communities across the nation. While the national projects, rallies and publications were most important in providing an overriding framework for the organization, it was the local chapter and council activities that had a lasting influence on thousands of young conservatives. YAF's anti-communism came to the fore in several local chapter activities that took place in the Fall of 1961. In November, the Greater Washington Council organized a counter-demonstration outside the White House responding to students against nuclear testing. YAF members held signs proclaiming "I Like Nike," and "Test Si – Disarm No" while showing the media that there were students who supported continued efforts to ensure a nuclear defense. [131]

Indianapolis YAF members noticed that a local auto dealer had begun selling Skoda cars imported from Czechoslovakia where they were made by the Skoda

Munitions operations of the Communist government. They confronted the dealer and told him, "As Young Americans for Freedom we are opposed to the sale of Communist-made goods in the United States and feel that you are, perhaps indirectly, assisting the Communist in his goal of world conquest." When this did not deter the sales, thirty-five YAF members picketed the dealership on Saturday, October 28th with signs including "Protest the sale of Communist cars" and "Foreign trade yes, Communist trade no." [132]

The Greater New York Council, along with similar groupings in Boston, Washington, Philadelphia, Indianapolis and other metropolitan areas, was aggressive in promoting YAF and its conservative principles. After forming a Greenwich Village YAF chapter, the next task for these young conservatives was to invade enemy territory. Chairman of the chapter was Rosemary McGrath who was described as a sandal-shod ex-model and actress who could pass for a Village "beat" but in reality was the wife of a surgeon and mother of two small children. [133] The White Horse was a well-known gathering spot for left-wing radicals in Greenwich Village and Dan Wakefield, a White Horse regular reported,

> *These card-carrying, flag-waving members of YAF were suddenly appearing with greater frequency in the press, and now they were showing up at the White Horse. Just like Bill Buckley, they turned out to be perfectly pleasant, witty, intelligent people, and we lefty liberals and right-wing conservatives found we had more common ground of conversation and interest with one another than with all those people who didn't give a hoot about politics, the great yawning masses of the middle.*
>
> *Most notable was Rosemary McGrath, a tall beauty who was president of the YAF chapter in Greenwich Village...With her long black hair, bright red lips, soulful dark eyes, and Goldwater rhetoric, Rosemary soon became known as "La Pasionaria of the Right," giving conservatives a heroine to match the legendary Communist orator of the Spanish civil war.* [134]

Stressing the dual need to raise funds and create a community of conservative activists, the Greater New York Council held a "Young Conservatives Ball" at the Waldorf Astoria Hotel to commemorate the first anniversary of YAF.

Similar events were occurring on college campuses with some 180 college conservative clubs listed in a directory published by YAF in the Spring of 1961. [135] One young college student expressed the outlook of many early YAF members when she wrote to her parents, "Wow! Is politics ever fun, and ever time-consuming! The conservatives on campus are gradually coming out of the walls. Right now we have seven definite joiners – all really swinging top-rate kids – and we've by no means even begun to scratch the surface." Working closely with the Greenwich Village chapter, students at Hunter College organized an active campus chapter led by Myrna D. Bain, one of a small number of African-American leaders in the conservative organization.[136] Ivy League campuses were a focus of attention for YAF. At Dartmouth, Tom Phillips formed a chapter in 1961 and then went on to help establish outposts on other campuses in New Hampshire. Meanwhile, Alan MacKay, Dick Derham, Danny Boggs, and Howard Phillips had established a presence on the Harvard campus. [137]

Yale University was the home for several early leaders of YAF, producing not only its first National Chairman but also several inventive leaders. To dramatize their opposition to the calls for unilateral nuclear disarmament, a dozen YAF members undertook a fifty-five mile walk from New Haven to Groton, Connecticut in support of the submarines based there that were capable of firing Polaris missiles. The missile site previously had been the target of protests by groups of pacifists. The Yale students' efforts gained substantial media attention. As they arrived in Groton in December 1961 to show support for continued nuclear testing other YAF members and supporters greeted them.[138]

At Boston University, Donald Lambro helped to establish a YAF chapter and was its first chairman in 1961-62. "I was very much influenced in my freshman and sophomore years by Barry Goldwater's *Conscience of a Conservative* but first read about YAF in the *New York Times* when National Chairman Bob Schuchman was leading protests against communism at the United Nations." Campuses from New England to the Midwest to the Middle Atlantic states saw the founding of YAF chapters. Several national YAF leaders could be found on the Northwestern University campus. YAF members at the University of Michigan outlined how they had organized on their campus with plans for an "anti-communist week" to coincide with May Day and the showing of "Operation Abolition" and "Communism on the Map." [139]

The various rallies, demonstrations, and meetings sponsored by local YAF chapters provided members with a valuable training ground for developing leadership skills. Beginning in the first year and continuing on for several more, these local chapter activities helped build a young conservative community with a shared group identity. This would be the beginning of a network of contacts and political allies that would last a lifetime for many of those who first became active in Young Americans for Freedom in the early 1960s. Just as important were the great and lasting friendships made while engaged in the common task of building a new organization.

1961 was also the year in which the left-wing media took note of the new conservative organization. Seth Offenbach surveyed the coverage of YAF in five national newspapers – *New York Times, Washington Post, Los Angeles Times, Chicago Tribune,* and *Wall Street Journal* – from 1960 to 1968. He found that ninety of the 283 articles published about YAF during this time frame portrayed the organization in a negative context.[140] Frequently the media would describe YAF as a conservative or right-wing group while not placing any ideological labels on left-wing groups. As Offenbach notes, "When the national press began writing about YAF in the early 1960s, the press was merely expanding upon their opinions about the conservative movement in general. The press had already labeled Buckley an ideologue, an extremist and a radical. Thus, it was easy for members of the press to expand their negative views of the conservative movement to encompass YAF."[141] In this manner a mainstream and generally non-political publication, *Mademoiselle,* selected Tom Hayden, a leader in the new Students for a Democratic Society, to write an article on student activism. Hayden was described as editor of the University of Michigan student paper rather than as a leader in a left-wing organization.[142] Likewise, *Nugget,* a men's magazine of the early 1960s, featured a critical essay on the growth of campus conservatives.[143]

Not to be outdone, the professional left publications joined in the attack with articles on YAF and the young conservative movement in *The Nation, The Progressive,* and *The New Leader.* [144] One writer for the leftist *National Guardian* gave faint praise before criticizing the methods of the YAF members when she said, "The meticulous grooming of the young conservatives seems to make them well-behaved in the minds of some observers. But behind the calm and reasonable exteriors of the standard-bearers is a rank-and-file of dirty in-fighters."[145] Similarly, Arnold Forster and Benjamin Epstein described YAF as a "bouncy, energetic, chesty, and somewhat ruthless outfit."[146] These comments were mild compared to the description of YAF as "racist, militaristic, imperialistic butchers" made by Al Haber of SDS in a June 1961 memo.[147]

Some of the commentators on the left more accurately perceived what was happening on the college campuses of the early 1960s and its subsequent impact on the political scene. As Forster and Epstein concluded, "They may not be the wave of the future, but these youngsters of extreme conservatism are already a detectable ripple. Their energy, their dedication, and their talent for the written and the spoken word appear to overshadow anything that the more liberal youth on or off the campus can offer."[148]

The year ended with Young Americans for Freedom on its way to establishing a broad-based grass roots organization of young conservatives and building public acceptance of its place in the political arena. It was being taken seriously not only by conservatives but also by the liberal media and especially the White House.

One of several organizations opposing the New Frontier policies, YAF was closely watched and monitored at 1600 Pennsylvania Avenue. YAF had established chapters on a number of college campuses and in major metropolitan areas, it had begun publishing a magazine of news and opinion on a regular basis, and it had pulled off a successful rally in Manhattan Center with thousands attending. A structure had been established and a staff hired. But there was much more still to be done and, as the new organization entered 1962, it was making plans for the most ambitious undertaking yet.

— 3 —

A Presence in the Room

THE YEAR 1962 PROVED TO BE A PIVOTAL turning point in the development of Young Americans for Freedom both as a significant campus and community presence as well as a major player on the national political scene. It was during this year that YAF held the largest rally of young conservatives ever held, weaned itself away from "adult supervision," conducted its first national convention, and moved its headquarters to the Nation's Capital. While nationwide projects and events coordinated out of YAF's headquarters continued to provide a focus for effective action, college and community chapters were springing up in more areas of the country. These chapters, often acting autonomously, brought with them involvement in local issues, diverse approaches to advancing the cause, and the creativity and vigor present in those launching a new undertaking.

By the end of the year, the focus of all political action remained the effort to promote the selection of Barry Goldwater as the GOP presidential nominee in 1964. Truly, as William F. Buckley, Jr. observed, Young Americans for Freedom was now recognized by much of the media simply as YAF and had become "a presence in the room."

Foreign policy and specifically opposition to communism continued to be a major focus of YAF attention as 1962 began. Local YAF chapters took the initiative in organizing a number of petitions, protests, speeches and demonstrations. While clearly opposed to much of the Kennedy Administration's domestic and foreign policies, YAF did support the President when they believed his policies correct. When the pacifist organization "Turn Toward Peace" organized demonstrations to protest the nation's defense policies and any resumption of nuclear testing, YAF was there to show an alternative perspective. In February, some 200 Washington area YAF supporters marched with picket signs across the street from the White House. Recruited on short notice from DC and Maryland campuses, the YAF members effectively responded to the "Peaceniks" and obtained media coverage for their position. When a few dozen "Turn Toward Peace" supporters marched in Austin, Texas, they were confronted with YAF members holding signs proclaiming "Pacifism Means Surrender: What Price Life?" and "Neither Red Nor Dead nor Under the Bed."[149] Some months later, during the Cuban Missile Crisis, when another pacifist group, Student Peace Union, organized a protest in front of the White House, YAF was there with more than 200 picketers supporting a strong response by the President to the Soviet placement of missiles in Cuba.[150]

Building on the previous year's success at Manhattan Center, the YAF leaders took the bold step of renting the historic Madison Square Garden with its 18,000 seats. When it was held not an empty seat could be found while hundreds stood outside trying to gain entrance. College banners vied for space and attention with those proclaiming "Better dead than Red," "Down with the UN," and "Staten Island YAF." [151]

As the crowd settled in, the evening began with the presentation of awards to a number of distinguished Americans. Those accepting awards and making brief remarks included Senator Strom Thurmond (D-SC), former Governor Charles Edison (D-NJ), New York University Professor of Economics Ludwig Von Mises, *Indianapolis News* editor M. Stanton Evans, and author John Dos Passos.[152]

Among the evening's speakers were Senator John Tower (R-TX), Congressman Donald Bruce (R-IN) and *National Review* editor L. Brent Bozell. Perhaps the most memorable of the remarks before the keynote speaker were those offered by Bozell who ended his speech by listing the orders that would go out in a conservative administration.

> *To the Joint Chiefs of Staff: Prepare for an immediate landing in Havana. To the Commander in Berlin: Tear down The Wall. To our chief of mission in the Congo: Change sides. To the Chairman of the Atomic Energy Commission: Schedule testing of every nuclear weapon that could conceivably be of service to the military purposes of the West. To the Chief of the CIA: You are to encourage liberation movements in every nation of the world under Communist domination, including the Soviet Union itself. And you may let it be known that when, in the future, men offer their lives for the ideals of the West, the West will not stand idly by.[153]*

The crowd went wild with excitement and approval. Starting slowly, Bozell had reached a crescendo with his call for action.

When Senator Goldwater was introduced an eight-minute demonstration erupted. Goldwater's speech topic was "To Win The Cold War" and he made clear that the enemy was not the Soviet Union but rather the ideology of Communism. Goldwater's speech closed out the night on a high note as the thousands of conservatives left Madison Square Garden feeling a little less lonely and a little more secure in their beliefs.

The Madison Square Garden rally established YAF as a national political force with news coverage in most major newspapers and weekly newsmagazines. Just as important as the increased media attention and the recognition from the political establishment was the emotional impact of the rally on YAF members and potential members. As one historian concluded, "In the months that followed, YAF members exhibited a confidence (some might say naivete) that would help sustain their organization for the next few years."[154]

The historic nature of this one event was perhaps best summed up by Richard Viguerie, then Executive Secretary of YAF, and David Franke, chair of the Greater New York Council, when they noted many years later, "If you are looking for a birth date when the conservative movement emerged out of the womb and announced itself to the public, no other event would qualify better than YAF's Madison Square Garden rally."[155] Vigucrie noted that YAF was the first major grass roots conservative organization and its success with the rally in the middle of Manhattan showed the nation that a conservative movement really existed, was a truly national effort, and would from that point on have a major influence on American politics and society for the remainder of the century.[156]

The YAF members left Madison Square Garden with excitement and enthusiasm and commitment, ready to organize new campus and community chapters. YAF now claimed 310 chapters throughout a growing number of states and a National Advisory Board that included 38 sitting Members of Congress.[157] One of those advisory board members was a movie actor who had most recently made a career as host of a television drama series and as a motivational speaker at General Electric plants across the country. To help raise badly needed contributions, Richard Viguerie wrote to Ronald Reagan and asked for his help, enclosing a fundraising letter to be signed by Reagan. In words few knew at the time to be so predictive of future events, the letter had Reagan proclaiming,

> *I know of no other group in the nation which is going to be more effective in preserving and extending our cherished goals. There is no need to emphasize that these young people are the future leaders of the nation. As they grow and develop, so will our country.*

Weeks went by without a response until one day an envelope came in the mail with the proposed fundraising letter enclosed. All over the letter were crayon marks and attached was a note from Reagan: "I just found this in Ronnie's toy chest. I'm sorry it's late but if you think my name would help, go ahead and use it." With that, the relationship between Ronald Reagan and Young Americans for Freedom was established and the political career of the future President had begun.[158]

This was a time of developing experience for the young conservatives now responsible for the expansion and administration of their organization. As one leader explained "you grew up very quickly putting things together. You exposed yourself to risk and failure."[159] From an early point in the organization's history, local chapters were encouraged to publish their own newsletters and eventually independent newspapers for distribution not only to members and supporters but to be used as a recruitment tool with a broader audience. By the end of the spring 1962 semester, over fifty chapters had their own publications. Not only did these publications inform members of political opinion and events but they also provided an opportunity to obtain experience in public relations and journalism, experience that would be valuable later in their political and community involvement.

Local chapters undertook a wide range of projects and activities to promote conservatism, express their opinions on specific issues, and build a sense of camaraderie and community. While regarded as a bastion of liberalism, the New York City area proved to be the strongest area of YAF support in the organization's early years. David Franke claimed that in one year the Greater New York Council had grown from 17 members to over 3,000 and from one central chapter to a council of 50 local chapters. Meanwhile, throughout 1962 YAF was expanding its presence geographically beyond its initial base in New England, the Middle Atlantic States, and the Midwest. Through building local chapters, developing programs, recruiting members, and raising funds, literally thousands of young conservatives gained the knowledge that would benefit them later as they assumed roles in American society and government.

On campuses across the country, YAF continued its campaign against the liberal domination of the National Student Association by taking a two-pronged approach: encourage schools to disaffiliate or not join NSA while at the same time organizing conservative support at the NSA Congress. Prior to the 1962 NSA National Student Congress, YAF was involved in organizing opposition to NSA on several campuses. Among those voting not to join or remain in NSA were the universities of Iowa, Missouri, Nebraska, Oklahoma, and Virginia, as well as Kansas State, Ball State, Northwestern, Earlham College and Gettysburg College.[160]

When the 1962 Congress was held at Ohio State, YAF attempted to organize an effective conservative floor leadership and had an unexpected degree of success. YAF helped to defeat several resolutions and for the first time elected a YAF member to the NSA National Executive Board. In future years, YAF would send key volunteers to the NSA Congress and publish a detailed report of their experiences in the *NSA Report* booklet that was distributed to student leaders on various campuses. First to turn down membership after the 1962 NSA Congress was Texas Christian University where the vote was five-to-one against joining. Then came the vote to disaffiliate at Ohio State University, site of the most recent NSA Congress when, with 8,300 students participating, the margin against continued membership was two-to-one.

YAF's STOP-NSA committee continued to have success in convincing schools to withdraw or never join the organization. By 1966, an official of NSA had to admit that only about 280 of the 1700 eligible schools were members, adding "This number represents a significant drop in membership from 1961 when about 350 schools belonged to the organization."[161] The most significant controversy surrounding NSA developed, however, in February 1967 when a leftist magazine disclosed that since 1952 the Central Intelligence Agency had been providing substantial funding to the organization.[162] The reaction from YAF was swift and even more critical of the government than the recipient organization. In response to the NSA-CIA disclosure, Barry Goldwater took the occasion to both praise YAF and criticize the CIA.

In addition to expanding its base on campuses and in communities, working to elect conservative candidates for public office, and establishing its presence as a major player in the political arena, YAF had some internal work that needed attention. With a growing membership spread across the country in local chapters, the organization needed to ensure that its leadership was representative of its membership and that its members had an opportunity to select those leaders. Thus, in September 1962 YAF held a gathering at the Commodore Hotel in New York City where YAF premiered its new recruitment film, "A Generation Awakes," and held a series of seminars.

Robert E. Bauman was selected as the new National Chairman as were five regional chairmen. Bauman, had served on the YAF Board of Directors since 1961 but his wife, Carol Dawson Bauman, had taken part in the Sharon Conference and served on the initial YAF Board. Bauman was a native of Maryland who had graduated from Georgetown University and was currently a Georgetown law student.

The YAF members then moved on to what motivated many of them – taking stands on the issues of the day. Resolutions were passed advocating the blockade of Cuba, opposing the Supreme Court decision banning school prayer, supporting the fraternity system, and opposing participation in the NSA unless it adopted democratic reforms.[163] Nearly five hundred took part in the closing banquet on Saturday night where the organization's new officers were installed. The keynote speaker was William F. Buckley, Jr. and new National Chairman Bauman gave an acceptance speech wherein he pledged to expand the *New Guard* magazine, build more state organizations, establish a speakers' bureau, and move the national offices to the Nation's capital. A few months later, YAF's headquarters would be located on Capitol Hill in Washington, DC.

Two years after its founding, Young Americans for Freedom had held two successful rallies, made the transition to new leadership among its officers, and established itself as a presence in the room. But many on the left refused to face this reality and believed that the organization would soon die out. Writing in *The Nation*, Robert Martinson claimed "much of YAF strength is ephemeral and will disappear."[164] Murray Kempton predicted "our children will remember Young Americans for Freedom, if at all, as part of a time sadly deficient in opportunities of self-expression for ordinary young men."[165] Steven V. Roberts, then editor of the *Harvard Crimson* and later with the *New York Times*, claimed that YAF was all public relations and image with little real support among students and likely not to have any lasting impact. But not all on the left were convinced that YAF and the conservative movement would die out. Irving Howe related his experience on the West Coast which convinced him that "after living in California only a few months, one discovers that the upsurge on the political right is a more serious matter than anyone in New York or Boston is likely to suppose…"[166] Many years later, Harvard Professor Lisa McGurr summed up the problem, "By failing to take into account the deep-seated conservative ideological traditions on which the Right drew and by refusing to closely examine the ideological universe of conservatives, liberal intellectuals underestimated the resilience and staying power of the Right in American life."[167]

That resilience and staying power was a major concern of the *New Guard* editor as he expressed his views in an article published in the June 1962 issue. Lee Edwards cautioned his readers that short-range efforts would not rid the nation of a welfare philosophy that had become too prevalent. What YAF needed to do was construct not a five-year plan but rather a twenty-five year plan. To change the direction of the country "Conservatives must begin to place themselves not only in the United States House of Representatives, but in the television networks, in the universities, in corporations and companies and perhaps most important of all, in the Federal government."[168] What Edwards wrote as a projection into the future is, of course, exactly what Young Americans for Freedom did over the next twenty-five years. When the decade of the 1980s arrived, those young conservatives who had grown and developed their political skills and philosophical grounding in YAF were ready to join in the effort to impact American government during the Reagan Administration as well as influence the direction of American society through their involvement in so many other areas of American society. Two difficult years had brought about a permanent organization under new leadership and set the path for future success, some of which would not come until the twenty-five years that Edwards described had passed.

Calendar year 1963 brought with it an increased emphasis on the upcoming presidential campaign. While it was not quite all-Goldwater, all the time, the thrust of much activity in Young Americans for Freedom centered around promoting the candidacy of Barry Goldwater for President. When there were anti-communist demonstrations and protests against the Kennedy Administration foreign policy, the Goldwater alternative of *Why Not Victory?*[169] was always present. When they involved themselves in Young Republican contests, it was always to elect the Goldwater loyalist to office. When the campus chapters published their newsletters and newspapers, there was always some article promoting Barry and his views on national issues. They were preparing the way for the grand campaign of issues and ideologies, the great debate between Barry M. Goldwater and John F. Kennedy.[170]

Before that great debate could take place there was much work to do. As it had in previous years, foreign policy with a strong anti-communist outlook was a major focus for Young Americans for Freedom as 1962 came to a close and the new year began. They continued using many of the techniques developed over the past two years designed to gain media attention and public support for their positions. In February, some 200 New York YAF members protested the Soviet occupation of the captive nations, walking from the Soviet Consulate some sixty blocks to the United Nations. The protest took place on Human Rights Day that commemorates the signing of the UN Declaration of Human Rights in 1948. Meanwhile, in Houston, YAF members picketed a hotel where Secretary of State Dean Rusk addressed the Texas Daily Newspapers Association. The signs read: "Tear Down the Wall," "Stop the Sellout," and "Better Brave than Slave."[171]

Captive Nations Week provided another opportunity for several YAF community Chapters to express their anti-communism. Georgia YAF organized a march in Atlanta with signs proclaiming "YAF Wants Freedom for Red Slaves" and "Tear Down The Wall."[172] Closer to home, National Chairman Bob Bauman and Executive Secretary Richard Viguerie sent a letter to all YAF members in February 1963 criticizing the Kennedy Administration's settlement of the Cuban missile crisis. The letter claimed "The plain truth is that Cuba is today just where it was prior to President Kennedy's 'strong stand' – under the control of a Communist dictator armed and garrisoned by Soviet aid. Only this foreign intervention in Cuba sustains this horrible suppression of a once free people."

Meanwhile, YAF college chapters were also expressing their anti-communism through the sponsorship of various speakers on campus. Among the speakers presented by YAF chapters were James Burnham and Frank Meyer of *National Review*, Dr. Fred C. Schwarz of the Christian Anti-Communism Crusade, and Herbert Philbrick, author of *I Led Three Lives*.

Although Indianapolis YAF had demonstrated against the sale of Communist cars in 1961, the issues of exporting American goods or building manufacturing plants in Communist countries were still on the horizon. Yet, in 1963, YAF's magazine published a critique on the sale of high technology equipment to Soviet bloc nations. According to the author, "While the Communists are waging a total cold war against our very way of life, we are shipping them vitally-needed electronic and industrial equipment to build up their economy, and, therefore, their war potential."[173] Two years later, YAF would launch one of its most successful campaigns against the construction of an American manufacturing plant in Romania.

During the summer of 1963, diplomats for the United States and the Soviet Union agreed to a nuclear test ban treaty. Once the text of the treaty was released, the Senate Foreign Relations Committee held hearings on its merits. Chairman Bauman testified that the treaty was a "grave threat to the national security of the United States and a threat to freedom everywhere."[174] In response, YAF chapters across the country issued news releases and circulated petitions opposing the treaty. Just before the Senate vote, Bauman held a news conference outside the Capitol with Senator Strom Thurmond. The YAF Chairman presented the Senator with petitions signed by some 15,000 Americans from every state. Both NBC and CBS television covered the presentation. Although not successful in stopping the treaty, YAF had shown its ability to produce grass-roots organization in every state on short notice and, in turn, impressed leaders in Congress with the strength of their organization.

When three American flyers were shot down by Russian planes over East Germany, Bauman sent a telegram to then-President Johnson asking that the new wheat deal with Russia be renounced.[175] Chapter leaders released similar statements and wrote letters to their local newspaper.

Later that year one YAF leader put forth the possibility that the United States should take a more pro-active role in assisting people under communism to throw off their oppressors. He argued that a cautious use of guerrilla techniques could put the Free World on the offensive against the Communist bloc. It might take a long-term perspective and was not without dangers, but such a change in policy, it was maintained, could result in freedom advancing around the world. "We must approach the subject with caution and with the realization that success will not come overnight. Any guerrilla war must take time, but if we have the strategic patience of the Communists, we can achieve some significant results."[176] Some twenty years later, President Ronald Reagan would follow similar policies, especially in Nicaragua, Angola, Afghanistan, and to some extent in Poland, designed to put the Soviet Union on the defensive.

Meanwhile, YAF was continuing its efforts to expand the conservative presence on America's campuses and in communities large and small. Writers Stephen Hess and David Broder labeled YAF "the most robust group on the right" during this period of time.[177] Promote, publicize, and proselytize were the goals of the YAF chapters in the early sixties. The number of YAF college chapters publishing weekly or monthly newspapers continued to grow. Local chapters used the new YAF film, "A Generation Awakes," as a recruitment tool. Each issue of *New Guard* included three to four pages of a "YAF Roundup" that featured local chapter events and happenings. This section not only provided suggestions for local projects but also helped to create a sense of community and belonging among the YAF members.

YAF was also making a presence on a number of high school campuses. James and Mary Louise Lauerman were high school students in Belleville, Illinois who organized the Nathan Hale chapter in 1963. As James Lauerman recalls "They were some of the most interesting times of my life and the highlight of my high school years." For his sister, YAF "gave me a sound economic, free-market education which has helped me understand and analyze current events over the years. My belief in freedom, in our Constitution, in the Founding Fathers is deep and abiding and YAF was a part of my education in freedom."

At the same time, community chapters remained active on local issues as well as on anti-Communist causes and on projects involving direct political action. One example was the Bay Ridge YAF chapter which circulated petitions to oppose tax-supported construction of high-rise apartments in their community in Brooklyn, NY.[178] The Greater Boston Chapter of YAF not only sponsored monthly meetings with guest speakers but also was very much involved in political campaigns, backing both some of their own members as well as other established conservatives.

Throughout 1963, YAF chapters attempted to rally support behind Barry Goldwater in anticipation of a campaign that would focus on the philosophical contrast between liberalism and conservatism. None of the various events sponsored by local YAF chapters was as dramatic and successful as the Goldwater speech before 3,000 fans at Indiana University in March. The Senator was introduced by Bill Jenner, Jr, president of the Indiana University YAF chapter. In speaking of the President, Goldwater declared that, "up to the first of the year I had grave doubts that he could be beaten. But now I think he can be beaten and beaten heavily." One school official described the event as the most enthusiastic rally on campus in years.[179] The next month, Peter O'Donnell, Texas Republican State Chairman, officially announced the formation of the National Draft Goldwater committee. While the Senator still refrained from making a formal decision, the unofficial campaign was underway.[180]

Independence Day in the Nation's Capital was to produce the next important event in YAF's involvement towards the development of the Goldwater candidacy. Officially sponsored by the Draft Goldwater Committee and held at the DC National Guard Armory, it was coordinated by YAF National Board Member Don Shafto, empressario of the 1962 Madison Square Garden rally.[181] YAF groups chartered buses and came from Boston, New York, New Jersey, Alabama, Florida, and the Midwest. It was labeled "the most impressive display of growing conservative influence." Estimates of the crowd ranged from 8,000 to 10,000 cheering fans, a huge turnout for any event in sweltering July in the Nation's Capital and a time when Congress was not in session.[182] Perhaps what was most impressive about the event, however, was that it took place without Senator Goldwater being present. The major political leaders making remarks were Governor Paul Fannin of Arizona, Senator Carl Curtis of Nebraska, and Senator John Tower of Texas who had the crowd chanting "We want Barry!" The demonstration started after Tower's closing speech and did not end for several minutes thereafter.[183] Once again, YAF had played a critical role in showing the growing support for Barry Goldwater and especially his appeal to young Americans.

When the Fall semester began, YAF members on campuses and in communities across the nation were geared up to promote a Goldwater candidacy. As the organization's magazine summarized the situation, "Name a place Goldwater has been in the last two months and YAF was there – New Jersey, Oregon, Boston, Massachusetts, Texas, California, and Pennsylvania." According to the *Newark Star-Ledger*, when he arrived at Newark airport in September, Goldwater was greeted by "an astonishing turnout of young supporters who chanted the now-familiar 'We Want Barry!'" Meanwhile, the Greater Grand Rapids Chapter of YAF staged a "Goldwater in '64" motorcade with more than forty cars over a sixteen mile route. When the North-South football game was played at the University of Alabama, the local YAF chapter entered a Goldwater car in the pre-game parade. Iowa State University YAF had its own float with the theme "Drown the Hoosiers in Goldwater" in its annual Homecoming parade.

At the Republican Issues Conference held at Mackinac Island, Michigan YAF members met every boatload of attendees with Goldwater paraphernalia and promoted his candidacy among the Republican activists. Two hundred cheering Oregon YAF members met Goldwater's arrival at the Western States Republican

Conference in Portland. In Boston, on October 16th, the Arizona Senator was greeted by "20 young ladies in white cowboy hats, red Goldwater sashes and blue shirts," representing the Greater Boston YAF Chapter. As one Republican official noted, "We were trying to keep this from becoming a Goldwater rally, but the Young Americans for Freedom seem to be running away with it."

These events all took place before Barry Goldwater had made a commitment to seek the Republican presidential nomination. But, as he indicated in his remarks at Indiana University, the Arizona Senator was becoming convinced that a serious effort could defeat President Kennedy in 1964. Just as important to him, he believed that it could be a campaign of ideas and political philosophy, emphasizing those basic principles that separated him from Kennedy. It would be a choice for the American people between liberalism and conservatism, not simply between two candidates or two political parties. The month of November 1963 was to change all those plans.

And then it happened. YAF and the entire nation were not prepared for a tragedy that no one then living had ever experienced. On that fateful 22nd day of November, Lee Harvey Oswald gunned down the President of the United States, the one nationally elected officeholder in our political system, the symbol of the nation. With the rest of the country, the young conservatives grieved. How could this happen to our country, to our President? No longer would there be the great philosophical contest between two men who held differing positions but greatly respected each other. The world had changed.

The political climate heading into 1964 was not the one that everyone anticipated. There would be no Goldwater-Kennedy debates across the nation modeled after the Lincoln-Douglas debates of a century earlier. America and the free world would need to become acclimated to a new President from Texas who talked and acted quite differently from the one they had elected in 1960. The New Frontier was over and, with it, perhaps the presidential campaign of Barry Goldwater. It would take much thought and reflection now before the Arizona Senator would be convinced to run against Lyndon Johnson.

To help convince him that he should become a candidate for the presidency, Chairman Bauman wrote to all YAF members in December, urging them to "WRITE A LETTER TO SENATOR GOLDWATER URGING HIM TO RUN FOR PRESIDENT AND TELL HIM HOW IMPORTANT HIS CANDIDACY IS TO YOUNG CONSERVATIVES." All across the country, YAF members responded by the thousands with messages to their political hero.

After the tragedy that impacted all Americans, the task ahead for Young Americans for Freedom was to remain dedicated to the principles that had brought them together in 1960.

As 1964 began, YAF members were becoming involved in a number of other activities and projects to advance their conservative philosophy. Many chapters sponsored speeches by conservative elected officials. Still others brought to campus conservative writers and professors to discuss the philosophy of conservatism or the principles of free market economics.[184]

YAF chapters also attempted to publicize their organization before audiences of likely supporters. In this fashion, Texas YAF sponsored a booth at the National Junior Chamber of Commerce convention in Dallas to spread the conservative message and recruit new members. It was reported, "models from Neiman Marcus Dept. store and 'Miss Dallas' were among those who helped staff the YAF booth."[185] In Fairfield County, Connecticut, the YAF chapter carried out its "project gutter" in various towns each Saturday. Volunteers would occupy a parking space, fill the meter with the appropriate coins, and then pass out literature to pedestrians. As one YAF leader noted, "this way they don't block sidewalks, and merchants and on-beat policemen are kept happy while YAF members continue their work."[186]

As had been the case during its first year, YAF continued to pick up chapters when independent local groups affiliated with the national organization. Ron Docksai and Dan Levinson were among a group of high school students in Queens, New York who organized themselves under the name "Young American Conservatives" before the 1964 presidential election. Docksai and his associates joined a growing body of YAF members who would make New York one of the strongest state organizations in YAF's history. Across the continent in Glendale, California, high school student Allen Brandstater picked up his grandfather's copy of *National Review* and saw an ad for an organization of young conservatives. "I responded and joined YAF in 1963 when Goldwater had not yet announced for president. When I was a junior in high school I joined Youth for Goldwater. After the election I formed Foothill YAF comprising mainly fellow students from Glendale Union Academy, a Seventh-day Adventist prep school."

Maurice Franks decided that while campaigning for Goldwater was fine, he would go all the way and become a candidate himself. The 22-year-old student at Harding College filed for the office of Justice of the Peace as an independent in a totally Democratic county. His campaign was successful and he became the youngest judge in the State of Arkansas and the first independent elected to the position.

Vietnam and the New Left were only beginning to surface on a few campuses in 1964. When the Penn State Socialist Club sponsored a Viet Cong propaganda film, the YAF chapter under the leadership of Carl Thormeyer objected. They declared "we didn't hear anybody yell for 'academic freedom' for the Nazis during World War II." Yet, while YAF strongly backed the war in Vietnam they also defended the right of anti-war activists to speak out against the war. They drew the line, however, at outright propaganda from the enemy. At Penn State, Berkeley, and other campuses in 1964 there was a high degree of debate and discussion involving YAF members and leftist advocates since both groups consisted of political activists who distinguished themselves from the larger body of apathetic and apolitical students.[187] Penn State YAF's Thormeyer also recalled lively debates with various peace organizations on campus, especially as the two groups set up their weekly recruitment tables in the university student union. These were the times before the Left took to violence and closing down colleges, when rational debate could occur on ideological differences.

YAF's anti-communism was reflected in more than the early conflicts over Vietnam; Cuba and Castro remained a major concern also. At the Massachusetts Institute of Technology, YAF leaders David Nolan and Mike Leavitt had one of the more active chapters in the state. One Spring 1964 program featured a lecture by Professor Ernesto Blanco of the MIT Mechanical Engineering Department. A former Director of Research in Castro's first cabinet, Blanco had fled the island in the early Sixties. His topic was "The Truth About Cuba and our Foreign Policy."[188] Chapter Chairman David Nolan, after graduating from MIT, became the major force behind the creation of the Libertarian Party, which ran its first candidate for President, Dr. John Hospers, in 1972 and remains a consistent third party in American politics.[189]

All across the nation, activists they were, and activists dedicated to proselytizing and organizing and influencing the direction of campus and community policy. Matthew Dallek concluded that "From the outset, YAFers did not defend the status quo; they attacked it. On campus they decried the liberal economic theories of their professors. At rallies, they inveighed against the *New York Times* and other establishment media for one-sided reporting. And in letters to financial backers, they denounced thirty years of liberal rule."[190]

Serious and committed though they were, the YAF members could also have fun. It was not just the left that could produce songs. Not to be outdone in musical creativity, in April 1963 the Boston College and Boston University YAF chapters combined to sponsor a New Frontier spoof called "The Mikado of Bravado." As Castro invades Florida, negotiations are undertaken by the Kennedy State Department and then freedom is finally saved with the rebirth of a nation under Barry Goldwater in 1964.[191]

Drawing on some of the left-wing songs of the thirties and the songbooks of the "Party of the Right" at Yale University, the tradition of satirizing the left as well as themselves is one that would continue throughout the organization's history. At some point in every YAF gathering, small groups could be found imbibing and carrying on the tradition of oral story-telling. The year 1964 produced a little booklet titled "Folk Songs for Conservatives by Noel X and his Unbleached

Muslims."[192] Among the collection were "Cool Goldwater," "Won't You Come Home, Bill Buckley," "Let's Test Again," and the ever-popular "Orally":

> *"Don't put fluoride in our streams, Don't spray our willow tree*
> *It's a Commie plot it seems, To get us orally*
> *Orally, Orally, Please don't poison me*
> *Cast aside your pesticide and down with DDT."*

The authors continue on to warn us "eternal vigilance is the price of a good set of choppers." Little did Parmentel and Dodge know that their efforts at writing, collecting, and publishing satirical political songs would be repeated many times over. The tradition of song books and satirical songs would continue with a YAF songbook compiled by various YAF members over the years.

As 1964 began there was still some uncertainty as to whether there would be a Goldwater candidacy. If Goldwater were to seek the nomination, campaign organizations had to be built, strategy developed, and advertisements secured.

Some 22 years later, in his last days as a United States Senator, Goldwater sat down for an extended interview with John Kolbe. Kolbe was one of the founders of YAF and at that time in 1986 was a political columnist for the *Phoenix Gazette*. Kolbe asked the Senator about his decision to run.

> *...when Jack was shot, I just thought I don't want to run against Lyndon Johnson. I had looked forward to running against Jack Kennedy. I think it would have been a real change in campaigning in this country.... Well, we would have debated. We had talked together about just going across the country – maybe using the same airplane – but stopping at a town and standing up in the old Stephen Douglas way and debate.. But I just decided not to run when he was killed. And then, right here in this room, I think it was around Dec. 15 or 16 of that year, they put the pressure on me. They said there were hundreds of thousands of young people that were looking forward to my running.*

Kolbe went on to ask "And they told you there were all these young people out there waiting for you?" Goldwater responded "And on the strength of that responsibility I felt for young people, I said, 'OK, we'll go.'"[193] On January 3, 1964 in Phoenix he formally announced his candidacy for President of the United States.[194]

Finally, this was what the YAF legions had been working for, hoping for, organizing for. Now they had an official candidate for President who reflected their conservative philosophy. One can accurately say that while Bill Buckley was the impetus and mentor for the organization, the person and political philosophy of Barry Goldwater were the major uniting factors in Young Americans for Freedom. It was Goldwater who epitomized the anti-communism, traditionalism, and free market economics that were the pillars of YAF as expressed in the Sharon Statement. There were few members who did not support the Arizona Senator. Wherever the Senator spoke during 1961 to 1964, he would be greeted by YAF members bearing the ever-present "YAF Backs Barry" signs. Lee Edwards summarized this serendipitous relationship when be noted some years later, "Barry Goldwater made YAF but YAF also made Barry Goldwater – made him a national political figure and then the Republican nominee for President in 1964."[195]

The cover story for the March 1964 issue of *New Guard* was an exclusive article from Barry Goldwater titled "Why I'm Running" and its presence was an indication of the significance of Young Americans for Freedom to the entire Goldwater effort.[196] But the campaign effort by YAF had already begun as in late January New England YAF held a regional conference in Concord, New Hampshire, bringing more than 150 YAF members into the site of the nation's first primary. In addition to hearing speeches and attending workshops, those present received an orientation into campaign work for the Arizona Senator. Over the following weeks until the primary on March 10th cars and buses filled with YAF volunteers from the Northeast would descend on the Granite State to campaign for their candidate.

To make sure that local YAF chapters and members were using every technique available to advance the conservative cause, National Secretary Marilyn Manion authored an article on tips for effective political action.[197] All across the country YAF chapters accepted the challenge. Reporting on the efforts of YAF during the campaign, writers Stephen Hess and David S. Broder noted "their presence at countless demonstrations confirming that right-wing girls are prettier than their left-wing counterparts."[198] Whether it was New Hampshire, Illinois, Indiana, Oregon or California, the YAF troops were present. As one historian later wrote, "At every stop photographers and cameramen were taxed trying to keep the ubiquitous "YAF Backs Barry!" banners out of their shots." [199] Through victory and setback and ultimate success in the nominating battle, YAF produced an essential element of the grass-roots support for Goldwater.[200]

How important was YAF's support to Goldwater's obtaining the Republican nomination? Perhaps Bill Buckley best put it in perspective years later when he observed,

> *There is absolutely no doubt that the intensity factor of the Goldwater campaign was vividly affected by YAF. If YAF had not*

> *existed, with the huge amount of money spent by the Rockefeller*
> *people, plus also the feeling that the Republican party's moderates*
> *had to rescue it from decrepitness, it might very well have tipped*
> *California to Rockefeller.... I don't think he (Goldwater) could*
> *have won that nomination without the youth enthusiasm.*[201]

It was YAF members who directed the Goldwater campaign at numerous college mock conventions and elections throughout late 1963 and early 1964; it was YAF members who worked to convince college Republican clubs and conventions to endorse Goldwater; it was YAF members who trudged through the snows of New Hampshire and continued on to the California primary, ringing doorbells, addressing envelopes, making phone calls, and attending campaign rallies; and then it was YAF members who organized the youth support and the rallies and the demonstrations that summer in San Francisco.

The Republican National Convention in San Francisco would end up being the ultimate high point of YAF's campaign to elect Barry Goldwater. Culminating years of work, YAF members came from all parts of the country to help nominate their chosen candidate. [202] The Youth for Goldwater chartered train arrived Monday under the leadership of National Board Member Tom Phillips. Then came busloads from Montana under the direction of Board Member Jim Dullenty and from Arizona coordinated by State Chairman Norman Wycoff. Next, a chartered plane touched down bringing 116 New York YAFers ready to do battle.[203] Hundreds more from all over California took part as active foot soldiers with many coming from Bay Area campuses such as Stanford, UC Berkeley, San Jose State, Foothill College and others.

Even before these volunteers arrived, YAF members from the West Coast were already at work led by National Board Member Jack Cox. Cox, a student at San Jose State, had established a Western YAF office that would serve as the mobilization center for YAF operations until YAF moved into a hotel suite in the Hilton Hotel in downtown San Francisco. When Nelson Rockefeller arrived at the San Francisco Airport, crews of YAF members were there and when the New York Governor stepped off his plane, "YAF Backs Barry" signs greeted him. YAF even had a Dixieland band on a pickup truck, plastered with Goldwater signs, which included many YAFers from northern California as band members. With Bob Bauman and Jack Cox on the back of the truck, it was driven right into the middle of a televised Rockefeller rally in the courtyard of the Mark Hopkins Hotel to the consternation of the Rockefeller campaign.[204]

A YAF led crowd of 4,000 waving "YAF Backs Barry" signs met Goldwater's arrival at San Francisco on Saturday. It was Executive Director Dave Jones' idea weeks before that this should be the YAF slogan consistently used in San

The Great Elm at the Buckley estate in Sharon, Connecticut, where Young Americans for Freedom was formed.

The rafters were full and thousands were turned away as YAF held its second awards rally in New York City less than eighteen months after the organization's founding.

The NEW GUARD

THE MAGAZINE OF YOUNG AMERICANS FOR FREEDOM   MARCH 1962

CONSERVATIVE RALLY FOR WORLD LIBERATION FROM COMMUNISM

MADISON SQUARE GARDEN, NEW YORK, MARCH 7, 1962

★★★★★★★★★★★★★★★★

2nd Annual Awards Presentations

★ HON. HERBERT HOOVER

★ JOHN DOS PASSOS   ★ SEN. STROM THURMOND

★ PROF. RICHARD M. WEAVER   ★ JOHN WAYNE   ★ HON. CHARLES EDISON

Addressed by **SEN. BARRY GOLDWATER** *and* **SEN. JOHN TOWER**

Special Award To

MOISE TSHOMBE

Katangan President

★★★★★★★★★★★★★★★★★★★★★★★★★★★

In This Issue:

THUNDER ON THE LEFT
by George McMurray, Jr.

THE TRUMPET THAT SOUNDS ATTACK
by Robert E. Bauman

'62 IS THE YEAR
by Douglas Caddy

YAF AND THE NEW CONSERVATISM
by Robert Schuchman

POLITICS AND THE POPULAR THEATRE
by Kenneth Paul Shorey

The March 1962 issue of The New Guard *served as the program for the rally at Madison Square Garden where an overflowing crowd showed the media that the young Conservative Movement had arrived.*

Ronald Reagan joined the Young Americans for Freedom advisory board in 1962 and was named honorary National Chairman. President Reagan was involved with YAF throughout his career.

Ronald Reagan is surrounded by Young Americans for Freedom activists, while stumping for Sen. Barry Goldwater outside San Francisco's Cow Palace on July 15, 1964. (Photo courtesy AP)

YAF had a major presence at the Republican National Convention in San Francisco as shown by the signs on the Cow Palace convention floor.

In the Fall of 1964, YAF members campaigned across the nation for Barry Goldwater. One of the more successful YAF rallies for their presidential candidate, with more than 3,500 attending, was held at O'Hare Field in Chicago. (Photo from Jameson Campaign)

New York YAF Chairman Don Pemberton headed up Youth for Buckley in the 1965 campaign.

"Sock it to the Left" was the theme of the 1969 YAF National Convention. Here David Keene addresses the delegates while Michael Connolly and Randy Goodwin are shown on the right. (Photo by Tom Dey)

In 1969, YAF was featured in an article on student resistance to the New Left that appeared in the Sunday supplement of Parade. *Here New York YAF State Chairman Jim Farley is shown in the organization's headquarters at 25 Jane Street, Manhattan.* (Photo by *Parade* Magazine)

YAF high school leader John W. Tower of Rockville, Maryland, reads an issue of The Alternative *published by the YAF chapter at the University of Maryland. From the mid 60s onward, many YAF chapters started their own independent campus newspapers.*

California YAFers burned their social security cards at a protest in Orange County. Ken Grubbs, Cal State – Fullerton YAF chairman, called the system "a fraud and not a proper function of the government." Shown here torching a card are John Schureman, Mike Johnson, and Dana Rohrabacher.

Outgoing executive director Frank Donatelli and National Chairman Jeff Kane were honored by the organization at the 1977 convention while Congressman Bob Dornan looks on.

Fifteen years after its initial national convention, Young Americans for Freedom returned to New York for the 1977 event. The roast of Bill Buckley was for many the highlight of this year's event. The theme, Freedom Not Socialism, is a timeless message YAFers of today are promoting on campus.

YAF chapters and individual members went all out for Ronald Reagan and other conservative leaders in 1980. Here California YAFers Dean Campizzi, Jon Garrison, and Sergio Picchio show their support for Reagan and Congressman Bob Dornan. (Photo by Sergio Picchio)

YAFers were a major presence in Dallas at the 1984 Republican National Convention as their favorite President was renominated for a second term.

Francisco and before the week was over it would become a household phrase. Still other YAF members were organized into a major distribution network to reach every delegate. Sunday saw teams of YAF members visit the 28 hotels where the delegates and alternates were staying. Each delegate received a personally addressed letter from Senator Tower with a copy of the special convention edition of *New Guard.* In the letter, Tower commended the organization and testified that YAF has "provided the muscle that is vitally needed in political organizations for sound, conservative politics."[205]

Also on Sunday, Bill Buckley arrived to be greeted by 200 YAF members shouting "We Want Buckley" as a band played "Won't you come home, Bill Buckley?" One sign held by a YAF member testified to his critical role in the effort when it said, "You Made It Possible, Bill!"

It is not surprising that at a time when most states set a minimum voting age of 21, few members of a relatively new youth organization had been elected as delegates to a national nominating convention. Moreover, in 1964 the size of the national convention was much smaller than those in the 21st century, with only 1,308 delegates seated. Nevertheless, five YAF members had been successful and were there as delegates: National Chairman Bauman from Maryland; Richard Plechner of New Jersey, a Sharon attendee who was later to serve on YAF's National Board; Fred Ackel from Florida, who would become a successful dentist in Fort Lauderdale; Ted Humes of Pennsylvania; and Morton Blackwell of Louisiana, the youngest delegate, who would go on to found the Leadership Institute and serve for more than twenty years as National Committeeman from Virginia.

On the second night of the convention, YAF held a rally for Goldwater at the Herbst Theater with Ronald Reagan as the master of ceremonies.[206] Bill Buckley recalled the event as one of the highlights of the entire week. "Five thousand persons were turned away. The auditorium was jammed with excited people, mostly under thirty years of age. The press was there in force. The professionalism of the physical arrangements was impressive."[207] The following day's *New York Times* gave front-page coverage to the rally. Referring to his closing speech at the theater, the paper reported, "Senator Goldwater told a cheering stomping audience last night that the country was caught up in a wave of conservatism that could easily become the political phenomenon of our time."[208] While Goldwater was correct, it would take another sixteen years before his prediction would come true.

Prior to Goldwater's nomination on Wednesday YAF sponsored another rally, this time outside the Cow Palace. While almost a thousand YAF members shouted for Barry, they also heard from Bob Bauman and Ronald Reagan. Speaking from a flatbed truck, Reagan told the crowd, "You were at this long before many, and God bless you for it.[209] With Goldwater nominated, the YAF members left San Francisco with what many of them viewed as their dream ticket. It was their greatest moment. They had captured the nomination; now they had to convince the American people and capture the White House.

Immediately after the convention and as the general election campaign began, YAF's initial National Chairman, Robert Schuchman, tried to put into perspective why so many young people were attracted to the Goldwater candidacy.

> *The great appeal of Barry Goldwater to our generation is that he represents the America of the future in which we want to live. He symbolizes a nation and a world in which the individual is free, free to make his own way without the government punishing him for his successes and rewarding him for his failures... Thus, it is not merely dedication to an individual, but also dedication to principle which motivates the young conservative movement.*[210]

Part of his appeal was personal and part of it was what he typified in terms of the ongoing regional and class divisions in America. As another young conservative later claimed, Goldwater "represented a rebel. He represented a challenge to the Eastern Establishment. He represented West versus East. He represented a new approach toward international communism. He represented freedom from the growth of the Federal bureaucracy. And he represented my personal freedom."[211] The commitment and excitement of the YAF members as they went forth from San Francisco to wage a war for the minds and hearts of the American people was hard to measure.

Writing many years later, Rick Perlstein summarized the outlook of these young conservatives who had climbed the mountain and could see the peak of victory before them.

> *They were now a force to be reckoned with. They marched at the head of a presidential crusade... It was indescribable, the exhilaration they felt those long days, exhausting themselves for the highest cause they could imagine. It remade you; it made everything else seem small. They had no words to describe it... They were young, idealistic; triumph was inevitable, for they were battling for the Lord.*[212]

Sociology professor Rebecca Klatch conducted a series of in-depth interviews with a number of YAF members some thirty years after the 1964 campaign. In attempting to analyze and identify the significance of various events on their political development she concluded that the Goldwater campaign had the greatest impact, acting "as a beacon for young conservatives much in the way the civil rights movement did for young leftists…For both traditionalists and libertarians, the Goldwater campaign was a primary route to activism and to YAF."[213] Whether one was mainly an anti-communist, traditionalist, libertarian or Objectivist – all could agree that the election of Barry Goldwater would turn the country around and make America a better place.

It was an exciting time for the young conservatives just days before the reality of election day would set in. Unfortunately, not all would go as wished. So much attention had been focused on gaining the Republican nomination that little planning took place for winning the general election. Political scientist John Kessel described the situation at the campaign office after the San Francisco convention as one where all the attention had been directed towards obtaining the nomination and no master plan existed for the Fall campaign.[214] Nevertheless, at the grass-roots level YAF members were dedicated to bringing about a Goldwater victory. They rang doorbells, stuffed envelopes, distributed flyers, organized and attended rallies for the ticket. Optimism and enthusiasm were outweighing reality. But for some YAF members, the cold truth would soon confront them.

On September 11, some two hundred YAF members gathered at the Commodore Hotel in New York City for the annual meeting of the organization. They approved a series of resolutions that included commending Senator Goldwater for his support of human rights, supporting the House Un-American Activities committee, and opposing participation in the National Student Association. The next day a pilgrimage was made to Great Elm to commemorate the fourth anniversary of YAF's founding. The events at Sharon, provided a glorious occasion reflecting on the accomplishments of the past and the plans for the future. It was good to be young and to be in YAF.[215]

Without question, however, the most memorable event of the conference was not the trip to Sharon but the address by Bill Buckley. Buckley spoke of the obstacles confronting Goldwater, not the least of which was that sufficient groundwork had not been completed to prepare the public to receive the Senator's message. He then spoke the words that stilled the audience: "I speak of course about the impending defeat of Barry Goldwater."[216] Much of the audience was in shock. They had expected to hear a speech calling them to increased campaign work and they were being told that their efforts would not result in victory. As Bob Bauman noted, "There were kids who came and expected to be told, 'You are going to win, here we are going to win the battle for the Lord,' and here they were told that that wasn't the case, and that we weren't going to win the battle for the Lord."[217] But Buckley went on to put the situation in perspective,

> *If it were not for the presence of Goldwater as a candidate for the Republican party our opportunity to proselytize on a truly national scale would not exist…The point of the present occasion is to win recruits whose attention we might never have attracted but for Barry Goldwater; to win them, not only for November the third, but for future Novembers; to infuse the conservative spirit in enough people to entitle us to look about us, on November 4th, not at the ashes of defeat, but at the well-planted seeds of hope, which will flower on a great November day in the future, if there is a future.[218]*

While depressing the immediate enthusiasm of some in attendance, it refocused the attention of many YAF leaders to what came next, to the continuing battle for conservatism after election day and reinforced Lee Edwards early observation that there needed to be a 25 year plan to bring about a more conservative America. Taking the initiative, YAF launched a major membership recruitment drive that produced some 2,500 new members in October and a like number in November – young people who were committed to the long-term effort to advance conservatism.

When the votes were counted some 27 million Americans had voted for Barry Goldwater, far less than those who voted for Lyndon Johnson. The Republican candidate had carried only six states. Some years later Goldwater reflected back on the 1964 campaign and was asked if he were simply ahead of his time: " No, I think the basic reason was that the country wasn't ready, and I don't think they'd ever be ready, to have three presidents in two years. I've come to that conclusion a long time ago. I think that was the main reason."[219] The candidate, not the philosophy, had lost the election. Yet, on further reflection, it was the campaign that had failed the candidate as much as the candidate had failed the campaign.

Whatever the reasons, the Goldwater campaign had failed and the impact of that failure would have consequences for Young Americans for Freedom. The optimism of youth had to be tempered by the reality of defeat. To some, the defeat was demoralizing and their political involvement came to an end.[220] According to Board Member Alan MacKay, however, "there were very few people, despite their disappointment, who said 'That's it for politics.' The almost universal reaction was 'By God, we're not going to let that happen again. We're going to go out and take control of the Republican Party.'"[221] Just as MacKay recalled, the campaign itself brought a significant increase in YAF's membership, many of whom were high school students attracted to the Goldwater campaign and determined to continue their involvement.

YAF provided a melding together of the philosophical and the political. More than merely the temporary, there was a lasting impact that would be felt throughout the careers of many YAF alumni from that era. The long-term impact of the campaign was positive in other ways also. As Lee Edwards later noted, "Thousands of young conservatives entered politics because of Barry Goldwater's run for the presidency. Today they sit in Congress or head think tanks or manage government agencies or edit magazines. They form a national network committed to conservatism."[222]

The campaign had been a baptism by fire, the first important effort to leave the notion of the "remnant" behind and build a mass movement for conservatism. It had shown that, properly approached, there were millions of Americans who could be rallied behind the banner of conservatism, not merely a small band of ideologues and true believers.[223] Young Americans for Freedom had established itself as a national organization comprising dedicated members who were rebelling against the status quo and attacking entrenched elites – an approach that would continue for the remainder of the decade on college campuses. YAF had made conservatism exciting and produced a generation of activists who would go on to lead numerous conservative organizations and fight for an endless number of causes.

Writing prior to the 1980 presidential election, political columnist David Broder claimed that

> YAF has unquestionably been the primary breeding ground and training ground for the new generation of conservative leaders.... What struck me is that the YAF alumni have profited from the losing battles they have been engaged in. I'm sure some got discouraged and dropped out along the way but those who survived have been toughened by the experience and have put the lessons they learned to good use.[224]

Many of those YAF alumni of the Goldwater campaign went on to assume leadership positions in the Reagan Administration and continue even today at the forefront of conservative organizations, in state and local government, and as a conservative presence in Congress and the Federal government.

The Goldwater campaign also brought to the forefront a new spokesman for conservatism and hero for the YAF members. Throughout the entire Fall campaign, the one successful element appeared to be a thirty-minute television appeal by a Hollywood actor, Ronald Reagan. Although some in the Goldwater campaign tried to stop it from ever being aired, "A Time for Choosing" raised nearly $600,000 for the national campaign through a brief plea for funds.[225]

Reagan was on his way to becoming the leading political personality for the conservative movement, the Governor of California, and eventually the President of the United States. As Reagan noted in his autobiography, "Of course, I didn't know it then, but that speech was one of the most important milestones in my life – another one of those unexpected turns in the road that led me onto a path I never expected to take."[226]

It was in this context that YAF took the Goldwater campaign not as a defeat but, rather, as an organizing tool and a framework on which to build for future efforts. It worked at promoting a conservative alternative for American society as well as developing new leadership and in so doing would help to transform American politics. Historian Jonathan Schoenwald noted,

> *Only YAF successfully bucked the trend of declining grassroots activism among conservative groups, and in the wake of the John Birch Society's demise, YAF filled in as the one group through which young people could meet, work together to achieve results, and then move on to another project, staying busy in their fight against the Left.[227]*

In the post-Goldwater period, YAF continued to recruit young people, training them in activist tactics and responsible conservatism, providing them with a means to work towards the victories that would come some fifteen to thirty years later, first with the election of Ronald Reagan to the presidency and the eventual Republican majority in Congress in 1994.

The first word in the organization's name indicated an age limit to active involvement and it had developed an image as a predominantly student organization. Thus, YAF's older members and the now developing alumni core needed an outlet for continued activity reflecting the responsible conservative position they had worked hard to develop and maintain. Such an outlet would provide a means for them to work as equals with other more senior political activists. To accomplish this, Bob Bauman contacted Marvin Liebman during the Fall of 1964 and proposed an organization for YAF graduates and others. Liebman suggested that they meet with Bill Buckley and when they did Buckley enthusiastically supported the idea.[228] Buckley agreed to host a planning meeting at his office on the Saturday after Goldwater's defeat. Agreement was reached among those present and the new effort was underway.[229]

On December 18th, the initial Board of Directors for the American Conservative Union (ACU) met at the Statler-Hilton Hotel in Washington. Members included Buckley, Bauman, and Liebman along with several other conservative leaders. Congressman Donald Bruce was designated to serve as

Chairman and for the next twenty years a Member of Congress would hold this position. The following day forty-seven leading conservatives joined together with the new Board for the founding conference. As Liebman recalls, "the efforts to create a conservative organization to counter the powerful influence of the Americans for Democratic Action were finally bearing fruit. We aimed to be the ADA of the Right. The American Conservative Union was well on its way." [230] The name was chosen because it had "the ring of permanence" and would be representative of an inclusive responsible conservatism. Its mission was to consolidate conservative support, mold public opinion, and encourage political action.

The ACU provided a place for continued activism by those who had graduated from YAF or from some of the smaller groups that did not survive after the Goldwater loss. ACU gave conservatives a home separate and apart from the regular Republican Party organization.[231] Throughout its history, YAF alumni have been at the forefront of the American Conservative Union's leadership. Just as YAF had helped create the ACU, the new organization in turn went on to become the source for the creation of the Conservative Victory Fund, the National Journalism Center, and the American Legislative Exchange Council – all of which continue to contribute to the conservative movement in the 21st century.

When 1964 came to a close YAF could look back with pride on its role in the Goldwater campaign and its contribution to the development of the conservative movement. By the mid-60s some of the original leaders would move on to new challenges, including helping to build the American Conservative Union. Still others would assume positions in government, law, business and the academy. But the impact and influence of Young Americans for Freedom on their lives would be felt for many years. As writer Niels Bjerre-Poulsen noted, "student politics provided a field of practice for a new generation of political activists who would in time take their place in the emerging conservative counter-establishment."[232] Some would fade away from YAF or from direct political involvement but the impact of those years of involvement would remain with them throughout their careers.

The lasting influence of the Goldwater campaign would be felt in American politics for the next forty years as conservatives began the takeover of the Republican Party structure, gained the nomination and election of Ronald Reagan and thirty years after the Goldwater campaign took control of both chambers of the United States Congress for the first time in more than forty years.

Looking ahead, YAF had recruited thousands of new members and expanded its operations to more campuses and communities. Working with others, it had created an organization to keep its alumni active and involved. It had gained the respect of the Republican Party organization and the recognition of the national media as a major player in the political arena. Now it was prepared to move on to newer and much different challenges involving both foreign policy and campus issues. There was much yet to be done for conservatism.

— 4 —

The Cause Must Go On

THE DEFEAT OF BARRY GOLDWATER DID NOT DETER the YAF leadership from its commitment to advance the principles outlined in the organization's Sharon Statement. There were thousands of additional young people now committed to the cause who were seeking ways to continue their involvement. Young Americans for Freedom would be the vehicle for their efforts in high schools, on college campuses, and in communities across the nation. The emphasis on conservative principles remained important to YAF and to its members. Whether dealing with campus issues or national defense, holding educational seminars and distributing books and articles on philosophical points or training members in political and organizational techniques, YAF would continue to expand its programs and its membership.

Despite his defeat, Barry Goldwater remained committed to Young Americans for Freedom and the conservative movement he had led into battle in 1964. In what was one of his first speeches after the election, Goldwater spoke at an event sponsored by the YAF chapter at Northern Arizona University with more than one thousand in attendance. Goldwater would continue to support YAF in many ways over the next several years, signing letters of support, speaking on campuses and appearing at many YAF national conventions. Ten years later, in 1974, it would be Young Americans for Freedom that would sponsor, with Goldwater as the honored guest, a ten-year reunion in San Francisco commemorating his presidential nomination victory.

Buckley for Mayor

No single individual reflected the conservative movement in America more than William F. Buckley, Jr., always ready to launch a new publication, organization, media program or campaign to advance the conservative philosophy he so deeply held and effectively advocated. With the defeat of Barry Goldwater there was a need to rally conservatives and expand the base, not so much around a candidacy as around a set of policies and programs that applied the conservative philosophy. Once again, Bill Buckley would be the central figure in another critical time for conservatism.

By early June of 1965, rumors began to surface that Buckley might run for Mayor of New York City, viewing the campaign as both a vehicle for spreading his conservative philosophy as well as standing in opposition to the liberal dominance of the New York Republican Party. While the party primary elections would not be held until September, it became apparent by June that the Republican Party would nominate Congressman John V. Lindsay as its candidate for mayor. Lindsay had developed the reputation as perhaps the single most liberal Republican in the House of Representatives and, along with several other New York Republicans, had refused to support Barry Goldwater's candidacy for President the previous year. In addition to the Republican nomination, Lindsay received the Liberal Party's support for Mayor.

On June 24th, Buckley made it official as he announced his candidacy for Mayor on the Conservative Party ticket. In so doing, he laid out a number of general principles upon which his later policy positions would be based. The candidacy would be a campaign of ideas as the author and editor spelled out his specific proposals to deal with the many problems confronting the city. Over the following weeks Buckley issued numerous positions papers covering topics as diverse as crime, drugs, pollution, water, education, welfare, taxation, housing, and on and on.[233]

The Buckley campaign became a crusade for young conservatives throughout the Greater New York City area. One week after Buckley announced his candidacy, a group of YAF members and supporters displayed "Buckley for Mayor" signs and chanted "We Want Buckley!" as John Lindsay opened his Richmond Hills, Queens campaign headquarters.[234] Heading up the "Youth for Buckley" effort was Don Pemberton, New York YAF State Chairman, while another YAF member, Neal Freeman, served as a personal aide to the candidate. It was Staten Island YAF that opened the first Buckley for Mayor storefront. From all parts of the City as well as from neighboring areas of New Jersey, Connecticut, and Long Island, YAF members worked to promote the campaign.[235]

The impact of the campaign was substantial. Pemberton, the YAF State

Chairman, explained that the campaign provided an avenue for the organization into more liberal campuses in the City, surfacing the conservative students who were present and interested in an on-going political involvement. As it developed, the Buckley campaign reflected a recognition of the changing dynamics of American conservatism. By the mid-1960s, YAF's membership, much as the support for conservatism in general, became more middle-class and ethnic than Ivy League. Thus, while the WASP Lindsay retained the support of his Silk Stocking district voters in Manhattan and most Protestant Republicans, Buckley's appeal was to the outer boroughs of the City, especially Queens and Staten Island.

When Election Day came and the votes were counted, Buckley received 341,226 votes on the Conservative Party line in a city with only 15,535 registered Conservative Party members. His total represented 13.4% of the vote, ranging from a high of 25.2% of the vote in Staten Island down to only 7.2% in Manhattan, home to the Silk Stocking Republicans to whom his appeal had originally been directed. Although one of the objectives was to prevent a liberal Republican from being elected, in the end, Lindsay received the most votes and became Mayor.

No one had expected Buckley to win. His famous response to the question of what would he do first upon election was that he would demand a recount. But this campaign of ideas, issues and philosophy had caught national attention and rallied his young supporters for future battles. Across the continent, a similar campaign was taking shape; this time it would be with a candidate and in a political environment where victory was indeed possible.

Although it was several months after the original founding date of September 11, Young Americans for Freedom took note of its 5th anniversary with a "Salute to YAF" banquet at the Shoreham Hotel in Washington, DC on May 9, 1966. Some 1,300 people, including YAF leaders, alumni, and National Advisory Board members were in a celebratory mood. It was a night for honoring the young conservative organization, but also for stressing the bi-partisan nature of mid-century conservatism in America. Appropriately enough, it was the senior Democratic Senator from Florida, speaking before Goldwater, who reminded the audience that there were conservatives in both political parties who deserve the support of YAF members. Spessard Holland told those present that "not all who love the Constitution and conservatism are in one party. You must pick out the people you believe in and the causes you believe in and fight for those people and causes. Pick your shots."[236]

Then it was time for the 1964 Republican presidential candidate. As writer James Jackson Kilpatrick observed, "When Barry's time came at last, they brought down the roof. For a couple of minutes, we were back in San Francisco."[237] Goldwater told them that his dedication was not to elective office or to party politics but rather to the cause he shared with those present. As he said, "I wouldn't be here tonight if not for the fact that I'm worried for our country. I could sit on my hill in Arizona, but I'm concerned about freedom."[238] He went on to remind those present that their task was to advance a philosophy, a task that involved much more than political action. "You are not a political party, not even a second cousin to a political party. You are conservative and there's nothing wrong about being conservative."[239] To Goldwater the need was essential and the reason obvious: "Conservatism remains today the only successful political philosophy ever known by man. Let's make progress on the proven values of the past. Freedom is our only cause."[240]

As summer 1966 approached, YAF's attention turned to developing new leadership and building a presence in more communities and on more college and high school campuses. To accomplish this, the organization undertook a number of programs including a summer Leadership Conference held at Franklin & Marshall College in Lancaster, Pennsylvania, designed to produce more articulate spokesmen, better coordinated efforts, and more effective conservative activity on the college campuses. More than 175 YAF campus leaders from 32 states attended representing a large cross-section of the 192 college chapters of Young Americans for Freedom at that time. Each morning during the eight days of the summer school the students heard lectures on conservative philosophy; workshops on chapter activities and programs were held in the afternoon while evenings were devoted to speakers on Communist ideology and practice followed by lengthy "bull sessions" with speakers and other participants.

The summer school was highly successful in producing a new cadre of trained leaders for the organization, individuals who were only in elementary or middle school when YAF was founded in 1960. Many of these younger members were introduced to their first direct education on the techniques of public relations, the tools of debating, and the directing of issues to serve one's overall philosophical objectives. Out of this experience would come the leaders that would carry Young Americans for Freedom not only through the remainder of the 1960s but also into the next decade of its history.

Reagan as Candidate

Only a few months after the Goldwater defeat, YAFers were already promoting the possibility of a Ronald Reagan candidacy for Governor of California. On January 4, 1966, he formally announced his candidacy for Governor in a statewide television special followed by a news conference. YAF members were ecstatic. The February 1966 cover article in the organization's national magazine was titled "The Republican More Like JFK Than Any Other," a characterization that would be viewed as prescient several years later when Reagan entered the White House. Even before he had been elected Governor, a number of YAF activists were focusing on Reagan as a future presidential candidate. In a poll of 175 YAF members at the Summer 1966 leadership conference, the preference for 1968 was Reagan 53%, Goldwater 30%, Nixon 15% and Romney 1%. The torch had already been passed.

California YAF was to play a major role in Reagan's campaign for the Republican nomination against George Christopher, former Mayor of San Francisco, and in the general election against incumbent Governor Edmund "Pat" Brown. It was a reciprocal relationship with several young Reagan workers being brought into the YAF organization just as YAF members assumed leadership roles in the campaign.

By the end of 1966, YAF clearly had a new hero who had become the Governor of the largest state. Bill Saracino noted, "After he became Governor, Reagan was a shorthand way of describing what YAF stood for." While especially true in California, this was becoming ever more accurate all across the nation. After all, Reagan had joined the YAF National Advisory Board in 1962, had signed a fundraising letter for the organization that same year, and had appeared at various YAF rallies, especially during the Goldwater campaign. While Bill Buckley remained the intellectual and organizational godfather, and Goldwater was the candidate of the past around whom they had united, Reagan now represented the political future for those in Young Americans for Freedom.

Beginning as early as 1967, thousands of Californians attempted to convince Governor Ronald Reagan to move from being merely a favorite son in 1968 to a serious candidate for the presidency, encouraging him to use the large bloc of delegates from the Golden State as leverage. California YAF members were in the forefront of this effort. As Congressman Dana Rohrabacher recalled, "We served as the advance guard for Ronald Reagan's gubernatorial campaign and again in 1968 during his first faint-hearted try at the Presidency."[241] When the YAF National Board of Directors was polled on their presidential preference, only two (David Keene and Gerald Plas) of the 21 members at the meeting supported Richard Nixon, with the other nineteen all backing Reagan.[242] While the leadership of YAF was clearly behind the California Governor, the membership was more evenly split. Reflecting that closer division among the membership at large, the Summer 1968 issue of *New Guard* featured two competing articles advocating the candidacies of Reagan and Nixon. [243] This level of support for Nixon among YAF members, however, was transitory. By the time of the Summer 1969 membership survey one year later, after Nixon's election as President, when asked with which political figure they most closely identified, the results were Goldwater 39 %, Reagan 37%, Nixon

9%, Wallace 6% with 9% scattered among others.[244]

One fact was clear from both surveys, however. There was little support among YAF members for Alabama Governor George Wallace. As early as 1966, Robert Schuettinger, one of the founders of YAF, concluded, "Wallace's supporters are united only in a common pursuit of power, jobs, and favors. There is absolutely no cohesion of principle or ideology in his ranks."[245] YAF National Chairman Alan MacKay, while recognizing that Wallace could be an appealing speaker, called him a "Pied Piper of pseudo-conservatism."[246] YAF's magazine, *New Guard* declared "The small percentage of Wallace supporters – which is 100 percent too large – is an official embarrassment to YAF leaders. The former Alabama Governor is typically referred to in the national office as a 'populist demagogue' who exacerbates racial prejudice for personal gain, and who would destroy conservative politics."[247] Clearly, the leadership of Young Americans for Freedom was not disposed to support Wallace, especially when contrasted with a conservative such as Reagan or, in the 1968 presidential election, a less-than-conservative Nixon.

While YAF had played a central role at the 1964 Republican National Convention as essential supporters of the Goldwater campaign, the organization's involvement in Miami Beach in 1968 would be substantially different. Once again, hundreds of YAF members gathered in the convention city and were treated to a series of meetings and speeches directed to them but this time most of those politically involved were supporting an outsider candidate who would fail to win the party's nomination. One of the most unforgettable experiences took place when a group of some thirty Youth for Reagan students welcomed Reagan to his headquarters hotel. Youth for Reagan leader Mike Thompson recalled, "Reagan came in, sat with us in the lobby, talked to us for about twenty minutes, thanked us. Quite a guy!"[248]

While Reagan maintained that he never wanted to be an actual candidate and "never believed that a former actor who had only been a governor a matter of months could suddenly say he wanted to be president," his name was placed in nomination and he received 182 votes. As one writer noted, "Reagan had the support of the grass roots, but Nixon had the backing of conservative political leaders, which was enough in 1968."[249] Still others postulated that had emotion ruled, nearly ninety percent of the delegates from the South would have gone to Reagan.

Despite the disappointment of not seeing their candidate win the nomination, there were meaningful experiences for many of the young Reagan supporters, experiences that testified to the character of Ronald Reagan. Mike Thompson recently recalled two post-nomination incidents involving the candidate and his young supporters.

When Reagan lost the nomination, out of the arena came groups of YAF kids with Reagan signs, disheartened for the loss but excited nonetheless. Up to one group of these young Reagan supporters came a black limousine and stopped. Down came the back window and there was the Governor and Mrs. Reagan. They chatted with these kids, thanked them, etc.

The next day, a group of students with Reagan bumper stickers all over their car are parked at a traffic light and they hear a car honking next to them. There was Reagan, window down in his limousine, and he thanks the kids.[250]

It was experiences such as these that endeared Ronald Reagan to these YAF members, many of whom would go on to play critical roles in future presidential campaigns, including those of Reagan himself in 1976, 1980 and 1984.

As the YAF members left Miami Beach and eventually headed back to campus for the Fall semester, they remained optimistic about the future of their organization and their country. Nixon would go on and win the election in November 1968. YAF's relationship with the new administration started on a positive note but would soon develop into a problematic relationship as the new decade began.

Beyond its involvement in the Reagan effort at the Republican National Convention and the subsequent general election, much of YAF's activity during 1968 was focused on supporting the effort in Vietnam, combating New Left violence and disruption on campus, and engaging in political action. As might be expected, with its Governor a prominent member of the YAF National Advisory Board, California was a hotbed of YAF political activity. The organization's 1968 state convention was attended by over 250 students and featured speeches by Governor Reagan, United States Senator George Murphy, and Superintendent of Instruction Dr. Max Rafferty who had just obtained the Republican nomination for the United States Senate.

But YAF was more than an organization committed to electoral politics. It was committed to opposing communism in all forms, to advancing the principles of limited government and free market economics, and to ensuring the opportunity for all students to receive an education in a campus environment conducive to learning. These three concerns: the communist challenge, the proper role for government, and the threat of New Left violence were to consume much of YAF's attention over the next few years.

The Communist Challenge

Over the last half of the decade, anti-communist activity became even more important to Young Americans for Freedom. Two actions by the Johnson Administration were the cause for this increased focus: the determination to "build bridges" to Eastern European Communist countries and the decision to escalate American involvement in the Vietnam conflict.

The anti-communism of YAF was clearly dominant in the organization's views on world trade. One of the major political and public relations successes for YAF, not simply in 1965 but historically as to the lasting contribution of the organization, was its efforts against East-West trade and, specifically, the Firestone Tire and Rubber Company's plans to build a synthetic rubber plant in Romania. During what would be the last year of his presidency, John F. Kennedy promoted increased trade with Eastern Europe as part of an overall policy of "peaceful coexistence."

Upon assuming the office of President, Lyndon Johnson continued this policy but added "differentiation" by which the United States enhanced its relations with Communist states that sought greater autonomy from the Soviet Union. In early 1964, Secretary of State Dean Rusk outlined this policy in a speech, "Why we treat different Communist countries differently," in which he put forth specific measures to enhance trade relations with Eastern Europe. This was followed by President Johnson's May 1964 address at Virginia Military Institute outlining his "bridge building" policy. The President declared "We will continue to build bridges across the gulf which has divided us from Eastern Europe. They will be bridges of increased trade, of ideas, of visitors, and of humanitarian aid."[251]

Romania was one such country ready to take advantage of this outreach from the United States. With Romania wanting to build up its industrial capacity and needing access to advanced technology and the Johnson Administration wanting to increase relations with Eastern European Communist nations, the essential elements of a trade deal were present. Discussions began for Romania to purchase American synthetic rubber technology.

In late May 1964, immediately after the President's "bridge building" address, formal talks began between the United States and Romania. Communist officials submitted a list of fifteen manufacturing plants they wanted to buy, topped by two synthetic rubber manufacturing plants. The Defense Department expressed concern due to the possible military applications and export to the USSR which then had a shortage of synthetic rubber used for aircraft tires. Nevertheless, the State Department saw this as an opening for American business to Eastern Europe and the United States government agreed to license the sale of eleven of the fifteen plants requested, including the two synthetic rubber plants and a nuclear electric power station.

Shortly after general approval was granted, Romanian officials visited several firms that expressed interest in building the rubber plants, including Firestone, B. F. Goodrich, and Goodyear. By the first week of January 1965, Firestone had come to an agreement with Romania to sell two synthetic rubber manufacturing plants. The deal was cut and it had the clear backing of the Johnson Administration. As the media became aware of the Firestone deal, *Human Events* published an article on the topic. Among those who read the article was David Walter, treasurer of Philadelphia YAF, who contacted his fellow members and prepared a plan of action. Walter and Philadelphia YAF Chairman Jay Parker began to draw up their plans for local action and consider how best to involve others in their efforts.

By March, the United States escalation in Vietnam had begun and with American troops battling Communist forces in Southeast Asia, the reasons for opposing East-West trade had increased. That same month, Philadelphia YAF started demonstrations outside Firestone dealerships. The picketers' signs proclaimed: "Firestone Sells the USA Down the Red River," "Scrap Iron for Japan, II World War, Now Synthetic Rubber for Soviets" and other similar messages. Their handouts claimed that Romania supplied China with heavy-duty trucks that were then provided to North Vietnam with whom the United States was at war.

On April 14th, a memo was sent to all YAF chapter chairmen explaining the reasons for opposing Firestone's sale of two synthetic rubber manufacturing plants to Romania and calling upon them to join a national protest against the company. That launched a nationwide campaign of picket lines, demonstrations, letter writing campaigns, and news releases against Firestone and its local dealers. Pickets started appearing before Firestone stores in Brooklyn, Cleveland, Atlanta, Los Angeles, Providence, Indianapolis, Miami, and other smaller communities.

While the picketing received significant local media coverage and resulted in complaints by several local dealers to Firestone claiming lost business, the corporate officials were not deterred. It would take more drastic action by the national organization to squash the deal. That came when National YAF told Firestone that it was considering handing out 500,000 pamphlets at the "Indianapolis 500" race on Memorial Day. The pamphlets would explain Firestone's plans to build a plant in Romania at a time when Americans were fighting Communist forces in Vietnam. The kicker came when YAF officials said they might hire an airplane to fly back and forth over the race site with a banner opposing the Firestone deal. YAF also made plans to set up a "Committee Against Slave Labor" booth outside the Indianapolis 500 to expose labor practices in Communist countries.

On April 20th, one month after Philadelphia YAF had begun its picketing at area Firestone dealerships, the corporate office in Akron, Ohio sent out a brief but historic news release: "The Firestone Tire and Rubber Company has terminated negotiations for a contract to design and equip a synthetic rubber plant in Rumania." [252] While Firestone took the heat for attempting to implement Johnson's "bridge building" policies, the Administration was reluctant to criticize YAF because it did not want to alienate YAF as a supporter in the Vietnam War.

Although some in the Administration wished the entire issue would simply go away, that would not be the case. The media picked up the story and then various members of Congress on both sides got involved. Young Americans for Freedom was seen as the responsible (or irresponsible) party in ending the deal with Communist Romania. As Bernard Gwertzman reported in the *Washington Evening Star*, "the conservative Young Americans for Freedom almost single-handedly caused giant Firestone, the nation's second largest rubber manufacturer, to drop the deal." It was, he claimed, "a severe embarrassment to the State Department."[253]

Newspapers on both sides of the ideological spectrum took note of YAF's success. The *Washington Post* editorialized against what they called a "slashed tires" campaign by YAF. Calling Romania "Westward moving" they were conveniently overlooking the fact that it was then headed by Nicolae Ceausescu, who would become the most brutal of all East European dictators. [254] From the other side came praise for YAF's actions. As the *Richmond News Leader* editorialized, "The YAFers were right to show Firestone the fallacy of strengthening the dedicated enemies of our system."[255] This media coverage heightened the interest of left-wing members of the Senate whose vitriolic comments would keep the issue alive for the next two months.

The Firestone effort was only one of many campaigns undertaken by YAF in opposition to trade with Communist countries, although clearly the most successful. YAF pledged to focus on contracts "which plainly give aid and comfort to the Communist enemy by building up their military power." The statement made it clear that YAF's opposition to such trade would continue and realized that this would put them in opposition to the President with whom they agreed on Vietnam.

The following year YAF was confronted with another major United States corporation attempting to trade with a Communist nation. This time, it was the Soviet Union and the company was American Motors whose former head, Governor George Romney of Michigan, was rumored to be considering a candidacy for President of the United States in 1968. In November 1966, A.M.C. sought to become the first United States auto firm to sell cars directly in the Soviet Union or other Communist nations in Eastern Europe.

Once again, direct action developed from the local chapter level. Ted G. Carpenter, chairman of the University of Wisconsin-Milwaukee YAF, sent a letter to National YAF announcing the chapter's plans to boycott American Motors and urging other chapters to join them. By mid-December, YAF pickets appeared at A.M.C.'s Rambler agencies in Indiana as well as at the American Motors plant in Milwaukee. On January 3, 1967, YAF's Executive Director, David R. Jones, sent a detailed memo titled "National YAF Opposition to American Motors Communist Trade Deal." Jones pointed out that YAF's long-standing opposition to trade of strategic goods with Communist countries was even stronger now because of the war in Vietnam. Selling autos to the Soviet Union was viewed as allowing them to divert metals, rubber, and other materials into military industrial aid to the North Vietnamese and the Viet Cong. YAF chapters were asked to establish picket lines outside American Motors dealerships beginning Monday, January 9, 1967. The purpose would be to inform the public about the negotiations to sell cars to the Soviet Union – not to encourage a boycott.

On January 9th, pickets appeared before A.M.C. dealerships in several cities across the country. One week later, less than two months after its original decision to sell cars in the Soviet Union, American Motors wired YAF and declared that, "American Motors has no plans, programs, or intentions to trade with Communist bloc nations… Our intentions are to continue our growing trade with our traditional customers all of whom would certainly be numbered as traditional allies and not members of the Communist bloc."[256] A second major American corporation had backed down under pressure from Young Americans for Freedom.

YAF organized a similar campaign in opposition to the sale of computer technology but in this instance the company, International Business Machines, had little direct competition and dealt mainly with corporations rather than consumers. Unfortunately, unlike the Firestone and American Motors campaigns, this one did not turn out as well for YAF. IBM continued to sell its various computers to Eastern European nations, maintaining they were of low capacity and not of significant military value. Nevertheless, YAF did receive ample publicity for its position opposing East-West trade. The setback with IBM only convinced YAF that a more concerted and focused educational and public relations campaign was needed. To help achieve this, National YAF prepared and distributed an "East-West Trade Information and Action Kit." Two years later in 1970 Ford Motor Company announced that it planned to build a truck factory in the Soviet Union.[257] The proposed plant would produce 150,000 heavy-duty trucks a year, compared to total U.S. production of only 125,000 heavy-duty trucks in 1969. According to an article in *Human Events*, "If Ford concludes a deal with the Soviets, YAF will almost certainly engage in a massive campaign against the company, though the activist youth organization is holding fire pending an inquiry into the entire matter."[258] This time YAF had a powerful ally in Defense Secretary Melvin Laird who made known his opposition to Ford assisting in the construction of a Soviet truck plant. Shortly thereafter, Henry Ford II announced that the company had rejected the Soviet proposal and a letter to that effect was delivered to the Soviet Embassy in Washington, D.C. This time, YAF's pickets, petitions, and demonstrations had been kept in reserve and were not needed to achieve their objective.

The Mack Truck Corporation was the next object of YAF's concern when it announced plans in 1971 to build what would be the world's largest truck manufacturing plant in the Soviet Union, basically a proposal that Ford had turned down the previous year.[259] The organization's protests started in July when Texas YAF learned that the company intended to negotiate with the Soviets for constructing the heavy-duty diesel truck plant in the Kama River area east of Moscow. State Chairman Jack Gullahorn noted that the vast majority of trucks supplying the North Vietnamese and Viet Cong were Russian built.

Houston YAF began picketing a local Mack Truck dealer on July 8 after local officials refused to meet with YAF. Following up on the local efforts, the national YAF office called on local chapters to become involved in the project and issued a news release announcing the campaign against Mack Truck. Soon thereafter, pickets appeared in California, Maryland, Washington, Pennsylvania, and other states. While Pennsylvania YAF leaders Bob Moffit and Tom Walsh had a lengthy conversation with Zenon C. R. Hansen, the Mack Truck President, refused to back away from the proposed deal. However, on September 15th, President Hansen announced that Mack Truck's letter of intent to build the plant had expired. The three month campaign had succeeded.[260] Pennsylvania YAF State Chairman Frank Donatelli noted "YAF played the major role in this campaign and pledges to take on any other American company in the future that wishes to trade with the Reds."

YAF's position on trade remained consistent from the presidency of John F. Kennedy forward, while both Democrats and Republicans occupied the White House. During the mid-60s to the mid-70s, an essential part of that argument concerned the conflict in Vietnam where the Soviets and their surrogates were supplying the force allayed against American troops and our allies. It was this linkage between East-West trade and the Vietnam conflict that together reflected the strong anti-communism of YAF as originally expressed in the Sharon Statement. But even after the Vietnam war, the organization maintained its opposition to East-West trade until the demise of the Soviet Union in 1991. YAF favored free trade among free nations but not trade with those aligned against freedom and the United States.

Vietnam: the Early Years

Long before the American public became aware of the scope of the conflict in Southeast Asia, Young Americans for Freedom was taking note of the Communist challenge to the independence of South Vietnam. In late 1961, one writer for *New Guard* favorably reviewed Bernard Fall's *Street Without Joy* and cited his critique of France for failing to invade guerilla sanctuaries in China during the 1954 war. A few months later, Robert Harley, recently returned from a tour of Southeast Asia, stressed the need for continued American involvement in assisting the South Vietnamese defeat the Communist attempt to dominate Indochina. [261] By 1964, one YAF National Director was advocating the United States undertake a coordinated effort to sponsor guerrillas and guerrilla warfare around the globe in opposition to Communist regimes. By seeking out and supporting counter-revolutionaries, the United States could launch a positive freedom offensive against world communism.[262]

The conflict in Vietnam became a major focus of activity for Young Americans for Freedom soon after the Goldwater defeat. In March 1965 the Johnson Administration began its escalation of troops in Vietnam. On April 7th, President Johnson delivered a major speech on Vietnam at Johns Hopkins University. He outlined the reasons for a commitment to Vietnam and said the United States would enter unconditional discussions at any time but would continue bombing while the discussions continued.

The following month, *New Guard* editorialized that "it was a masterful stroke of foreign policy." Despite their differences on trade and domestic issues, YAF was willing to credit Johnson for his policy on Vietnam. To back up their support, National Chairman Bob Bauman called on the "overwhelming majority of the young people in America who support President Johnson's policy" on Vietnam to "make their support known....we must not let it seem for one minute that the small cliques of pacifists, left-wing extremists and beatniks calling for retreat speak for our generation."

Responding to Bauman's call for action, across the country YAF chapters circulated petitions in support of the President's policy and forwarded them to the White House. On May 24, 1965, Carl E. Jaske, chairman of the University of Illinois YAF, wrote the President and enclosed petitions signed by 1,522 persons who supported the Vietnam war. At Michigan State University, YAF worked with others to collect signatures from 15,872 student, faculty, and community members on a petition of support. [263] From the State University of New York at Buffalo came petitions signed by 3,200 students and faculty in support of the war effort. Then in November, the White House received a telegram from Charles Hanson, YAF chairman at the University of Minnesota, with a petition signed by 9,000 students and faculty supporting the war effort. [264] Meanwhile, on April 24th, some 150 Chicago area YAFers countered a peace march by carrying replicas of black coffins, each representing a captive nation.[265]   Even more dramatic statements were made at some schools. Tim Hunter recalls his demonstration at the University of New Mexico where " I burned a Vietcong flag in front of the student union building in 1965 at the request of a U.S. Army Captain serving in combat in Vietnam."

Working with College Republicans and some local College Democratic chapters, YAF helped form a National Student Committee for the Defense of Vietnam that circulated and collected petitions on more than three hundred campuses. With nearly 500,000 signatures on the petitions, representatives of the committee met with Vice President Hubert Humphrey in January 1966.

Circulating petitions was not the only project undertaken by YAF members during the Fall of 1965. Local chapters also sponsored clothing and food drives for South Vietnamese citizens, mailed Christmas cards to American troops, "adopted" Vietnamese orphans, and undertook other similar projects to show support. These and other projects developed at the local level were designed not only to show support for the war effort at home but also to provide some meaningful assistance to those engaged in the battle against communism in South Vietnam.

As one young activist not involved in YAF noted, "By this point in the war, conservatives were providing the only real leadership on the campuses for the proposition that we should defend South Vietnam against Communist aggression."[266] After reviewing material from the time, historian Greg Schneider concluded that YAF had become "the most capable and the most vocal of conservative organizations in its denunciation of communism and its support for the U.S. war effort in Southeast Asia." [267] This analysis was supported by other scholars of the period who analyzed both support and opposition to the war by American students.[268]

It was a commitment to freedom, not only in the United States but throughout the world, that led many YAFers to rally behind the cause of South Vietnam. But also present was a skepticism about liberal politicians, those who were developing and executing the American strategy for dealing with the Communist aggression in Vietnam, that was leading more and more in YAF to question the Johnson Administration's determination and direction. In a *New Guard* editorial titled "No More Koreas!" YAF called for more intensive bombing of missile sites in North Vietnam and industrial complexes around Hanoi and Haiphong as well as the mining of Haiphong harbor. Many in YAF were convinced that the Johnson Administration's objective was not victory but negotiations with the North Vietnamese.[269]

By Fall 1966, YAF had launched a new ad hoc committee, Student Committee for Victory in Vietnam, under the leadership of Michael Thompson, a student at the University of Missouri and National Director of YAF. Thompson made clear the outcome sought by the members of his committee. "By victory we mean the pacification of the Viet Cong, an end to communist terror, the withdrawal of the North Vietnamese invaders from South Vietnam, and the creation of a climate of law and order in which a South Vietnamese government can function."[270] The creation of the "Victory" committee reflected a shift in the campus environment regarding the war as well as a move by YAF to slowly disassociate itself from the Johnson Administration.

For the first part of this divided decade, political debate and discussion on campus normally occurred in a civilized manner. Unfortunately, by the latter part of the 1960s, all this was to change on most campuses as debate was replaced by confrontation and violence became a tool of the left on campus. As the left became more violent, YAF served for some as an oasis of sanity. Mel Davey of the University of Rhode Island recalled, "I was a Vietnam Vet so it was nice to associate with people having acceptance and respect." Meanwhile, as the Vietnam protests gained in support and intensity, YAF began attracting more high school and college students on the appeal of patriotism as well as conservative philosophy, a pattern that would intensify as the so-called New Left began to broaden its areas of concern to the takeover of college campuses.

While YAF was becoming increasingly critical of the Administration's Vietnam policy, its members were even more critical of left-wing protesters, many of whom wanted the communists to succeed militarily. Thus, Tom Stokes of New York University YAF led one hundred students from NYU, Fordham, and Suffolk Community College to counter a demonstration by left-wing protesters outside a speech by Secretary of State Dean Rusk. YAF might have serious concerns over the policies being implemented by Rusk, but those concerns reflected tactical differences towards a common objective and not a desire to see the United States defeated.

1968 was also a year dominated by many other issues and concerns, including the murders of Martin Luther King, Jr. and then Robert F. Kennedy, the various urban riots that engulfed cities across the country, the intensification of New Left protests on campus, the announcement by President Johnson that he would not seek re-election, and the Republican presidential nomination battle that involved California Governor Reagan and New York Governor Rockefeller as well as the eventual nominee and successful candidate, Richard Nixon. There was hope that Nixon, with a strong record of anti-communism and a pledge that he had a "secret plan" to successfully end the war, might actually produce victory not only for the American troops but for the South Vietnamese who cherished their freedom from Communist domination.

In June 1969, President Nixon met with President Thieu of South Vietnam and announced the first phase of a withdrawal of American troops with 25,000 to be repatriated by August. Thus began the policy shift towards "Vietnamization" of the war. Nevertheless, this change in strategy did not deter the left from its efforts at pushing for total American withdrawal. The Student Mobilization Committee to End the War in Vietnam announced in July that they were planning a nationwide student strike on November 14th.[271] Meanwhile, another organization led by Sam Brown, the Vietnam Moratorium Committee, was organizing protest events on campuses to be held on October 15th.[272]

When the left conducted anti-Vietnam teach-ins and boycotted classes, YAF chapters made their pro-Vietnam positions known. At the University of Minnesota, YAF members held a pro-victory rally and burned a North Vietnamese flag.[273] When students arrived to attend the Moratorium rally outside the University of Maryland library, they were greeted by a YAF banner quoting President Kennedy's support for the battle against aggression in South Vietnam. Meanwhile, at Mount St. Mary's College, students saw "The NLF Wants You" posters appear on campus to reinforce the words of support given to the Moratorium by Hanoi's representative at the Paris Peace Talks.

While opposing what they viewed as a "sell out," by the Fall of 1969 YAF was becoming more uncertain as to President Nixon's objectives in Vietnam. An editorial in the November 1969 issue of *New Guard* advocated using only volunteer American troops in Vietnam, using the Navy and Air Force to bomb and blockade North Vietnam and to set the American objective as one designed to "end the war – win it – now."[274]

November brought about a joint effort by the two leading anti-war forces as the Vietnam Moratorium committee launched protests, teach-ins, and class boycotts on November 13 and 14 while the New Mobilization Committee to end The War in Vietnam (New Mobe) held a rally at the Washington Monument on Saturday November 15th. When the rally took place, some 250,000 listened as various speakers called for a rapid withdrawal of all U.S. troops from Vietnam.

Realizing that they could not match the crowd gathered in Washington by the New Mobe, the national office of YAF determined that they would sponsor a series of rallies, "teach-ins" and demonstrations across the country in December. The thrust of the YAF campaign was a simple message: "Tell It to Hanoi," emphasizing that those who wanted peace in Vietnam needed to direct their efforts at the aggressors who had started the war and continued to stymie efforts at a lasting peace agreement.[275]

Boston was the site of one of the first and also more successful "Tell It to Hanoi" rallies as the YAF organizers decided to hold it on Sunday December 7th, Pearl Harbor day. The centerpiece of the activities was a rally on Boston

Common that was preceded by a candlelight march from the State House and ended with the burning of a Viet Cong flag.[276] David Brudnoy titled his column in *National Review*, "This Time, *Our* Side in Boston Common," in describing the events of December 7th where "four or five thousand were in the field, to stand freezing for two and a half hours." The evening began as "candle-carrying students trooped behind a hundred-piece band and circumambulated the Commons, singing Woody Guthrie's 'This Land is Your Land' and shouting 'To Hell with Ho.'" According to Brudnoy, "Harvard YAFer Doug Cooper gave the evening's most thoughtful speech: ' The war is not hurting us as much as are its critics, who clamor only for material things; we need more than just a higher standard of living; we need a higher standard of character in America.'"[277]

Most YAF activities to counter the New Mobe took place, however on December 13-15, "Vietnam Alternative Weekend". As YAF National Chairman David Keene explained, Vietnam Alternative Weekend had two purposes, "to promote on college and high school campuses an understanding of the realities of the conflict in Vietnam and to demonstrate to the American people and to Hanoi that the majority of American students do not favor U.S. defeat." On more than 600 campuses across the nation, YAF presented speakers, conducted pro-Vietnam teach-ins, distributed one million copies of the tabloid, and circulated a petition.

Unfortunately, for some on the left, the right to protest was available only to those who agreed with them. Towson State College YAF decided to hold its Vietnam Alternative Weekend demonstration outside the Baltimore Peace Action Center headquarters. When the YAF members attempted to burn a cardboard replica of a Viet Cong flag, it was torn from the hands of Michael Davis. One police officer was pushed to the ground and others grabbed when they went to rescue Davis from the peace supporters. Davis later observed, "You can burn the American flag in this country but you can't burn the National Liberation (Vietcong) flag."[278] Meanwhile, at Purdue University leftists smashed a window and scrawled, "Die fascist pigs!" in the student center offices of Purdue YAF after the chapter distributed copies of the "Tell It to Hanoi" tabloid. Other pro-Vietnam efforts also met with violence as YAF attempted to counter the various "peace rallies" conducted in cities and on various campuses. Many, if not most, of these were in reality pro-Communist and pro-North Vietnam rallies rather than simply efforts to end war. When New York YAFers attempted to counter a peace rally in Central Park, they were met by leftists intent on physically silencing them. One more time, the point had been made that the so-called peace activists were intolerant of dissent.

With 1969 coming to a close, Young Americans for Freedom had shown that while they questioned the commitment of the Nixon Administration to victory in Vietnam, much as they had questioned the tactics of the Johnson Administration, they still believed in defeating communist aggression in Southeast Asia and helping to ensure the independence of South Vietnam. Once again, it was a difficult balancing act between support of the goal of defeating Communism in Vietnam and opposition to the administration in Washington on its policies in many other areas. As historian John Andrew noted, "Founded as an organization determined to launch a conservative crusade against the Establishment, ... the war had led YAF to defend the Establishment, even when it opposed some of its policies.[279] As the end of the decade approached, YAF would be challenged further on its policy towards Vietnam as well as its approach to the Nixon Administration in general.

In addition to its efforts against East-West trade and in favor of the battle against communism in Southeast Asia, Young Americans for Freedom launched a number of other anti-communist efforts throughout the latter half of the decade. YAF chapters sponsored appearances by a number of anti-communist speakers. A number of local chapters also entered anti-communist themed floats in community parades and distributed literature at civic gatherings. The plight of the Cuban people under Castro's communist regime was a recurring concern of many YAF chapters with programs and speakers featuring individuals who had escaped from Cuba.

The Eastern European nation of Czechoslovakia experienced serious change during the latter part of 1967 that resulted in the selection of Alexander Dubcek as the First Secretary of the Communist Party in January 1968. To the surprise of some, Dubcek turned out to be a reformer who thought he could produce "socialism with a human face" and began a process of liberalization known as the Prague Spring. For the first time since Communist occupation, Western publications were circulated and ideas could be expressed freely.

Two YAF leaders, Dana Rohrabacher and David Keene traveled to Eastern Europe during the late Spring and summer of 1968, spending three weeks in Czechoslovakia. Their experiences were recounted in *New Guard*. As Rohrabacher described the situation he found when meeting with Czech and Slovak students, "Everyone had great hopes for the future. More freedom was present than in thirty years. I even participated in a student demonstration to recognize Israel."[280] It was a time when the word freedom was taking on a new meaning as hope overcame despair. But the thaw came to an end as Soviet tanks and troops and those of four other Warsaw Pact countries invaded Czechoslovakia and once again the country was under the thumb of the Soviets.

The Czech crisis spurred nationwide protests by YAF chapters but, of course, the Left in the United States saw this as another opportunity to "blame America first." Two days after the invasion Senator George McGovern of South Dakota charged that the Johnson administration must bear "a considerable part of the blame" for the Soviet takeover of Czechoslovakia.[281] If only the U.S. government had taken a more positive attitude towards the Soviets they would not have felt threatened by the Prague Spring actions in Czechoslovakia. In support of the Czechs, YAF chapters picketed Federal buildings in Detroit, Atlanta, Honolulu, and Pittsburgh as well as in the Nation's Capital

YAF would continue to view Communism as the greatest threat to individual liberty and believe that the United States should stress victory over its ideological and political foe. Over the next few years, however, other challenges would confront the organization. On college campuses across the nation, New Left organizations began to resort to violence and destruction. In many cases, only YAF would stand against this nihilism and represent those students who were attending college to attain an education. While some of this leftist agitation used the Vietnam war as an issue around which to rally student opposition, it was clearly an organizing tactic for these radical organizations whose leadership was promoting not peace, but revolution on campus and in society at large.

The New Left and Campus Conflict

Not the least of the many changes underway during the 1960s was the choice of strategy and tactics by left-wing organizations, especially on America's college campuses. Left-wing student activity focused initially on promoting a foreign policy supposedly emphasizing peace and the advocacy of various schools of Marxism, moved on to assisting in the struggle for equal rights by Blacks in the southern United States, shifted to efforts to abolish university policies of "in loco parentis," and then moved to an all-out assault on American society and government. Throughout these developments, Young Americans for Freedom became the major campus organization opposing the excesses of the New Left and defending the rights of students to an education free from disruption and violence.

Begun in many instances as a protest to seek remedies for perceived grievances – often as mundane as dormitory regulations and the quality of food services – a shift in emphasis was occurring. By the mid-60s, "an increasing number of confrontations were based on the principle that students should govern their own affairs and should participate in making the policies of the institution."[282] This shift to a demand that students determine the rules on campus would lead to many subsequent confrontations and violent incidents.

Those active in Young Americans for Freedom were also concerned about the ability of students to make decisions for themselves and to experience the freedom implicit with becoming adults. As one college administrator commented about YAF's involvement on student issues, "they tend to be quiet in their style, and they have a disposition to work through regular channels." He went on to say, "they share with their peers on the Left an interest in student power, and they have worked hard on some campuses for a higher degree of involvement by students in the decision-making processes of the institution."[283] YAF chapters, in fact, often spoke out against many of the "in loco parentis" policies that restricted the freedom of individual students while defending their right to voluntarily enroll in Reserve Officer Training Corps courses and meet with recruiters from the military and private industries.

The New Right and the New Left, while both expressing concern over the quality of education and the rights of students, were moving in quite different directions. The left was moving its focus to a new target, one brought to the fore by the Johnson Administration's decision to expand the American involvement in Vietnam. In March 1965, anti-war faculty and SDS leaders at the University of Michigan organized the first "teach-in". Thirty-five other universities soon followed suit. When two speakers attempted to speak in favor of the war at the Berkeley teach-in, the same students who months earlier were protesting as part of the Free Speech Movement booed and harassed them.

Although started as an independent movement on the Berkeley campus, the protests were soon to be coordinated by one major national organization. Begun as the Student League for Industrial Democracy, the organization changed its official name in 1960 to Students for a Democratic Society (SDS) and was reformulated at its Port Huron conference in 1962. Leaving its anti-communist socialist roots behind, SDS increased its ties with the various Communist and Marxist groups then active, removing bars to Communist Party members. As one former leftist noted, by 1965 "it is now fashionable in Communist circles to belong to both SDS and a Communist organization."[284]

David Keene was a student at the University of Wisconsin at Madison during the mid-1960s and recently noted the change in attitudes among the left. "This was a time of growing foment on campus, but it didn't begin to turn violent until late 1965 and continued as the anti-war movement grew at Wisconsin over the next few years, culminating in a series of student strikes, the bombing of the 'Army Math Research Center' and the killing of a student." Madison became a focus for leftist activity over the next several years. Wisconsin SDS captured the university administration building, heckled Ted Kennedy and tried to prevent him from speaking on campus. When Lady Bird Johnson planned a visit to Madison, university officials, fearing what SDS might do, would not permit her on campus. The message to one observer was clear: "the Madison left had successfully given notice in 1966 that the right to free speech did not extend to anyone who took Lyndon Johnson's side."[285] What had begun two years earlier as a movement for free speech had degenerated into a campaign to prohibit speech by those with whom they disagreed.

No longer were demonstrations regarded by the left as a means to bring about specific changes on campus or in society. Rather, they were designed to create violent responses by the authorities that, in turn, would serve to radicalize even more students. To the leadership of SDS, violence did not beget more violence; it produced more recruits for the cause of overthrowing the dominant, repressive forces in society. As SDS and other New Left groups became more violent, YAF's appeal as a rallying point for the anti-protester began to take hold. According to Keene, "YAF's growth beyond the hard-core intellectual/activists that made up its membership from 1960-64 began as students reacted to the growth of the activist left as many saw YAF as the main opponent on campus of the SDS and similar groups."

The Left began to turn its attention to preventing Dow Chemical Company, maker of napalm and many consumer products, from recruiting on college campuses. In the Spring of 1967, University of Wisconsin SDS conducted the first sit-in to disrupt Dow recruiting efforts on the Madison campus. On other campuses, protests developed against research projects funded by the U.S. Department of Defense and in opposition to the Reserve Officer Training Corps programs.

At the same time, 1967 saw a long, hot summer of urban riots starting in Newark, spreading to Detroit, and then on to a hundred other cities. SNCC Chairman H. Rap Brown called it a "dress rehearsal for revolution" while SDS President Greg Calvert boasted that, "We are working to build a guerrilla force in an urban environment. We are actively organizing sedition."[286] Although the cities were aflame with destructive actions, mainly by Blacks encouraged by leftist groups, most campuses remained quiet as the majority of students were on summer break.

That Fall, the opposition to Dow's recruiting on campus became even more violent. On October 17, 1967, SDS launched its campaign on the University of Wisconsin Madison campus to prevent the company from meeting with students. According to one historian,

> *Three hundred SDSers grabbed and choked the students who were trying to get to the interviewers. Campus police officers attempted to rescue them but were beaten back by SDS. At that point the city police arrived. They were immediately hit with bricks and stomped on... Enraged, the Madison police fought back, injuring 175 SDSers*

and arresting anyone they could catch… After the Dow protest,
SDS vowed to "destroy" the University of Wisconsin.[287]

By the time of the anti-Dow confrontations David Keene was both a student at the University of Wisconsin and National Vice Chairman of Young Americans for Freedom. From his perspective, "the basic issue, put simply, was whether one group would be allowed to impose its values and desires on another by force."[288] YAF's magazine claimed that the issue was not Dow Chemical since defense contracts were only a small portion of its sales. If the issue were the war, SDS would be picketing large defense contractors. Rather Dow was only the start to a larger attack on American industry.

The first protest actions by SDS at Columbia University began in 1965 when the organization obstructed the annual Navy ROTC review. By the Spring of 1967, SDS organized a sit-in to protest CIA recruiting and the efforts of the Marine Corps to recruit on campus. By the Fall of 1967, those in favor of allowing recruiters of all kinds on campus formed the Students for a Free Campus (SFC) and distributed information in advance of an undergraduate referendum on the issue. When the votes were counted, open recruiting was endorsed by 67.6% of the vote. The Columbia SDS chapter continued to oppose recruiting by Dow and the military but began to shift its focus to the university's affiliation with the Institute for Defense Analysis (IDA) and the university's decision to build a new gymnasium in Morningside Park between the Columbia campus and the Harlem neighborhood of Manhattan. These two issues allowed SDS to rally additional support and attack the Columbia University administration as an evil instrument of the "white, racist, capitalist, imperialist, warmongering, power structure of the United States."[289]

On March 27, 1968, SDS launched a demonstration against the IDA by briefly occupying the administration building that included the office of the President. On Monday morning April 22nd SDS distributed a leaflet calling students to a mass rally on the following day at the Sundial outside Low Library. YAF leader John Meyer recalled what happened,

> *After a long, tense, but nonviolent confrontation SDS withdrew and moved onto the site of the controversial gym, where SDS enthusiasts tore down an iron fence and had a brush with the police. Frustrated there, SDS returned to the campus and seized Hamilton Hall, a classroom building, and held the Dean of the College, Dean Coleman, a prisoner in his own office.[290]*

The number of protesters grew in Hamilton Hall while the administration did nothing. By Thursday, three more buildings were "liberated" by SDS. Meanwhile, three students crept through the tunnels that link university buildings and found the master fuse box for Hamilton Hall, broke the lock, and turned off the power. As one writer later described them, "They were guerrillas of the right, engaged in the war against the radical left."[291] Shortly thereafter, his captors released Dean Coleman.

Meanwhile, opposition to the SDS was building with the formation of a Majority Coalition. In a joint statement, the participating groups made clear, "Despite our differences we stand united on one principle: There shall be no use of coercion, disruption, or blackmail to influence the future of this great academic institution." The group circulated a petition condemning the SDS tactics and obtained 2,600 signatures from concerned students and faculty. SDS leader Mark Rudd would admit only a few months later in a speech before activists at Harvard "We manufactured the issues."[292] To Rudd and his followers, the issues were immaterial, the radicalization of the student body and the demand for political power were the real motivations for the SDS takeovers of the buildings.

Over the next few days, SDS rejected all attempts at compromise and remained in possession of the campus buildings. By Sunday afternoon the Majority Coalition agreed on a plan to blockade the west side of Low Library where SDS was located, given that the administration was totally incapable of removing the SDS protesters and restoring order to the campus. At 5 p.m. that Sunday, the Majority Coalition began its blockade of Low Library. The Majority Coalition established a successful blockade that continued overnight and into Monday. At peak moments, seven hundred students could be counted on the line outside Low Library organized by the Coalition.[293] Despite various attempts by SDS members to break through and aid their fellow leftists in the building, the blockade remained firm.

The SDS leaders were becoming frustrated and then came the violence. Meyer recalled the incident, "After marching three times around the line, about fifty of them, mostly non-students penetrated the lines by throwing ammonia in the faces of those opposing them. A struggle ensued and the invaders were repulsed before they could enter Low."[294] Monday night the police were called in, the SDS supporters were removed from Low, and the Majority Coalition's 33-hour vigil ended.

Mark Rudd and the other SDS leaders immediately claimed police brutality as they were removed from the administration building they had been occupying. An SDS-called student strike was held and lasted for some four weeks. When the strike began to fade out, SDS decided to take more extreme action. First they occupied a Columbia building, were arrested, but gained little support or attention. On May 21st, SDS again occupied Hamilton Hall and were peaceably removed by the police with 148 students arrested. Then fires broke out in the building and also in Fayerweather Hall, bringing the police back on campus and the resumption of violence. This led the administration to decide to clear the campus entirely, effectively ending the Spring semester.

There were several lessons to be learned from the experience at Columbia University, lessons that would be important for YAF over the next few years as it continued to battle SDS and other New Left organizations on campuses across the nation. Meyer believed a successful resistance could be developed when it is broad-based, inclusive, and focused on the specific objective of keeping the campus open and free debate and discussion allowed. What was needed is "the presence of an organized opposition, which could serve as a focus and rallying point for latent anti-SDS feeling." To Meyer "even on a campus as far left as Columbia, the majority of the students are neither ideological liberals nor radicals. They are non-political, usually with vague Liberal leanings."[295] Historian Kenneth Heineman echoed this analysis of the situation when he claimed, "two thirds of Columbia's undergraduates opposed the SDS and Afro-American Society sit-ins and supported the efforts of the Young Americans for Freedom to oust the radicals."[296]

The efforts at Columbia convinced YAF to launch a nationwide program to encourage the creation of Majority Coalitions on campuses. Through effective training and guidance, YAF members could take the lead in such efforts, although the organization itself would not always gain credit for stopping SDS. An additional outgrowth of the Columbia resistance was the decision to use blue armbands, or what soon became blue buttons, as a symbol of peace on campus and opposition to SDS demands. Finally, YAF members learned that they would need to assume leadership in keeping their campus open since unfortunately, in most instances, they could not rely on the university administration and especially not the faculty to do so.

On January 9, 1969, twelve Columbia students filed suit in New York Supreme Court to remove the Columbia Board of Trustees for breach of contract, contributing to the riots by not taking a firm stand, and depriving the students of the education for which they had paid. Moreover, they sought an injunction "against political discrimination in the hiring of faculty members." While the students realized they had no hope of winning, their goal was to bring pressure on the administration, to better ensure the protection of all students' rights.[297] Just as with the coalitional approach and the use of blue armbands, legal action would become a method employed by YAF members on other campuses in responding to what they viewed as the insensitivity of university administrations to ensuring free access to classes and an education.

While Columbia was gaining much national attention it was by far not the only campus where SDS and other New Left groups were causing disruptions. At Arizona State University, SDS students occupied the administration building. Michael Sanera was leader of the YAF chapter and noted that they were able to rally opposition forces: "YAF members picketed the building with signs such as 'The Hitler Youth is alive and well in the SDS.' We got a lot of press coverage because the TV cameras were rolling when the state Highway Patrol arrived to arrest the SDS students." During the Fall of 1968, the Student Peace Union at Purdue University organized a sit-in to disrupt the CIA and other agencies from recruiting on campus. Purdue YAF took the initiative in condemning their action and, on the day before a trustees meeting where the school's policy on recruiters was to be discussed, held an anti-anarchism rally attended by 400 students.

The national YAF office prepared and distributed a new issues paper titled "Student Subversion: The Majority Replies," which was geared specifically to attracting moderate and apolitical students who were finally being activated by their opposition to the leftists' actions. YAF was now committed to rallying those students who opposed SDS violence and making direct action against the left a weapon in the organization's arsenal.

At Penn State, YAF leaders became enraged by the increased militancy of the Left and its threats to close the campus down. They warned University President Eric Walker that they would file suit against the University if disruptions prevented classes from taking place.[298] Under the leadership of Chapter Chairman Doug Cooper, YAF's Student Committee for a Responsible University (SCRU) sent a telegram to Walker in the Fall of 1968, "By accepting our tuition, this university has entered into a contract with us... If the actions of a belligerent minority deny us our rights by interrupting classes, we will bring suit, if necessary to have the university live up to its contractual obligations."[299] The wording was to be used over and over again by other YAF chapters and was incorporated in YAF's Majority Coalition Campus Action Kit.

Indeed, at Penn State it was not an idle threat as in the Spring semester of the following year, Penn State YAF decided to take direct legal action. YAF's Laura Wertheimer and two other members obtained a court injunction to stop radicals from demonstrating against recruiters on campus. This was the first time one student group had obtained an injunction against another and resulted in President Nixon sending a letter of commendation to Doug Cooper, Penn State YAF's Chairman.[300]

As the Vietnam Moratorium committee attempted to shut down colleges and halt classes, YAF chapters at more and more campuses sought injunctions or issued threats to sue the administration. Their argument was that the suspension of classes was a breach of contract resulting in the YAF members and others losing the option of attending classes. As Sheldon Richman of Temple YAF put it, "We pay our tuition, which entitles us to an education. If Temple should close down as a result of campus disorders, then YAF will not hesitate to bring suit against a negligent administration."

On October 3, 1969, YAF leaders held news conferences in 57 cities to announce a campus legal offensive against leftist radicals while reaffirming their support of legitimate free speech for all individuals and groups. As Ron Docksai noted, "YAF will force the New Left onto the defensive. YAF will no longer sit back and allow administration buildings to be burned, students to be blackmailed and beaten, buildings to be burned down, or fear and intimidation to replace academic freedom." The targets of the legal offensive "would be both university administrations that failed to act against 'disruptive students' and the students themselves."[301]

To assist local YAF chapters, national YAF prepared and distributed a 54-page document, "Legal Responses to Campus Disorder," that was to be used in preparation of court cases. As the preface explained, while school administrators and civil authorities have been relied on to maintain order and protect student rights to an education, too often these officials have not provided that protection. The document described various legal arguments that could be employed by students with citations of relevant court cases. It outlined the relationship between student and university, possible causes of action by students against the university, actions against disruptive students, and other possible legal actions.[302]

Spring semester 1969 saw an intensification of the violence and destruction on and off American campuses. During the first six months there were protests on 232 campuses with 20% of them involving bombings, arson, and property destruction. Perhaps one of the most dramatic and tragic of all was the burning of the Bank of America branch, viewed as "a symbol of imperialist finance capitalism," and the bombing of the faculty club at the University of California at Santa Barbara, resulting in the death of the club's janitor.[303]

San Francisco State College was the site of the longest student strike, lasting 134 days from November 1968 to March 1969. Each day, protesting students would gather at noon and march to the administration building where they protested outside the offices of President S. I. Hayakawa who became a national symbol of resistance to the student left. On other campuses YAF leaders also stood against the senseless violence and destruction that was being brought about and also preventing students from receiving their education. At the University of Maryland, YAF joined a group of veterans in blocking the entrance to the computer science building so that leftists, who were protesting government contracts and alleged war research, could not enter. At Michigan State University, YAF and others opposed to campus disorders collected over 10,000 signatures on a petition against the "atmosphere of intimidation, violence and disruption" they perceived on campus.[304]

Perhaps the most publicized example of YAF resistance to SDS actions in 1969 took place at Stanford University. Led by Harvey Hukari, the YAF chapter already was publishing its own weekly newspaper, *The Arena*, as an alternative to the official leftist-leaning campus paper. The Stanford YAF chairman did not appear to be your stereotypical conservative student. As writer George Fox described him in an article in *Playboy* magazine, "Physically, he looks farther left than Mark Rudd – shoulder-length hair, Mao jacket, cord bell-bottoms, etc. According to Hukari, 'It makes me a little more difficult for the SDS to attack.'"[305] When SDS held a rally and tried to take over the Applied Electronics Laboratory, YAF was there with signs reading, "SDS is Revolting" while Hukari, armed with a bullhorn, led cheers of "Pigs Off Campus" against the leftist demonstrators. The YAF effort was successful in preventing the takeover. As Hukari noted, however, "In the future one can expect to see more militancy develop (on our part) in various areas of the campus, as long as the Administration fails to act firmly with campus disorders."[306]

On February 17, 1970, California YAF launched a statewide blue button campaign with news conferences in San Francisco, Sacramento, Los Angeles, and San Diego. With the buttons, California YAF distributed a two-page flyer that explained its purpose was to support peace on campus. As the flyer stated, "We want the people of California to know that the student majority is with them, that we are not a lost generation, that there is an alternative to the militant leftists inhabiting the campus community." It maintained that terror is wrong, whether by a mugger or a student leftist on campus. A few days after the YAF news conferences, the *Los Angeles Herald Examiner* printed an editorial calling YAF the "unsung heroes."

Apart from the news conferences and the public relations push, something significant was occurring on campuses across America. New YAF chapters were being formed and existing ones were being reinvigorated. When the once-inactive chapter at the University of Michigan held a rally in support of ROTC classes and in opposition to leftist disruptions, 200 students took part.[307] At the University of Texas at Austin, 19-year old Mary Kay Davis resuscitated a dormant YAF chapter in her freshman year and made it into a major force on her campus. As a campus magazine noted, "On this campus she is a determined leader, an articulate opponent of liberal doctrine."[308] Freshman Laszlo Pasztor was determined to reorganize a YAF chapter at Harvard when he reached campus in the Fall of 1969. Pasztor had some significant help in the form of Doug Cooper, a new graduate student from Penn State where he had been YAF chairman, and in two outstanding faculty advisors, Professors Gottfried Haberler and Edward C. Banfield.[309] At the Massachusetts Institute of Technology, freshman David Horan stepped before 35 students to call to order the first chapter meeting in over a year.[310]

Meanwhile, more and more YAF chapters began to go beyond the official campus newspapers and started their own publications. As the *New York Times* observed,

> Dozens of conservative newspapers have begun competing with traditionally liberal dailies on such campuses as Stanford, the University of Wisconsin and the University of California at Berkeley. Last month, a student conservative weekly began distribution at Duke University, North Carolina State and the University of North Carolina. [311]

Bob Tyrrell continued editing his *The Alternative: An American Spectator* at Indiana University, *The Arena* kept publishing at Stanford, and the University of Maryland YAF started its second year of distributing its own *The Alternative* on the College Park campus and at Baltimore area colleges. The national organization assembled a handbook for local YAF chapters called "Do It! Or Publishing A Conservative Underground Newspaper." The 48-page manual covered all the basics of publishing from finances to staff to content to distribution. By the 1970-1971 academic year, seventy-one YAF chapters were publishing independent alternative newspapers.[312] For those chapters unable to publish their own independent newspaper, national YAF created the "Free Campus News" and shipped a total of 200,000 copies to various campuses for free distribution.[313]

From the perspective of years later, it is hard to realize the extent to which the United States was engulfed in serious societal breakdown and destructive behavior. According to one report, during the sixteen months from January 1969 to April 1970, there were approximately five thousand terrorist bombings in the United States, most of which took place on or near college campuses.[314] Several of these acts of violence ended in death for participants or innocent by-standers. After the conviction of the Chicago 7 in February, Ann Arbor witnessed destruction at the hands of the University of Michigan SDS led by Robert Meeropol, son of convicted Soviet spies Ethel and Julius Rosenberg. Under SDS direction, "five thousand Michigan students and campus hangers-on marched to the Ann Arbor city hall, breaking the windows of downtown businesses and wrecking a police car along the way."[315] One month later, in New York City, a bomb factory in the townhouse owned by Cathy Wilkerson's father blew up killing three members of the Weatherman Underground faction of SDS.[316]

Then on April 18th, radical leftists set fire to the temporary Bank of America building in Isla Vista, next to the University of California at Santa Barbara campus. This was the same bank that had been bombed by SDS one year earlier. Three students opposed to the terrorists left their apartment and went in the bank to put out the fire. As they emerged, 22-year old Kevin Moran was shot dead. It was later determined that Moran was accidentally shot by a policeman who thought he was one of the individuals responsible for the fire. Responding to the tragedy, Harvard YAF released a statement in which they said, "Kevin Moran's story doesn't fit, so it won't be discussed, no vigils held, no money collected, no outrage expressed. Kevin was on the wrong side."[317]

Dramatic as these events were, they were soon to be surpassed by what occurred in early May. On April 30th, President Nixon announced that American troops would be going into Cambodia to halt the continued infiltration into South Vietnam of North Vietnamese regular forces. [318] This action, viewed by the left as a widening of the war, set off major opposition on campuses and in the Democratic-controlled Congress. As the lead sentence in a *New York Times* article explained, "The national anti-war movement, drained of vigor in recent months, seemed yesterday to have found a new rallying point and an impetus to renewed protest in President Nixon's announcement of direct intervention in Cambodia by United States troops."[319]

On May 1st, ROTC buildings were firebombed at the University of Wisconsin and at Michigan State University. At Kent State, home to a radical wing of the SDS, students marched to the downtown area where a riot broke out and much property was damaged. One day later, the ROTC building was set afire and when the firefighters arrived, leftist students assaulted them. Soon thereafter, Governor James Rhodes called out the National Guard and ordered them onto campus. On May 4th, students called for a "peace rally" on the commons but then began attacking the National Guard with bottles, rocks, blocks of wood with nails and spent tear gas canisters. After much provocation, some of the Guardsmen began firing back. The end result was four students killed and nine wounded. From that point on, the Kent State disaster would move from impetus to action to myth to history.[320]

Over the next few days, anti-war protests occurred at more than one thousand campuses as students reacted to the deaths at Kent State. Leaders of the Student Mobilization Committee called for a student strike to oppose the Nixon Administration's move into Cambodia. Meanwhile, the violence continued. One hundred SDS members took over the president's office at Boston College while others broke into and destroyed the ROTC offices. At the University of Wisconsin, hundreds of students set fires and smashed windows on campus. At Boston University, administrators cancelled exams and commencement and urged all students to go home.[321]

Two days later, the number of colleges on strike had increased to 350.[322] At the University of Kentucky, students burned the Air Force ROTC building. Meanwhile, Black radicals were using the situation to make their own demands.

Students at New York University occupied three buildings and demanded a ransom of $100,000 to be paid to the Black Panther Defense Fund.[323] When it was all tallied, some nine hundred colleges shut down, many not opening again until the Fall semester. More than 160 bombs were reported to have exploded on campuses in reaction to the Cambodia and Kent State actions. [324]

The events of early May led YAF to take a number of stands against the violence on campus as well as in favor of ensuring that students continue to receive the education for which they had paid tuition. Ohio State University YAF won a temporary injunction against nine radicals designed to ensure the rights of the eleven student plaintiffs. At Wayne State University, eight YAF members convinced a Circuit Judge to order classes be reopened, a decision that was unfortunately overturned on appeal. Meanwhile, at George Washington University Randal Teague and 14 co-plaintiffs filed suit to get reimbursement for tuition spent for cancelled classes.[325] As one historian noted, "YAF's arguments were compelling and offered a contrary opinion to the growing tendency of universities to be arms of radical and social change."[326]

The New York area saw a number of threatened lawsuits by YAF members and chapters. At Adelphi University the YAF chapter obtained an injunction to force college administrators to open the campus. YAF members formed a group called "Strike Back" at Hofstra University, threatened a lawsuit, and negotiated with the administration to have the school opened again on May 10th. Classes also resumed at Nassau Community College after YAF instituted a lawsuit to force the reopening. The New York Institute of Technology reopened after YAF met with school officials and threatened to sue for $37,000, the tuition lost by students who could not attend classes because of the protests. Following a YAF threat to sue, Suffolk Community College resumed classes. [327]

The New York City Board of Education ordered all seventeen city colleges to hold regular classes while three other area colleges "reopened when the Young Americans for Freedom threatened to file suits for tuition losses."[328] At Marymount College in Tarrytown, New York, an all-female Catholic institution, six students charged the college administration with breach of contract for canceling classes in support of the student strike. After the school agreed to resume classes for the remainder of the semester, it was dropped.

YAF activity during the aftermath of the Cambodian incursion and Kent State was not limited to lawsuits and injunctions, however. At Towson State College, fifteen YAF members surrounded a flagpole on campus to prevent leftist students from lowering the American flag. YAF was attracting formerly apolitical students for, as Towson YAF leader John Malagrin noted, "We've got a lot of moderates in YAF now. Many of them are disillusioned students who were part of the silent campus majority before the tactics of the left opened their eyes."[329]

As colleges closed for the summer, the demonstrations and destruction died down but did not totally disappear. That August, one of the most destructive attacks took place on the University of Wisconsin campus. The "New Year's Gang" firebombed the campus ROTC building, the Selective Service offices, and even unsuccessfully tried an aerial bombing of a munitions plant. Then in August, the Gang attempted to bomb the Army Math building on campus with the equivalent blast of 3,400 sticks of dynamite. Instead of hitting their intended target, the bomb destroyed the Physics department, killing a graduate student and blinding a night watchman. Subsidiary damage was done to twenty-six campus buildings and a major cancer research project inside the Old Chemistry Building was destroyed. Despite the death and destruction, the New Year's Gang and the bombing was supported by Madison's alternative leftist newspaper and local SDS members. The left in Madison refused to cooperate with the FBI investigation and all four attackers escaped, eventually making their way to Canada.[330]

The violence on campus did not cease, nor did YAF's commitment to standing up for student rights and opposing the radical leftists in their actions. On October 14th, a bomb was set off and seriously damaged the Center for International Affairs on the Harvard campus.[331] Two days later, Harvard - Radcliffe YAF held a rally condemning the bombing and urging the University to prosecute those responsible. YAF chairman Laszlo Pasztor indicated that a telegram would be sent to President Nathan Pusey and YAF leader Doug Cooper said, "Unless we preserve a peaceful legal and rational framework to work in, we will not be able to produce meaningful change."[332]

Unfortunately, Spring semester 1971 saw a continuation of violent confrontations with the left on the Harvard campus. On March 26th, Harvard-Radcliffe YAF planned to hold a Vietnam Teach-In at Sanders Theater with speakers including the Royal Thai Ambassador to Canada, the Counselor for Political Affairs of the Embassy of South Vietnam, and Professor I. Milton Sacks of Brandeis University. Three radical leftist organizations on the Harvard campus vowed to prevent the speakers from being heard and they packed the meeting, attended by approximately one thousand students. When the meeting was called to order, militant demonstrators began 45 minutes of ceaseless chanting, clapping and booing. Archibald Cox, as a representative of Harvard's President, pleaded with the crowd for ten minutes "on behalf of the President and Fellows" to no avail.[333] At 8:45 pm, the university police chief informed Cox that a rowdy crowd outside was attempting to break in. Cox then met with moderator Lawrence McCarty and YAF chairman Laszlo Pasztor, and said, "In view of the crowds of people massing outside the building, I ask you to call off the meeting," and the program ended before it began.[334]

For the Left, the disruption was a resounding success. As one SDS member commented, "This was the largest mass action I've seen on this campus in my four years here. We should use this to build up a tremendous momentum to fight the war."[335] Two weeks later, a Harvard Professor of Philosophy was the speaker at a Progressive Labor Party "Forum on Free Speech" where he called the disruption a "genuine act of internationalism" and "advocated more militant actions in the future, suggesting a picket line around University Hall to force a confrontation with University officials on the issue of discipline in the wake of disruption."[336] Still other students interviewed by the *New York Times* approved of the disruption and maintained that the principle of free speech was not involved since those attempting to speak were not students but government officials.[337]

By the end of Spring semester in 1971, campuses were once again beginning to quiet down. But the left was still most active, even with the breakup of Students for a Democratic Society. Especially active in the early 1970s were the Trotskyite "Young Socialist Alliance" and the ultra-leftist Progressive Labor Party, the group that basically picked up the pieces of the dying SDS. As Phillip Abbott Luce observed, "I am convinced that this may very well be the lull period. The left-wing is obviously struggling to 'get itself together' and we should not view the present as a time of leftist impotence."[338]

While the organized campus left was in disarray, Young Americans for Freedom remained a strong presence on many campuses with a second generation of leaders ready to take on the decade of the 1970s. As historian Greg Schneider commented "… YAF survived the Sixties, even thriving during times when emotions ran the highest on campus. YAF made it through the decade intact as an organization – a testimony to the idealism and work of the hard-core membership who believed the time for conservative principles had come."[339]

The high school and college students who helped build YAF during those turbulent years, whether on campuses with active SDS chapters or not, did succeed and meet head on the challenge of the left. As Greg Schneider noted, "During a time when radicalism swept society and the very order of the nation was being challenged, YAF held its own against the tide. In so doing, YAF helped make possible for conservatives what only appeared to be a dream at the dawn of the 1960s – political power."[340] Looking back on that time several years later, historian Jonathan Schoenwald concluded, "the leaders always knew that demonstrations, press conferences, and the like were only means, not ends… understood that through these relatively insignificant activities they were building the basis of a long-lasting political movement.[341] As YAF approached its second decade, it's presence was being felt not only as an organization but as the birthing ground for political and community leaders who would begin assuming positions of leadership in American society. They had more than survived; they had grown, matured, and thrived.

An Educational Foundation Emerges

By the late 1960s at Vanderbilt University a group of students, mainly YAF members, under the leadership of Chuck Stowe, created an organization called University Information Services, Inc. as a tax-exempt educational foundation. Formed in reaction to the radicals who dominated campus, this new entity provided conservative speakers and literature to students at Vanderbilt. When Stowe graduated and entered the Navy, he approached the national office of Young Americans for Freedom to see if they would be interested in taking over the foundation and broadening its scope of activity.   By 1973, the name was changed to what is now known as Young America's Foundation.   Since then Young America's Foundation, under the leadership of President Ron Robinson, has grown into the premiere entry point for high school and college students into the conservative movement. Its current Board of Directors includes a number of former YAF members.

The goal of sponsoring conservative speakers on campus was now broadened to a national scope and over the years has included a wide range of speakers representing all facets of the conservative movement from Margaret Thatcher, Colin Powell, Pat Buchanan, Dan Quayle, Newt Gingrich, Michelle Malkin, John Stossel, and yes, Bill Buckley.   In 1974 the Foundation expanded its activities by initiating and financing a nationally syndicated radio program with messages from then-Governor Ronald Reagan. Young America's Foundation has sponsored annual summer institutes for high school students and for college students in Washington, DC for many years as well as regional weekend conferences in the Midwest and West Coast. In 1998, the foundation purchased the Reagan Ranch outside of Santa Barbara to preserve it for history and shortly thereafter opened the Reagan Ranch Center in downtown Santa Barbara as a focal point for West Coast conservative meetings and programs. Then in 2011 Young Americans for Freedom became an essential part of Young America's Foundation, bringing full circle the relationship between the two organizations.

— 5 —

Campus Initiatives

As Young Americans for Freedom moved forward, it faced a number of new challenges and opportunities. The campus scene of the early 1960s was quite different from that of the late 1960s and more change was to occur in the 1970s. While leftist organizations continued to be active on many campuses, Students for a Democratic Society and, to a large degree, the Black Panthers were no longer the forces they had been in the previous decade. The National Student Association retained affiliation on a small number of American campuses and YAF still had its STOP-NSA committee but, as the decade progressed, NSA lost most of its luster as a viable representative of American college students. Campus takeovers, moratoriums, and class shut downs became a less frequent method of protest for radical students. The draft became modified first by a lottery system and then abolished entirely. YAF continued to battle efforts by American corporations to engage in trade with the Soviet Union and its satellite nations but not to the extent of the 1960s campaigns against Firestone and American Motors.

With a Republican in the White House for the first six years of the 1970s, the organization confronted a changed political situation in which on many occasions it staked out a position of opposition to the administration, causing some fissures with a few members and a few more contributors. As the newly-elected Conservative United States Senator from New York, James L. Buckley, noted "YAF has never been afraid to stick its neck out when it thought principle was at stake. It has never feared to champion unpopular causes; and it has never had occasion to consult with George Gallup or the New York Times before acting."[342]

New issues would surface in the 1970s and older ones would come to the fore. Most of these were college issues as YAF turned more of its attention to the campus. Mandatory student activity fees, Public Interest Research Groups, the election of conservatives to student government, the publication of independent campus newspapers, unbalanced speakers programs, student government support for leftist demonstrations, and YAF's own "Movement for Quality Education" took precedence for many chapters. For the more active college chapters, the focus turned inward towards influencing the direction of thought on their own college campus.

Mary Fisk, later to serve on the YAF National Board and as editor of *New Guard*, appreciated the impact YAF had in helping her deal with a liberal campus environment. It was from YAF that she recalled"… benefiting from guidance in starting my own college newspaper, *Disrespect*, in opposition to official campus newspaper; having support to oppose antiwar and other left-wing activities on campus, including a lawyer to keep the campus open when the moratorium was proposed; finding other young conservatives at the campus, state, and national levels; general political companionship in the unwelcoming climate of the campuses – others with whom to share ideas, explore new approaches, discuss tactics, and so much more." Fisk's efforts were duplicated on numerous other campuses by YAF members, assisted by the Free Campus News Service sent out from the national office.

YAF was also willing to take on controversial topics where there were differences among conservatives. Under the general topic of "Privacy, the Rights of the Individual, and the Role of Government," the organization's magazine featured debates and discussions on what are now referred to as social issues. YAF's influence continued to grow, as did its involvement in youth affairs outside the campus. When writer Alan Rinzler put together a compendium of views from the youth of America, six of the twenty-nine authors featured in his book were YAF members. [343] At the 1971 White House Conference on Youth held in Estes Park, Colorado, the few conservatives present were YAF members. For Nixon and conservatives, the conference was a "White House Woodstock" as "the Nixon Administration, in another of its seemingly masochistic moves, had assured a radical and leftist orientation" to the conference. As Steve Frank observed, "we came here to unite as youth and all this conference has done is divide."[344]

Meanwhile, some areas of involvement continued into the early years of the decade. Vietnam was an issue that would not go away, but it was one whose focus and involvement would change as the 1970s began. For the first few years of the decade, YAF could not get beyond Vietnam, although downplaying the issue was a position which some in the organization's leadership wanted to see occur. While others in the organization continued to push for victory over communism, the policies of the administration and the conditions on the ground were moving more towards a hoped-for peace treaty, a treaty that would never be enforced as the forces of North Vietnam and the Viet Cong eventually overran South Vietnam after the pullout of American troops.

In March 1970, YAF sent a delegation of eleven members led by National Chairman David Keene on a fact-finding mission to South Vietnam. The trip was designed to check on the progress of the war in view of the Vietnamization process under way and the upcoming national student referendum calling for a unilateral withdrawal of all American troops from Vietnam. During their visit, the delegation met with college students, military officers, private citizens and government officials as well as United States diplomatic representatives, including Ambassador Ellsworth Bunker.

Upon their return, Keene spoke at a news conference in Honolulu and reported that the delegation was convinced that Vietnamization was working. Criticizing the previous policies, he maintained that fewer American troops would have been required "if we had gone in there with the attitude the Vietnamese could help us. We took the attitude that these guys don't have it, they are not up to snuff and pushed them aside."

YAF continued to use rallies and demonstrations to show support for the American commitment to Vietnam. YAF was a co-sponsor of a "Wake Up America" rally held in late April on Boston Common and City Hall Plaza. As Massachusetts YAF state chairman Dan Rea noted, "we are trying to use rallies, such as the one to wake up America to radicalize people to the Right, just as the Student Mobilization groups are trying to radicalize people to the Left." Rea added, however, that YAF was totally against violence and this distinction "will spell the difference in our attracting people to the conservative side."[345]

As the student strikes took place on campuses in early May after the incursion into Cambodia and the unfortunate student deaths at Kent State University, YAF ran advertisements declaring its support for American troops in Southeast Asia and "for a continued American presence in South Vietnam, for gradual Vietnamization of the war, and for victory over Communist aggression in Asia."[346] YAF pledged its support to the cause of freedom and peace in South Vietnam and urged Americans to "Tell it to Hanoi." Local YAF chapters used a number of different techniques to show support for the war and opposition to the student strike. The University of Tennessee at Knoxville hired a small plane to fly over campus pulling a banner calling on Americans to "Give Nixon a Chance." Meanwhile, at Mount St. Mary's College in Maryland, Michael O'Malley, sophomore and Vietnam veteran, held his own 72-hour vigil. As the *Baltimore Sun* reported, "A bearded sleepy and hungry Vietnam war veteran continued his watch over a butane flame at Mount St. Mary's College in a symbolic support of America's role in the Indo-China war." O'Malley, who had just been elected president of the junior class, explained "the purpose of my vigil is to draw interest to those students like myself who are supporting the President's commitment in Vietnam. There has been a disproportionate amount of attention already focused on the anti-war." Outside the Washington headquarters of the Student Mobilization Committee, twenty-five YAF members from two Virginia high schools and Notre Dame Academy in DC marched and demonstrated their support for the war.

On the campus of the University of Southern California, the administration ordered the American flag to be lowered to half-mast in honor of the four students killed at Kent State, without setting any end date. After a few days of the lowered flag, YAF activist Pat Nolan attempted to raise it and a tug of war developed with a student striker. As Marty Morfeld, USC YAF chair, indicated, "The incident wasn't planned. Some members became emotional. We just couldn't see the reasoning behind lowering the flag for four students at that time. They've never done it for the men killed in Southeast Asia, and we've had over 50 thousand killed there."[347] A short time later, YAF held a pro-Vietnam rally on the USC campus where Mark Johnson burned a Viet Cong flag.

Two YAF chapters in Arkansas co-sponsored a "Victory in Vietnam" rally with Mike Thompson as the featured speaker. Thompson, National Vice Chairman of YAF, praised Nixon's decision to go into Cambodia. The rally was co-sponsored by the *Jacksonville Daily News* whose city editor, Steve Collins, was also chairman of Jacksonville YAF. Thompson also spoke at a candlelight procession of one hundred YAF supporters that began at St. Louis University, an event that Thompson said was designed "not only to show that we are against the Moratorium but that we support our troops." National Chairman Keene was the featured speaker at a "Proud to be an American" rally sponsored by YAF in Minneapolis, an event brought about by the combined efforts of a number of Twin Cities high school chapters and the University of Minnesota.

The culmination of this approach was an event that was billed as non-partisan and not designed specifically to indicate support for the Vietnam war. "Honor America Day" was a huge rally in the Nation's Capitol led by entertainer Bob Hope and evangelist Billy Graham. YAF was one of the major sponsors of the day's festivities, which brought somewhere between 250,000 and 500,000 Americans to the Mall on July 4, 1970. Local YAF chapters joined in promoting the event and bringing their members and supporters to Washington. In New York, Great Neck YAF under the leadership of 16-year old Larry Penner, chartered two buses that left Long Island at 1:45 am on Saturday morning and returned back some twenty-four hours later with tired but proud rally participants.[348]

When President Nixon stepped up the bombing of North Vietnam in late

1972, YAF state organizations did hold a series of news conferences in support of the action. As Kirby Wilbur stated at the University of Washington, "President Nixon had no alternative but resume heavy bombing. The way to achieve a lasting peace is to convince aggressors that aggression does not pay." California YAF State Chairman Patrick Geary maintained, "the North Vietnamese Communists have shown that they respect only force and consider any conciliatory moves by the United States as a sign of weakness." Despite these statements, however, a shift in emphasis was already under way and YAF was focusing on other related but distinct issues. As historian John Andrew noted, "this shift was subtle but unmistakable. Although YAF still gave lip service to the concept of victory in Vietnam, it really longed for an honorable withdrawal as quickly as possible." [349]

One aspect of the war on which all YAF members could agree was concern over the treatment and return of American prisoners of war. As the war continued for several years, more information was becoming available on the mistreatment of prisoners by the North Vietnamese. Among those organizing tributes to the POWs and those missing in action was Senator Bob Dole of Kansas, a wounded veteran of World War II. In light of Dole's involvement in the issue, it was appropriate that one of the first YAF chapters to sponsor a rally in support of American POWs/MIAs was Wichita State University. According to Gary Leffel, chapter vice chairman, the rally was designed "to demonstrate to the wives and other relatives of American prisoners that Americans do care and to show the North Vietnamese and the Viet Cong that their conduct is not condoned by the American public." Speakers at the May 2nd rally included local Congressman Garner Shriver and Professor Dwight D. Murphey, faculty advisor to the YAF chapter.[350]

Later that Spring, the YAF national office prepared and distributed to local chapters and state organizations a Prisoner of War Action Kit with information on possible projects by chapters as well as by individual members. As the cover letter explained, "Note that several possible projects can be undertaken by individual YAF members. Efforts should be made to activate all YAF members in your state, whether or not they are active in a local YAF chapter."[351] National Director Mary Kay Davis of the University of Texas prepared most of the material in the kit and Texas YAF, under State Chairman Jack Gullahorn, had carried out an active campaign on the POW issue.

By the Fall of 1970, the prisoner of war issue had become a major focus of activity for many YAF chapters, involving high school and community chapters as well as those on college campuses. Greater Richmond Hi-YAF circulated petitions throughout the Virginia capital and presented them to Governor Linwood Holton, who added his signature to the sizeable list. University of Florida YAF members picketed outside Gainesville Mall when the management firm would not allow the Arnold Air Society to collect petition signatures calling for fair treatment of prisoners of war. According to mall officials, such an effort was a political activity not allowed inside the shopping area. However, after YAF's action and much bad public relations in the community, the mall officials backed off and allowed the ROTC members to circulate their petitions.

In October, a number of Boston area YAF chapters joined together for a fast and vigil in downtown Boston, gaining the attention of shoppers and office workers as well as the media. At the University of Texas as well as at Boston College, YAF members built POW cells to dramatize the conditions under which the North Vietnamese were holding Americans. LSU YAF made their major Fall semester activities an effort to inform students of the plight of American POWs. To this end they carried out a "Free The Hanoi 1600" publicity campaign.[352]

New York Young Americans for Freedom, coming off its successful involvement in the Buckley for Senate campaign, urged its chapters to take up the issue of American prisoners. Herb Stupp, New York YAF State Chairman, launched a campaign to inform the public of "these Americans who have received so little attention, especially among their own countrymen." National YAF leader Al Forrester spoke on campus and noted that "the North Vietnamese are not living up to the Geneva Agreement" concerning treatment of prisoners.

One of the major efforts to garner public support for the cause took place on December 6th as Massachusetts YAF, led by State Chairman Dan Rea, held a rally on Boston Common. David Brudnoy described the scene.

> *Young Americans for Freedom is one of the few groups at home which is sufficiently concerned about the plight of American prisoners in North Vietnam to do anything about it. Last night, in subfreezing temperatures augmented by a 35-mph wind, Massachusetts YAF staged a rally on Boston Common to dramatize the situation. Coming a year to the day after Mass YAF's first rally in support of America's role in Vietnam, this gathering on behalf of the prisoners was more moving, although the impossible weather kept the crowd small.[353]*

Among the speakers in that bitter cold were cartoonist Al Capp, YAF National Director Don Feder, and Commander Lloyd Bucher, who with his crew on the USS Pueblo had only recently been released from a North Korean prison. During the Spring semester, a number of other YAF chapters used the technique of showing the conditions in which POWs survived as a means of dramatizing the need for pressure on Hanoi. Creighton University YAF built a replica of a

POW cell in the State Capitol building in Lincoln, Nebraska and Governor J. J. Exon dedicated the exhibit. The project was coordinated by YAF member Bob Passavanti and Creighton YAF chairman John Scully.[354] Scully was one of many young conservatives who had first become active in YAF while a high school student. According to Scully, "although as a conservative we seemingly marched to the beat of a different drummer from most students, YAF gave me comrades in arms in the battle of freedom to march with and provided opportunities for my education as a conservative and to act on my principles."

Daniel Webster Hi-YAF erected a POW cage in downtown Astoria, New York. YAF member Jerry Gavin was "locked" in the cage while other members collected signatures on a petition calling for humane treatment. Shiloh Hi-YAF, headed by James O'Neill, demonstrated in front of the United Nations building with an all-night candlelight vigil in support of the prisoners of war and calling on North Vietnam to live up to its commitments under the Geneva Agreement. Meanwhile, in Hawaii the Honolulu Hi-YAF chapter was successful in having Mayor Frank Fasi proclaim "POW Day." [355]

During the late 1960s and early 1970s, YAF recruited a number of high school activists, especially in New York, Ohio, Massachusetts, California, and Maryland. There were several active high school chapters in the early 1970s, chapters that produced leaders for many years as the high school students went on to college and graduate school. At Lutheran High School South in Afton, Missouri, Walt Busch headed up the General "Blackjack" Pershing Memorial Chapter that helped out often at the Missouri YAF state headquarters in Kirkwood. YAF reinforced his conservatism and influenced him in other ways also. "I am the only public servant in the family and spent 32 years in law enforcement at least in part because of YAF… I teach history and state/local government at a junior college part time and some of my views definitely come across to students." In Ridgefield, Connecticut, James Farfaglia formed a chapter that obtained excellent coverage of its activities in the local media. Working with local veterans' groups, they rallied public support in their community for the prisoners of war. As he recently noted, "YAF gave me an opportunity to defend the values that have made America great and gave me the opportunity to fight against communism, to grow as a leader and stand firm in my convictions." Hollis Vasquez Rutledge was the founder and chairman of Mission Hi-YAF near the Texas border with Mexico. Encouraged by teachers who served as sponsors, it was his first political activity. Rutledge went on to become state chairman of his church denomination's high school group and then student government president at Pan American University.

Local YAF chapter efforts to provide support to American troops in Vietnam and those wounded and living in Veterans Administration hospitals began as early as 1965 with the escalation of troop assignments and American ground troop involvement in the war. Developing projects on their own, YAF chapters took a variety of approaches to showing support for American troops. During the Fall semester of 1968, the University of Colorado collected paperback books to be sent to servicemen in Vietnam while the University of Dayton chapter collected gift items and Christmas cards to be delivered to wounded veterans in VA hospitals. Likewise, Southern Illinois University YAF solicited donations for "Operation Buddy" to send Christmas gifts and cards to servicemen in Vietnam.[356] The Indianapolis Community YAF chapter sponsored a program to send messages to Vietnam. Anyone having a relative or friend serving in Vietnam was invited to send a taped Christmas message. The YAF chapter enclosed an American flag lapel pin and a blue button and then forwarded the recording on to the serviceman.

The national organization launched a major, coordinated effort to provide assistance to wounded veterans in the Fall of 1971 when it announced "Project Appreciation." Local chapters were sent Project Appreciation kits that included personal items such as toothbrushes and paste, after shave lotion, playing cards and dominoes, as well as copies of conservative periodicals such as *Human Events, New Guard,* and *National Review* and paperback editions of *Conscience of a Conservative.* Once they received their shipment, the YAF chapters would assemble the kits, organize a visit to a nearby Veterans Administration hospital, and present the kits to wounded servicemen. Project Appreciation was an important means for activating YAF community chapters throughout 1971 and 1972 but also attracted participation from campus groups.

Kings County YAF took on this project throughout the Spring of 1972, delivering Project Appreciation kits to those in the Brooklyn Veterans Administration hospital.[357] The District of Columbia YAF community chapter assembled kits and helped DC college chapters deliver them at Walter Read Army Medical Center. Canisius College YAF paid Easter visits to patients at the Buffalo VA hospital and presented them with Project Appreciation kits. The University of Akron and Kent State University YAF chapters joined together to work on the project. According to Brad Ellis, Kent State chairman, the YAF members wanted "to show in some small but meaningful way, that we appreciate these veterans and to make a public statement in opposition to those persons who want to write off our veterans as 'war criminals.'" YAF members distributed the Project Appreciation kits at the Brecksville and Cleveland Veterans Administration hospitals.

YAF's final involvement in the Vietnam war controversy was on the question of whether or not to grant amnesty to those who either avoided military service illegally or deserted from the military after induction. During the campaign, President Nixon took a firm stand against amnesty and continued to express that throughout 1973 but the public cries for amnesty continued, especially after the withdrawal of the last American troops from Vietnam in the Spring of the year. The national office also released a new "No Amnesty" issues paper for recruitment and distribution purposes.

Over the next several months, YAF chapters and state organizations took up the issue. In New York, eighteen YAF chapters in Nassau County made a concerted effort to influence their area congressmen on the issue. Ralph Munroe, State Vice Chairman of Virginia, held a news conference in Richmond to outline his state organization's opposition to blanket amnesty and called on the Old Dominion state's congressional delegation to stand against any unconditional and all-encompassing amnesty for deserters and draft evaders. State Chairman Pat Geary and National Director Pat Nolan led a similar effort in California.[358]

The most prominent YAF spokesman on the amnesty issue was Jerry Norton, YAF's publications director and a Vietnam veteran. Norton was the author of the brief YAF Issues Paper on amnesty where he summarized the organization's position by saying "For a democratic government to be viable, its citizens cannot pick and choose with impunity what laws they will obey and what laws they will ignore; that is why we oppose amnesty."[359] Norton made a tour of Maryland, including a talk on the issue at Towson State College and an appearance on Baltimore television. At the University of North Carolina – Greensboro, he debated the issue with UNC-G professor James Reston, Jr., son of the *New York Times* columnist. Other local YAF leaders also spoke out on the issue that Spring.

YAF continued to oppose amnesty, as did Richard Nixon while he remained in the White House. However, shortly after assuming the office of President, Gerald Ford issued a conditional amnesty offer in exchange for two years of public service work. Few of those eligible took advantage of the program and a report one year later showed that of those few who accepted, sixty percent evaded or deserted from their public service commitment.[360] Then, in the face of a failing program of conditional amnesty, one day after becoming President, James Earl Carter pardoned all who had illegally evaded military service. As of early 1977, the United States had removed all military personnel from Vietnam, the war against Communism in Southeast Asia had been lost, and those who had violated the draft laws of the United States had now been exonerated. It was the end of a long and contentious period in American history but one whose consequences would be felt for many years thereafter.

While it is true that many who were first motivated by anti-New Left and pro-Vietnam activities faded from involvement as the campuses quieted down, nevertheless YAF continued to produce effective future conservative leaders throughout the 1970s and 1980s. YAF was integrally involved in the political process but its objective was to advance conservative principles more than to promote individual personalities. Its standard was the Sharon Statement and its campaign efforts were directed towards assisting those who would advance conservative principles. Action, in other words, had a definite purpose grounded in philosophical roots.

Moreover, the leftist challenge to the American university system had to be opposed and only YAF was there to provide student opposition to their radical goals. Just as importantly, YAF provided an oasis of support for conservatives in a sea of liberalism. Jeff Kane remembers the impact this had on him and other young conservatives. "Everything was politicized on campus and I remember the ostracizing the left tried to do to all of those in our YAF chapter. The thought that anyone supported the war was so out there that we were branded as something less than human." This essential role of Young Americans for Freedom in standing up to the radicals who wished to destroy the entire system was noted by others also. Reporting on YAF's Tenth Anniversary celebration in 1970, C. S. Horn noted,

> *Again and again, the note was sounded: radicalism is fragmented,*
> *discredited, disordered, dying, and in its death struggle it will pull*
> *our universities and our political system over with it if it can; it is*
> *up to YAF –because YAF is the only organization available willing*
> *to do it – to make sure the universities survive.*[361]

Looking back on the conflicts and confrontations occurring on American campuses in the 1960s and the overwhelming campaign of the Left to defeat American efforts in Vietnam, one can surely ask, if YAF had not rallied those forces opposed to the Left on campus and garnered support for the Vietnam War among the youth of America, then who would have done it? In this respect, YAF's role was critical in showing support for American troops and a strong stand against the spread of Communism.

When Young Americans for Freedom was formed in 1960, the original members saw themselves in a philosophical and ideological battle against "the Establishment" – an establishment of Eastern liberal politicians in control of both national political parties, an establishment of liberal media forces, and an establishment of liberal administrators and professors on most American campuses. As the decade progressed, the expansion of the Vietnam war and the rise of radical leftist organizations occasioned a shift in focus for YAF. In national politics, their candidate had won the Republican presidential nomination and more young conservatives were assuming positions within the party structure. In defense of the effort to defeat communism in Southeast Asia, it became necessary to support many of the Johnson and Nixon Administration policies. On campus, when the radical leftists took over buildings, closed down campuses, and resorted to other forms of violence, YAF chapters were sometimes viewed as supporting the established order on campus.

By the 1970s, YAF was once again on the offensive against what they perceived as the establishment, a liberal establishment on most American college campuses. To battle this liberal establishment, consisting of administrators, faculty and fellow students, YAF chapters used a number of different approaches. Early on, YAF determined that an effective means of spreading the conservative message and recruiting new members was through the use of brief 8 ½ by 11 inch three-fold issues papers. The initial seven covered topics ranging from social security to student subversion. Periodically these issues papers were updated with more current information and supplemented with additional topics.

Beginning in 1969, national YAF packaged six programs under the title "Young America's Freedom Offensive" designed to allow individual chapters to select from the list and focus on those they believed more applicable to their situation. Initially, the six were (1) the Freedom versus Communism high school study course which YAF lobbied state legislatures for inclusion in the high school curriculum; (2) majority coalitions to combat the left on campus; (3) support for a voluntary military; (4) opposition to East-West trade in strategic goods; (5) youth in politics; and (6) member involvement in independent sector solutions to societal problems. Soon thereafter, YAF modified it to a more encompassing Campus Freedom Offensive that included possible legal action, campaigns against mandatory student fees, involvement in student government elections, a push for free market economics courses, and a commitment to open recruitment on campus.[362]

During the late 1960s and through the 1970s, the national office prepared and distributed a number of "how to" manuals for use by local chapters and state organizations. There were separate high school, college and community chapter organizational manuals that had initially been prepared in the early 1960s. These were updated and supplemented by a 112 page book, *The Complete Chapter Chairman*, written by Jerry Norton and distributed beginning in 1970. That same year saw the publication of Jim Hager's *Politics: Campus Style* and Bruce Eberle's *Direct Mail Fundraising for State Organizations* along with updated versions of *Film Programs for YAF Chapters*, *Speakers Program for YAF Chapters*, and *A Capsule Course in Communications*. The previous year, a rather comprehensive *State Organizational Manual* was made available and then revised and updated in 1972. Around the same time, Don Feder of Boston University and David Havelka and Paul Skocz of the University of Maryland co-authored *Do It! or publishing a conservative underground newspaper*, a 44 page manual that was printed and distributed by the national organization. All of these publications were designed to assist the YAF member and chapter in their efforts at becoming more effective agents for conservatism.

The national office supported a series of fourteen state leadership conferences during July and August, 1970 with an additional five as the Fall semester began.[363] Building on the success of the state leadership conferences, the national office sponsored "Freedom Offensive Conferences" during the 1970-71 academic year. These were designed to be one-day conferences focusing on one aspect of Young America's Freedom Offensive, conducted by YAF state organizations but with speakers provided by the national office.

While many YAF members had long expressed concern over the funding of leftist projects and speakers out of mandatory fees collected by student governments, no real organized effort to resist payment or simply abolish such fees took place until 1969 when separate efforts launched the campaign on both coasts. In May of 1969, the University of Southern California YAF chapter initiated a campaign to abolish the mandatory fee.[364] Two months later, on July 14, 1969, Judith Abramov, chairman of the YAF chapter at the State University of New York at Stony Brook, wrote to the student government executive committee, with a copy to the Chancellor and University President. She declared, "It is with great sadness and anger that I inform you of my intent not to pay the Student Activities Fee for the 1969-70 academic year. I have urged all those with whom I have come in contact to do the same in the hope of crippling – even if ever so slightly – student government."[365] Abramov went on to cite the use of mandatory student fees in printing "Dump (University President) Toll" bumper stickers and buttons, granting $4,000 to Black Students United for a planned trip to Africa, allocating funds for bail money for students indicted after a drug bust, and allocating $25,000 for "Stress Analysis Research." The letter was reprinted in *New Guard* and became the impetus for other chapters launching similar campaigns against mandatory fees.

Beyond raising public concern over the issue through news releases, independent publications, and appearances before student government, YAF chapters frequently used petitions and forced referenda on campus to measure student opposition to the continued imposition of mandatory fees. On several campuses, the fee issue was a spur to YAF involvement in campus politics, resulting in the election of YAF members to student government positions.

It took a while for the national YAF organization to launch a concerted campaign against mandatory fees but it eventually prepared and distributed a handbook on the student fees issue, providing examples and ammunition that could be used on any number of campuses. In the Fall of 1969 at the University of Tennessee at Knoxville, the YAF chapter launched an investigation into the use of student fees. Of particular concern was the speakers funded by such fees. UT YAF would continue its attack on fees and use it as a major issue in rallying support for conservative candidates for student government.

At the same time, Brown University YAF filed suit to prohibit tuition money being used for political purposes. YAF members at the University of Washington filed a similar suit while YAFers filed suit against the University of Nebraska at Lincoln. Following a similar path, the University of New Hampshire chapter launched a suit to enjoin the use of mandatory fees for political activities.[366] In April of 1973, the University of Texas chapter filed a petition for a temporary injunction against the *Daily Texan* newspaper for endorsing candidates. This was denied but the issue of state funds being used for political purposes had been brought to the public's attention.

At the traditionally radical leftist campus of San Francisco State College, Pat Colglazier led YAF in collecting 1,885 signatures against mandatory fees. The University of Arizona YAF criticized the use of fees to bring only liberal and leftist speakers to campus. On one occasion, those fees paid to bring Communist leader Angela Davis to campus. When she refused to debate Phillip Abbott Luce, YAF made an issue of it, pointing out the clear bias in the speakers program. Youngstown University YAF used the fee issue to elect several YAF members to the Student Senate.[367]

One of the campuses where YAF was successful was at the University of California at San Diego. YAF chairman Jim Sills led a referendum campaign in March 1972 that saw fees defeated in a vote of 1,387 to 516. [368] YAF leaders went one step further and attempted to "work out a complete alternative package of voluntaristic action... showing how our system might function in practice."[369] Grit and determination finally paid off at the University of Southern California where YAF overcame the opposition of university bureaucrats and student government "wannabees" when they won the final vote against fees. As two of those active in the effort concluded, "In February of 1975, six months after that vote and five and a half years after we had begun our campaign, the fee was collected on a voluntary basis."[370]

Over the next several years, both local YAF chapters and the national organization continued the campaign against mandatory fees. As a YAF publication stated in 1976, "Young Americans for Freedom is the only organization fighting to stop this liberal tyranny in higher education. YAF's position is that public institutions, especially institutions of education, have no business requiring students to subsidize opinions which some find abhorrent."[371] YAF also began distributing a light-hearted flyer in the 1970s titled "Are you old enough to make your own decisions?" with a drawing of a Linus-like character sucking his thumb and holding a blanket. The message at the bottom was "End Mandatory Fees."

While most of YAF's campaigns were not successful in banning mandatory fees, they did open up the system on some campuses by either requiring a vote of all students before fees could become mandatory or allowing some form of rebate or waiver to those who wished not to pay student activity fees. YAF's involvement on this issue did point out the use and misuse of funds by student governments, brought such funding under closer public scrutiny, and showed YAF's commitment to individual choice and free association as opposed to compulsory actions, whether by government or by student entities.

At least one aspect of the mandatory fees issue – the composition of the speakers paid with mandatory fees – is now addressed on a regular basis by Young America's Foundation. While encouraging pressure on college administrations and student governments to provide more balance in their speakers' programs, the Foundation has taken positive action by assisting students in sponsoring prominent conservative spokesmen. The Foundation has distributed a "Campus Conservative Battle Plan" to assist students determined to bring about change and it provides financial assistance or outright sponsorship of conservative speakers. William F. Buckley, Jr. was a frequent speaker on campuses at lectures sponsored by Young America's Foundation and believed that they were "experiences of infinite importance."[372] In addition to Buckley, some of the prominent political leaders sponsored by Young America's Foundation on American college campuses have included Margaret Thatcher, Lech Walesa, Colin Powell, Edwin Meese, and Steve Forbes.

Ever since it's founding, some YAF leaders had been actively involved in student government.[373] By the early 1970s, more YAF chapters and members were becoming involved in campus elections. Jim Hager's booklet, *Politics – Campus Style*, had been published and distributed by the YAF national office and influencing student government became a priority for many chapters. Over the remainder of the decade YAF members on a number of campuses continued to be involved in campus politics as candidates and office-holders.

For several years YAF activists at the University of Southern California held leadership positions in student government. Among them were Pat Nolan, who became California Assembly Minority Leader, John Lewis, who served in both the California Assembly and State Senate, and Jim Lacy, who served as Mayor Pro-Tem of Dana Point, California. YAF's success on the USC campus led Nolan to conclude in 1971 that, "YAF isn't so much concerned with the Left anymore. They're a thing of the past. The revolution is over. We're not out to make headlines anymore. We're putting people into areas of effectiveness rather than publicity."[374]

There were a number of other campus issues that arose in the early 1970s and attracted the involvement of YAF. Each chapter provided an opportunity for leadership development, consensus building, and effective organizational work. Out of all these diverse efforts, new leadership for the conservative movement was developing.

While YAF remained true to the core principles laid out in the "Sharon Statement, the 1970s brought to the forefront a number of what would subsequently be called "social issues" that showed division within the conservative ranks. Many YAF members welcomed the changing attitudes in American society as enhancing individual freedom and for them social change did not require acceptance of left-wing ideologies. As Kathy Forte, YAF chairman at University of Southern California in 1969, explained her position,

> *It seems clear that the cultural revolution which is now taking place in America will indeed succeed in changing America for the better; however, doubts emerge at the point where I am urged to take part in a more devastating political revolution.*
>
> *I will not join a violent revolution, I will not swallow Marxist ideology any more than I will follow the rantings of George Wallace… If a war is to be waged, it must be a war of the minds, in which a free interplay of ideas are interchanged and assimilated in the making of a better, more beautiful society.*[375]

Forte's differentiation between political revolution and social change was one shared by many in YAF, not merely those of a more libertarian persuasion. What began as a debate over the changing attitudes towards women, soon extended into a discussion of individual rights and the role of government.

First up in the period before the Supreme Court's decision on abortion was the question of women's liberation and what should be the appropriate conservative response to the movement. In April 1972, Carol Dawson Bauman, former National Director and editor of *New Guard*, presented what she called "A Conservative View of Women's Liberation." She came to the discussion as a life-long conservative who had been active in politics since her undergraduate days, as a Roman Catholic who had been educated at a Catholic college, and as a married mother of three at the time pregnant with her fourth child. Bauman began by asking and answering the question of why women had been willing to accept subservient roles in the past. "Why has it taken women so long to begin to demand equal treatment? Because of prejudice, and because of the attitude drummed into us for so many years: if you act too smart or display too much ability, men won't find you attractive."[376] Apart from the drive to achieve equal treatment, Bauman saw the women's liberation movement as awakening women to the possibility and the delight of interacting with other women on an equal and non-competitive basis. "Now women can assess one another merely as fellow human beings who happen to be members of the same sex. They make good friends, can hold intelligent conversations, and are every bit as interesting as men are." While disagreeing with some of the tactics employed by leaders of the women's liberation movement, Bauman saw its overall development as positive for all women.

It did not take long for an opposing view to surface. Two months later, the magazine presented a rebuttal by Kathy King Teague, a long-time YAF activist from Missouri and then Executive Secretary of the Charles Edison Youth Fund. Teague's response basically centered on defending the positive attributes of the traditional American female as wife and mother. She viewed the women's liberation movement as placing too much emphasis on equal work opportunities with goals that are short sighted and materialistic. "A human being's worth cannot be judged by how much the personnel department decides his wage should be," according to Teague. Viewing women's liberation as an attack on the traditional family, Teague noted, "as if Gloria Steinem and her contingent of braless spinsters aren't enough, we have one of our own conservatives, Carol Bauman, who has been taken in by their sharp-tongued assaults on marriage and the family."[377] The advice Mrs. Teague had for Mrs. Bauman and others who looked positively on women's liberation was clear: "What women's liberation should be fostering is more good mothers, who believe that their role as a mother is indeed a unique one."

Clearly, there were opposing views within the organization on this issue. YAF's willingness to bring up and debate controversial issues, especially those on which there was no unanimity of opinion in the organization, was evident throughout the early 1970s. In addition to the differences on women's liberation and the equal rights amendment, YAF's magazine launched a series of articles on the overall topic "Privacy, the Role of Government, and the Rights of the Individual." The series focused on six issues involving individual rights that were topics of popular discussion at the time: population control, childhood training, military conscription, religion and social values, privacy and surveillance, and victimless crimes.

While each of these topics generated a good deal of discussion among YAF members, both in terms of letters to the magazine as well as programmatic discussions for local chapter meetings, it was the "victimless crimes" article that generated the most debate. That Fall, Randy Goodwin and Jim Sills of California YAF responded to David Brudnoy's argument for decriminalization of marijuana by pointing out what they regarded as the dangerous aspects associated with its use. To them, marijuana was a harmful and addictive drug that, if made legal, would do irreparable harm to all of American society.[378] The letters, pro and con, came in to the magazine, over the next few months. Then came Richard Cowan's article in defense of decriminalization a few months later. Cowan, one of YAF's founders and a former National Director, had become a noted proponent of marijuana legalization and was active with the National Organization for the Reform of Marijuana Laws. In his article he stressed the medical uses for marijuana and disputed the claims of its harm and addiction.[379] The flow of letters began once again.

One point was clear. While there were differences and disagreements on important issues and concerns, the young conservative movement was alive and well in the 1970s. It had moved beyond Vietnam, had taken a more active role in campus affairs, and was willing to address controversial social issues even when no consensus was present on how best to deal with those issues. But the organization was also involving itself in a number of political battles as it entered the decade of the 1970s. These would test its strength as well as provide an opportunity for the development of new leaders, a second generation whose members would go on to assume leading roles in American politics into the 21st century. There would be victories in unexpected places, trials and tribulations with the downfall of a presidency, and excruciatingly close defeats that, over time, would turn into a historic victory. It was a new decade and a new era for politics and YAF was ready to assume a leadership role on the American scene.

— 6 —

A Decade of New Politics

T HE YEAR 1970 WAS A SIGNIFICANT ONE for conservatives and Young Americans for Freedom. That year marked the tenth anniversary of the organization's founding, an occasion that was recognized with a return to YAF's birthplace in Sharon, Connecticut. Later that Fall, two political victories showed the increased influence of the young conservatives who played major roles in the re-election of Governor Reagan and the election of James Buckley to the United States Senate. Soon thereafter, YAF and the conservative movement began a separation and eventual divorce from a Republican President, considered the possibilities of encouraging the formation of a third party, and led the challenge to a sitting President's nomination. Throughout the decade, YAF members played an important role in the political process and YAF was viewed as an essential element of the growing conservative movement. With stops and starts, the efforts during those ten years led to the eventual presidential victory of Ronald Reagan as another new decade was about to begin.

As the 1970s started, Young Americans for Freedom made a major commitment to expanding its members' involvement in political campaigns. While the right to vote for 18 year olds would not be extended to all elections until 1971, high school and college students could and did play essential roles in many campaigns. During the summer of 1970, national YAF sponsored twenty-two "Youth in Politics" conferences across the country, training young conservatives in the various techniques that could be employed to increase support for their candidate.[380] To increase their effectiveness, YAF published a booklet titled *You &*

Politics, showing members how to organize "youth for" campaigns, to maximize involvement of young people by combining practical projects with fun activities that would attract more participants, and to obtain media coverage for the youth projects and the candidate.[381]

Election year 1970 brought about YAF member involvement in several campaigns across the country from Ronald Reagan and George Murphy in California to Bill Brock in Tennessee and Harry Byrd in Virginia, to Jim Buckley and Jack Kemp in New York. YAF members were involved in each of these campaigns and many others. In a key Senate race in Tennessee, Bill Brock's youth campaign included YAF leaders Jim Duncan, Alan Gottlieb, Todd and Mary Gardenhire and many others while YAFers from throughout Virginia provided a base of youth support for Independent candidate Harry Byrd, Jr. It was the YAF members from Canisius College, led by Ron Robinson, and from SUNY-Buffalo, under Rick Gorsky and Jackie Davies, that provided youth support for Jack Kemp in his first campaign for Congress, a race won only due to the votes he received on the Conservative Party's ballot line.[382] Meanwhile, in suburban Chicago, Phil Crane won his first re-election after being victorious in a 1969 special election.

Of particular interest to conservatives was the re-election effort of Governor Reagan who was already being viewed as a future GOP presidential candidate. This was also the year in which Senator George Murphy was a candidate for re-election and YAF members were involved in both campaigns. Led by State Chairman Bill Saracino, YAF members volunteered for Reagan and Murphy and put in long hours stuffing envelopes, knocking on doors, and providing enthusiasm at campaign rallies. Saracino had been chairman of Youth for Rafferty in the 1968 contest for Senate and gained valuable statewide campaign experience.[383]

Patrick Geary was a student at the UC-Irvine who had joined YAF just before the Reagan re-election campaign, an experience he remembers fondly: "YAF enabled me to meet great Americans like Ronald Reagan and William F. Buckley. YAF helped me formulate and articulate the political beliefs which I still hold today." The Reagan re-election campaign was also the entry point into YAF for John Lewis while he was still a high school student. As he recently noted, "my entire life was shaped and changed by my involvement in YAF. Joining the YAF in the early 70s shaped my philosophy, led to lasting friendships and was a primary influence on my elected success." First elected to the California State Assembly in 1980, Lewis served there until 1991 and then for the next ten years was a California State Senator before term limits ended his career in the legislature. While Reagan would go on to a re-election victory by a margin exceeding 500,000 votes, liberal Congressman John Tunney defeated Murphy and captured the Senate seat.[384]

Perhaps the most significant victory for conservatives in 1970 took place in

New York as James Buckley became the junior United States Senator, elected on the Conservative Party line. The story begins, however, a few years earlier. The Buckleys were a unique family of ten children whose home became the birthplace of Young Americans for Freedom. Of the ten, Jim was the second oldest son, followed by Bill whose own campaign for Mayor of New York City some five years earlier had been the first family political campaign. In fact, the senatorial election of 1970 was not the first venture in politics for Jim, who had been his brother's campaign manager in that mayoralty race and also the Conservative candidate for United States Senator in 1968.

While the Conservative Party leadership had attempted in the Fall of 1967 to draft Bill Buckley as the party's candidate against liberal Republican Senator Jacob Javits, he believed that he had already fulfilled his duty and turned them down. The leaders then focused on Jim and asked him to be the candidate. When asked for advice, younger brother Bill urged him to run, noting that from his experience in 1965, "nothing is quite the same again. There is a certain exhilaration in making one's points well, in feeling the response of a crowd in reaction to one's own rhetorical arguments."[385] Jim Buckley succumbed and his first campaign for the United States Senate was underway.

Just as YAF had been integrally involved in the 1965 campaign for Mayor, chapters and members throughout the state and ultimately nationally played important roles in the 1968 Jim Buckley campaign for U.S. Senate against the Republican incumbent, Jacob Javits, who also obtained the Liberal Party nomination, and Democratic candidate Paul O'Dwyer. New York YAF state chairman Jim Farley held the additional position as chairman of Youth for Buckley and involved as many YAF members as possible in the campaign.[386] On several campuses, Youth for Buckley worked with College Republicans and the Youth for Nixon effort. At St. John's, the YAF chapter set up tables on campus for the "Nixon-Buckley" ticket.[387]

When the votes were all tallied, combining those he received on both the Republican and Liberal Party lines, Jacob Javits was re-elected, but with only 49.7% of the vote while Jim Buckley on the Conservative Party line received 17.3% of the total vote and pulled in 1,139,402 votes. Buckley's vote total was the most to that point for a Conservative Party candidate, more than twice the previous high of Paul Adams in his 1966 gubernatorial campaign. As Arnold Steinberg indicated, "the 1968 campaign was a campaign of impact but not one designed to win."[388] Yet, in many ways, the 1968 campaign helped make possible the victory two years later. To the media and conservatives nationwide, what it did was give a certain level of credibility to the 1970 campaign before it even began. Having campaigned statewide and having polled more than one million votes against a Republican incumbent, Jim Buckley could be viewed as a serious candidate when the 1970 contest started, if he could be convinced to run again.

Moreover, the 1968 campaign was, in many ways, a dry run for the young conservative activists who would be trained in the first campaign and go on to assume leadership positions in the 1970 effort. Jim Farley and Ron Docksai were already YAF leaders in 1968 and would play key roles in the subsequent campaign. But others were learning and gaining campaign experience. As Herb Stupp recently noted, "I was 18 and just getting involved in YAF. I was a basic volunteer in Jim Buckley's campaign, going door to door with literature in Queens neighborhoods like Rego Park and Middle Village." Donald Harte had just graduated from high school in Nassau County, where he had been a YAF high school chapter chairman, and became involved in the 1968 Jim Buckley campaign. When the next senatorial election rolled around, Harte was beginning his freshman year at Adelphi University and ready to put in more hours for the Buckley campaign. And there were many others.

It was the tragic murder of Robert F. Kennedy in June 1968 that produced the forces leading to a second Jim Buckley campaign for the United States Senate in 1970. When Governor Rockefeller appointed upstate Republican Congressman Charles Goodell in September 1968, he was perceived as a moderate conservative who had represented the Jamestown area for ten years. Upon becoming a member of the United States Senate, Goodell veered sharply to the left on a wide range of issues, including opposition to continued American involvement in the Vietnam war. With the election of Richard Nixon to the White House in November 1968, Goodell became a leading Republican critic of the Administration when he joined liberal Democrats in sponsoring legislation to cut off money for the war effort and in 1969 introduced a sense of the Senate resolution calling on the House to impeach Nixon for expanding the war into Cambodia. By 1970, when Goodell was in line to become the GOP nominee for a full term in the Senate, Vice President Spiro T. Agnew labeled Goodell a "radical liberal."[389] In fact, Goodell's ideological shift was sufficient to earn him the Liberal Party nomination in addition to the Republican nod.

The Democratic nominee was Richard Ottinger, a three-term Congressman. Ottinger had first been elected in 1964, ousting a conservative Republican after spending personal and family fortunes to finance it. Six years later, he was opposed in the Democratic primary by Congressman Richard "Max" McCarthy, Theodore Sorensen, a former speechwriter for President Kennedy, and Paul O'Dwyer, attorney and anti-war activist who had been the Democratic nominee two years earlier.[390] In the primary, Ottinger outspent his opponents seven to one to receive the party's nomination. In the pre-Watergate era without limits on contributions, Ottinger would go on to spend some five million dollars in the November race, most of it from his mother, who's wealth came from the

U.S. Plywood Corporation. While his official campaign slogan was "Ottinger Delivers," Buckley staffer Arnie Steinberg changed it to "Ottinger's Mother Delivers." Denied the Liberal Party endorsement, Ottinger did gain the backing of Americans for Democratic Action and the New Democratic Coalition. During the Fall, Goodell and Ottinger both battled for the desired label of liberal while criticizing each other's records in Congress.[391]

While Goodell was solidifying his Republican support and picking up the Liberal Party endorsement and Ottinger was fending off the challenge from his Democratic primary opponents, James L. Buckley was slowly starting to build a campaign team to seek victory on the Conservative Party line. As Arnie Steinberg recalled, "I flew into NYC on June 3, precisely 5 months before the election; there was no campaign; we arranged to borrow $50,000 in seed money; I operated out of Catawba (Buckley family company), and we slowly started to hire."[392] Having completed a "dry run" less than two years earlier, this time the Buckley team was determined to mount a serious effort to win in 1970.

What started with only two staffers in June, soon expanded into a team worthy of carrying a campaign to all areas of the geographically large and politically diverse state. Overall campaign strategist was F. Clifton White while the campaign director handling all day-to-day aspects of the effort was David Jones, who had recently left his post as Executive Director of Young Americans for Freedom.

On June 23rd, Democratic primary voters brought the November election contest into focus as they selected Richard Ottinger over his three opponents. Immediately, Ottinger began attacking Goodell as if it were a two-man contest. This perception of the almost irrelevancy of the Buckley campaign existed in the media for the early months of summer 1970. It was a misperception that shrewd political observers would have avoided. As one former reporter for the *New York Times* later noted, "Any sensible politician or thoughtful journalist should have remembered that in another three-way Senate race, just two years earlier, Buckley had polled 1.1 million votes while spending only $115,000."[393]

Once Ottinger became the Democratic nominee, the Buckley campaign strategy became evident. As Clif White recalled later, it was to "portray Goodell and Ottinger as birds of the same feather despite their party allegiances, and have them split the liberal vote evenly so that Jim could squeak in with a bare plurality."[394] The Buckley campaign was able to have their candidate participate in three debates including both Ottinger and Goodell. According to White, Buckley's standing in the polls went up after each debate as more New Yorkers became aware of him. On October 25th, the *New York Daily News* released its final poll: Buckley 37%, Ottinger 30%, Goodell 24%. Goodell considered dropping out of the race but then purchased a 30-minute spot on television to make his last appeal to the voters, vowing to stay in the race and win. On October 30th, the *New York Times* endorsed Goodell, a move that many believe prevented any significant seepage of liberals to Ottinger but also may have kept a number of upstate New Yorkers behind the candidate.[395]

As the campaign progressed, it became clear that other Republicans were beginning to vacillate in their support for Goodell. Rockefeller was running for his fourth term as Governor and did not want to be dragged down by the lagging support for the Republican Senate candidate. While remaining officially committed to Goodell, the existence of "Rockefeller-Buckley" bumper stickers and signs reflected the intentions of many New York voters. With Agnew criticizing the liberal voting record of Goodell, the White House appeared ambivalent also. In fact, Nixon advance personnel tipped off the Buckley campaign that the President would make a stop outside New York City on his way back to Washington. As YAF's magazine reported the events, "When President Nixon stopped at Westchester Airport, Youth for Buckley organized hundreds of youths with Buckley signs to greet him…The great bulk of the delegation were YAFers."[396] It was a "carefully advanced maneuver" with a "wordless endorsement worth a thousand words."[397] Clearly, at least some at the White House were not adverse to a Buckley victory.

When the votes were tallied, New York had a new United States Senator and the conservative movement had a new hero. Buckley received 2,288,190 votes running on the Conservative Party line while Ottinger as the Democratic candidate had 2,171,232 votes, a margin of slightly more than 100,000 votes. Combining his votes on both the Republican and Liberal lines, Senator Goodell had obtained support from 1,434,472 New Yorkers. The only counties carried by Goodell were rock-ribbed GOP counties upstate, especially in his former congressional district. At his celebration, Buckley made the now famous declaration: "I am the voice of the new politics." New York had elected not only a conservative, but a Conservative.

Beginning in the summer and throughout the Fall, the youth campaign was the essential secret ingredient of the Buckley effort. As Dave Jones observed, "They were our blitz squad. They distributed leaflets and performed tasks on a moment's notice, providing a solid base we could always depend on."[398] The Youth for Buckley effort came up with innovative ways of drawing attention to their candidate, using techniques that would make the voter smile with satisfaction. A most effective technique was to organize a group to head for shopping center parking lots armed with windex and paper towels. They washed more than 100,000 windshields, placing a circular under each windshield wiper reading: Your windshield has been washed courtesy of James L. Buckley. Now that you can see your way clearly, we hope you'll vote for Jim Buckley on November

3rd.[399] In the New York City metropolitan area, most young Buckley volunteers were students at commuter colleges who lived at home with their parents, many holding part-time jobs. Others were high school students from the City and its suburbs.[400]

The official campaign student organization, Youth for Buckley, was headed by Herb Stupp of St. John's University as Chairman with Rich Macksoud of Columbia as Vice Chairman.[401] Among those who were back again for their second Buckley campaign as volunteers were Jim Farley, who had headed up the 1968 effort, Ron Docksai and Don Harte, as well as Stupp and Macksoud. The number of future leaders who got their start in the Buckley campaign is impressive. Many went on to leadership positions in YAF and then outstanding careers in government, the media, academia and the business world. The enthusiasm of youth was critical to the success of the campaign. As Steinberg noted, "Basically, I was too idealistic and work-centered to believe that hard work would not pay off, and so were the YAFers. Had they been around politics for a longer period, they would have been jaundiced and skeptical. Not knowing they could not win, they did win."[402]

In fact, several of the Youth for Buckley organizers were high school students in the Fall of 1970. Ed Martin was a 16 year old student in Lynbrook, New York when he opened a storefront campaign operation for "Youth for Buckley and Lent," supporting both the senatorial candidate and a victorious Conservative-Republican candidate for Congress. Subsequently he became press spokesman for Senator Al D'Amato and also served as an appointee in the Reagan Administration. Chris Braunlich was a Nassau County high school student and later became YAF leader at Hofstra University.

The leadership of Youth for Buckley comprised almost exclusively members of Young Americans for Freedom. As Herb Stupp, Youth for Buckley chairman, summed up the situation, "Most YAF chapter chairmen formed their own clubs, most of the campaign county chairmen were YAF members, and a large proportion of the youth campaign's manpower was supplied by tireless YAFers performing thankless tasks."[403] Many of those YAF members involved in the campaign would go on to be candidates themselves. Three of the Youth for Buckley leaders later served in the New York State Senate.

Adrienne Flipse has fond memories of her time in YAF and the Buckley campaign. As she recalled, "It gave me the guts to speak up for what I believed, no matter how unpopular. It convinced me to go to law school; it gave me the tools to run for office. It gave me the skill to debate without rancor…It made attending a liberal institution bearable. It gave me friends for life." After graduating from Hofstra University, she received her law degree from St. John's University and, some twenty years later, a Master's of Divinity degree. She is now a partner in the law firm of Carway and Flipse as well as Pastor for Congregational Care at the Community Church of Douglaston.

Without a doubt, the key individual in the entire Youth for Buckley operation was Herb Stupp, a 20-year-old student at St. John's University who had been a foot soldier in the first Buckley senatorial campaign. From 1975-81, Stupp was editorial director of WOR-TV in New York City. During the Reagan Administration he was Regional Director of ACTION and then deputy and acting Regional Director for the Department of Education during the George H. W. Bush Administration. For eight years he was Commissioner of the New York City Department of Aging, serving in the cabinet of Mayor Rudy Giuliani. Looking back, Stupp concluded that "YAF was one of the most important formative experiences in my life, enabling me to become a "conscious" conservative more rapidly and giving me critical analytical skills – a gift for life. I would not be the person I am today without my experiences in YAF." Stupp is a classic example of the lasting contribution of Young Americans for Freedom in the development of leadership - leadership exemplified in his efforts in public service and non-profit community organizations. One could say that it all began with the challenge of the Buckley campaign and his performance in organizing and leading the Youth for Buckley effort.

How important was the Youth for Buckley effort? Shortly after the campaign ended, Arnie Steinberg put it all in perspective. "if there had been no state organization of Young Americans for Freedom, if YAF leadership past and present had not been building over the last years, it would have been impossible to create and carry out an undertaking of the magnitude of the Youth for Buckley effort."[404] The benefits were mutual. As Herb Stupp noted, there were 59 YAF chapters in New York before the election; by Spring of 1971 there were 121. New chapters had been formed but, just as importantly, new leadership had been identified that would carry New York YAF forward as one of the strongest state organizations. And, of course, the Buckley victory was a tremendous shot in the arm for the morale of young conservatives. If it could be done in New York State, well then, it could be done anywhere!

A few weeks after his brother's election to the United States Senate, Bill Buckley invited a number of YAF members to participate in a taping session for his television program, "Firing Line." On December 8, 1970, the YAFers served as an audience for the taping of a Buckley interview program with Vice President Spiro T. Agnew. The second program taped consisted of Buckley being questioned on a wide range of topics by the YAF members. Perhaps the most significant exchange centered on the question of why Buckley had not been as critical of President Nixon and his departures from conservative policies as he would have been with the same programs advocated by a President Hubert

Humphrey. Buckley's response was that "conservatism, as I understand it, is always about two things – its about the paradigm, how things ought to be, - and its about what can you wrest out of the current situation." While working with Nixon was viewed as better than nothing at all, Buckley went on to add, "I think that the conservative movement ought always to make clear what it is that is ideal." [405]

In the response to this one question, Bill Buckley had summarized the dilemma facing young conservatives, and the entire conservative movement, as they considered the Nixon Administration. Nixon was, indeed, on a wide range of issues better than any likely Democratic President. Yet there were so many issues on which he departed from the conservative position. Moreover, to many on campus, Nixon was perceived as a conservative and his policies as those supposedly supported by an organization such as YAF. Should they continue to wrest what they could out of the situation or stand boldly for the ideal?

By the start of the decade YAF was playing a more crucial role in the developing conservative movement in America. As early as January 1969, David Jones had proposed that YAF, the American Conservative Union, *Human Events*, and *National Review* co-sponsor a conservative conference in the Spring of 1969. [406] This memo was followed by a letter to Bill Buckley the following month. [407] While it would be five years before the first such conference was held, in 1970 YAF joined with the other three entities to sponsor an annual conservative awards dinner in Washington, DC, an event that was continued in 1971. During the Fall campaign of 1970, YAF proposed that representatives from the four entities who co-sponsored the awards dinner meet periodically to coordinate policy positions on major issues. The first meeting was held in January and those present expressed concern over the direction of the Nixon Administration but did not agree on any specific path to follow. [408]

By Spring, YAF leaders were searching for alternatives. National Chairman Ron Docksai launched a short-lived "Draft Reagan" movement. On May 21st, the California Governor wrote to Docksai and politely asked that he cease and desist in his efforts. "While I am naturally proud that you hold me in such high regards, I still must ask with all the urgency I can express that you desist. To publicly repudiate any activity of YAF is not something I'm eager to do but, in this instance, I'll have no alternative if this effort continues." [409] Docksai and YAF backed off, not wanting to lose the support of one of their most important advisors. A few days later, on May 25th, representatives of the four groups met and considered expanding their numbers. They would review their options and meet again in two months.

May 1971 also saw the appearance of a critical article on Nixon in YAF's magazine by Jeffrey Bell of the American Conservative Union. Bell's article predicted electoral defeat for the President unless he changed policies that were alienating his 1968 constituency. In words that some would say rang true again years later, Bell proclaimed, "Gone are the days when Republicans could excoriate big Government, high taxes, unbalanced budgets, welfare abuses, and Great Society scandal and profligacy. If Republican candidates tried to revert to these successful past themes now, they would be laughed out of the house."[410] It was a plea for the President to change direction and return to the conservative beliefs and policies that Bell saw as having brought about his victory in the election against Humphrey and Wallace.

With frequent state and regional conferences, YAF was an organization that provided opportunities for feedback from its members. Those members were more and more expressing their opposition to Administration policies and increasingly the President himself. Reporting on the seven YAF regional conferences of Spring 1971, a YAF publication noted, "hearts were not behind any massive effort to re-elect the Richard Nixon of March and April 1971. Their indecision as to the viable alternatives for conservatives in 1972 was a reflection of the dilemma facing all conservatives today."[411]

The time for indecision had passed and it was not only the young conservatives of YAF who were seeking a way to separate themselves from the Nixon Administration. As Jerry Norton, editor of *New Guard*, observed, over the remaining months of Spring 1971, "it became clear to leaders of other Movement elements that YAF's feelings were not unique. Conservatives in general were frustrated by the tendency of the media and public to classify them as supporters of an Administration that they were in fact dissatisfied with."[412] A growing number of conservatives became convinced that Nixon could be influenced more by direct, public criticism than by private pleas for a more conservative direction. It was time for a dramatic step and one that included more than the initial four groups.

On July 26th, a gathering of conservative leaders that became known as the "Manhattan Twelve" released a statement in New York and Washington announcing that they were suspending support of President Nixon. Among those signing the document was YAF executive director Randal C. Teague. While critical of several of the administration's domestic policies, the statement focused more on the overtures to Red China, the failure to respond to Soviet advances in the Mediterranean, and the perceived deterioration of the nation's military position. The statement proclaimed, "in consideration of this record, the undersigned, who have heretofore generally supported the Nixon Administration, have resolved to suspend our support of the administration." They would not be encouraging formal opposition to Nixon in the primaries but were keeping all options open at the time. The statement concluded by saying, "We consider that our defection is an act of loyalty to the Nixon we supported in 1968." The signers included individuals representing the original four entities as well as Anthony Harrigan of the Southern States Industrial Council, Neil McCaffrey of the Conservative Book Club, and J. Daniel Mahoney from the Conservative Party of New York.[413]

The most significant name among the signers was Bill Buckley, not only because of his public recognition but also due to the efforts of those in the administration, especially Henry Kissinger, to appeal for his continued support of Nixon. The following month Nixon added to the conservatives' consternation by taking the United States off the gold standard and imposing wage and price controls. By August, the young conservatives were even more convinced that a divorce from Nixon was needed.

Labor Day weekend 1971 saw some fifteen hundred YAF members and supporters converge on the Shamrock Hilton Hotel in Houston, Texas for YAF's sixth national convention.[414] The organization had, for the first time in its history, surpassed 800 local chapters and had a record number of state organizations in place. An article in the convention program saw the delegates confronting a "choice between principle and expediency, between the real and the ideal, between a commitment to conservatism or to normalcy... Conservatives – and the nation at large – are watching and waiting to discover in which direction the 'New Politics' of young conservatism will turn."[415]

In an effort to reflect its non-partisan nature, the second evening's featured speaker was Democratic Senator Robert Byrd of West Virginia, who had earlier in the year defeated Ted Kennedy for the position of Senate Majority Whip. Byrd, who at that time was considered more conservative than his later voting record reflected, accepted the invitation "to demonstrate that the Democratic party is broad-based enough to include both liberals and conservatives."[416] The YAF members warmly received Byrd's speech and beyond its content saw his presence as reinforcing the organization's independence from the Republican party.

Texas Senator John Tower was a surprise guest and spoke on the need for greater military preparedness. Along with both Bill and Jim Buckley and Barry Goldwater, Tower urged that the convention not make an open break with the Nixon administration. Goldwater's position was made known in a letter to all attendees as well as in the remarks of his former campaign manager, Stephen Shadegg, who spoke on Friday. A small coterie of YAF members supportive of the President opened a Nixon suite during the convention and attempted to quiet down the dissatisfaction with the administration. Also present, "doing missionary work for the administration" as one reporter described their activities, were two past National Chairmen: Tom Huston and David Keene.[417]

One commentator described it as "the largest convention ever and the most peaceful, intelligent debate on resolutions, a veritable era of good feelings." [418]

During the platform discussions, the sentiment against several policies of the Nixon administration became evident. The platform condemned the President's welfare reform plan as a step towards "a guaranteed annual income to a swollen welfare constituency" while another called on the President "to promptly terminate" wage and price controls and "restore freedom to the economy."[419] The platform also called on the President to take prompt steps to "return the United States to superiority in strategic weapons."[420] Another resolution called his scheduled trip to Communist China "morally offensive" and a threat to American alliances with free Asian nations.

One writer noted that "amid chants of 'Dump Nixon,' YAF members denounced administration policies on China, strategic nuclear weapons, welfare and wage-price controls and pledged to raise $750,000 to finance primary challenges to Nixon."[421] As Ron Docksai said in remarks the following day, it was evident to him that the young conservatives in YAF "feel disenfranchised. The man they helped elect President on a conservative platform seems instead to be carrying out the program of Hubert Humphrey. Young conservatives are not kids who can be satisfied with an occasional lollipop from the Administration."[422]

National political reporter David Broder noted, "The YAF delegates, who consider themselves the vanguard of the conservative movement, are realistic enough to know Agnew is not going to challenge Mr. Nixon for the nomination." The signal they were sending was that they want Agnew on the ticket and "to tell any possible conservative challengers for the presidency that they are willing to back a contest against Mr. Nixon in the presidential primaries, if anyone can be found to make it."[423] In what was a purely symbolic action, but one that reinforced their determination to back a serious effort for the nomination, the delegates also voted to raise $750,000 to support a conservative challenge to Nixon's re-election in 1972.

Sunday evening featured an address to the delegates by telephone from Governor Reagan. He commended the young conservatives for holding to their beliefs in the midst of great challenge: "When I think of the philosophy prevalent in so much of the intellectual community, I marvel at the way you have obtained an education yet remained steadfast in your beliefs, resisting the zeitgeist – the wind of our times." Reagan recited a brief overview of 20th century political history and then spoke to their concerns about the administration, "Be critical, be vocal and forceful in urging your views on the President. He needs that input to counter the constant pressure from the opposite side; he needs the arguments you can provide.[424] While acknowledging that Republicans would be horrified if Hubert Humphrey had announced a presidential visit to China, he nevertheless defended Nixon doing so on the basis of his long-standing support for the Republic of China and his actions as Vice President in standing up to Khruschev.

Nixon would remain strong in his meetings with the Chinese Communist leaders, according to Reagan. Reiterating his support for the organization, he concluded by advising the delegates to "consider very carefully the long hard struggle that lies ahead, and how far we've traveled together to reach this moment of hope for all the things we believe in. Weigh the alternatives, and use your strength wisely and well."[425]

The leaders of the young conservative organization would take Reagan's words seriously but their resolve to make evident their programmatic disagreements with the Nixon administration would not go away. As the YAF members left Houston, they were emboldened and encouraged. YAF's role as an essential element in the growing conservative movement would become apparent as they viewed the possibilities of a direct challenge to the re-nomination of the President.

Over the next few weeks, YAF leaders and those from other conservative entities weighed their alternatives and considered the unthinkable – a direct primary challenge to a sitting Republican President. Throughout the Fall, discussions were held among the Manhattan Twelve as to the next step to take after suspending their support of the President. Months earlier, Reagan had disavowed YAF's effort to start a draft movement and indicated his support for Nixon's re-election. Goldwater and Tower had both endorsed a second term for the President, conveying their decisions by letter and speech to the YAF members. Jim Buckley was a freshman Senator and both Phil Crane and Jack Kemp were serving their first full terms in the House.

On October 21st, the Manhattan Twelve hired campaign consultant Jerry Harkins to explore the possibility of primary opposition to Nixon. Five weeks later, on November 30th, he reported back on his initial soundings and concluded that a campaign in New Hampshire could achieve significant success.[426] After receiving Harkins' report, Bill Rusher, Ron Docksai, and Tom Winter met with Congressman John Ashbrook to discuss the possibility of a challenge to Nixon. Ashbrook was a former national chairman of the Young Republicans who had first been elected to Congress in 1960 and served as chairman of the American Conservative Union from 1965 to 1971. The Congressman listened to their appeals and promised a decision by late December. Quickly, the media picked up on his potential candidacy and heightened the interest in a possible challenge to the President.[427] While Ashbrook was weighing his options, the Conservative Party of New York added fuel to the fire when it announced that it would be officially suspending support of Nixon, a serious and practical action that directly challenged the ability of the President to retain a second ballot line in New York State that he had claimed in 1968.[428]

By the middle of the month YAF leaders had met with Ashbrook to discuss the ways in which they could help any Ashbrook campaign. Even before an official announcement YAF members were instrumental in lining up the needed signatures to place his name on the New Hampshire ballot. On December 29th, John Ashbrook announced that he would run in the New Hampshire and Florida primaries and the challenge had begun. A decision had been reached and a candidate had been recruited. Clearly, 1972 would be a volatile political year for conservatives and YAF would be in the midst of it all.

The effort would be known as "Ashbrook for America" and the slogan for the campaign would be "No Left Turn" with the international traffic signal identifying that prohibition as the campaign logo. Immediately upon the announcement of an Ashbrook campaign, YAF swung into action. Connecticut YAF chairman Jim Altham and National Director Dan Rea of Massachusetts moved into New Hampshire to organize youth activity. They were followed by literally hundreds of volunteers. As Lee Edwards recalled, "Ronald Pearson helped coordinate volunteer workers in New Hampshire, especially members of Young Americans for Freedom, which bused in hundreds of students from New England, New York, New Jersey and Pennsylvania."[429]

Essential to the Ashbrook youth efforts was Young America's Campaign Committee (YACC) which funded Youth for Ashbrook operations and provided travel, rooms and meal money for volunteers from Michigan, Ohio, Indiana, Virginia, Maryland, New York, New Jersey, Pennsylvania and the New England states, allowing those YAF members to spend weekends campaigning in New Hampshire. Nationwide, YACC printed and distributed thousands of Ashbrook for President bumper stickers, having them ready before the official campaign committee or anyone else. While technically a separate political committee, the ties to Young Americans for Freedom were obvious to the politically involved and aware. The address for both YACC and Youth for Ashbrook was the same as that for the national YAF office. Through the efforts of YAF and its political action committee hundreds of young conservatives stood for principle in 1972 and promoted a conservative alternative to Richard Nixon. [430] Unfortunately, it was a lonely battle and, in the end, a losing campaign.

Despite these electoral setbacks, the Ashbrook campaign was an essential element in both the maturation of the conservative movement as distinct from the Republican party as well as the role of YAF within that movement. Summing up the campaign, Lee Edwards concluded, "His campaign preserved the conscience of the conservative movement. It demonstrated that conservatives within the Republican party couldn't be taken for granted."[431] On June 7, 1972, John Ashbrook withdrew from the campaign for president but vowed to continue to work for the "principles that made our party great" and so carried forth his efforts in the platform committee deliberations in Miami Beach that August.

Not everyone in YAF, and certainly not in the conservative movement, was interested in supporting a candidate against the President. There were those YAF members such as former National Chairman David Keene and former University of Maryland chapter chairman Warren Parker who worked in the White House or held positions in other departments of the executive branch. There were those not directly involved with the administration who feared that a conservative challenge would harm the movement and the country. Larry Mongillo had published several articles in *New Guard* and claimed an unsuccessful challenge – as he predicted it would be – would be disastrous for conservatives, as a "Democratic administration would be virtually assured, and the conservative element within the Republican Party would suffer a severe loss of power and authority."[432] Mongillo maintained that conservative voices were being heard in the Nixon administration, a situation that would not exist with a Democrat in the White House. He reminded the magazine's readers that while not viewed as a conservative by those active in the movement, Nixon was thought of as a conservative by others. Finally, he pointed out that while the Left succeeded in bringing down Johnson, their effort resulted in Nixon as President, certainly not the left-wing Democrat that they desired.

Mongillo's advice became even more relevant as the Ashbrook campaign faded and Nixon was renominated in Miami Beach. YAF and other conservatives were present and played a role at the convention but their main focus was on the platform and on the rules committee.[433] In the battles over rules for future conventions, historian Theodore White claimed that "Young liberal Republicans, led by the ivory-tower men of the Ripon Society, matched wits with young conservative Republicans of the Young Americans for Freedom in an effort to sway the votes and opinions of their elders."[434] In the end, the conservatives prevailed by a margin of 910 votes to 434. However, as it turned out, Nixon ended up carrying every state except Massachusetts and the District of Columbia, thus negating any delegate strength advantage for traditionally Republican states at the 1976 nominating convention.

As the presidential contest shaped up between Richard Nixon and George McGovern, YAF took two complementary approaches to the election. One was to form a youth group geared to opposing McGovern's election and the other was to emphasize youth involvement in the campaigns of conservative candidates for Congress. To aid those who were concerned over McGovern inroads among young voters in the first presidential election that included 18 year olds in all states, YAF – through its Young America's Campaign Committee – formed "Youth Against McGovern" (YAM). YAM's Board of Directors consisted almost entirely of YAF members, although their titles for identification often indicated other groups in which they were active.

Rather than dedicated to the re-election of Nixon, Youth Against McGovern could be seen as ideologically partisan, with a goal to speak out on the issues. YAM was attempting to reach young people turned off by McGovern and his radical stands, hoping to move their gut reaction against McGovern into a conscious belief in conservatism. Across the nation during the Fall campaign, Youth Against McGovern formed "truth squads" to follow McGovern supporters and show what they perceived as the likely results of the Senator's policies were he to be elected.[435]   They attacked McGovern on a wide range of issues from national security to Vietnam to economic policies.

YAM members were encouraged to show up at McGovern appearances waving white flags. They distributed on campuses and at political rallies a biting tabloid that attacked the South Dakota Senator's far-left proposals. They printed and distributed "Misgovern with McGovern" buttons. Wherever possible, their goal was to show that not all young people were enamored with George McGovern and his liberal agenda. The cover of YAF's November 1972 magazine featured an Alfred E. Neuman-like drawing of McGovern with a caption of "What, Me Govern?" and the character wearing an "Eagleton for VP" button.[436] Whatever hopes the South Dakota Senator had for defeating President Nixon faded rapidly and on election day he was swamped in both popular votes and the Electoral College.

YAF was not focused entirely on the presidential election as it involved itself in the political arena. As one YAF leader pointed out, the members "are calling for, and participating in, a new politics of conservative principle based on ending big government bureaucracy, protecting individual rights, and preserving the national security… The new politics exemplified by YAF concerns itself with the course of our nation not only for the next two, but also the next twenty to forty years."[437]

Two months later, this approach was echoed in a *New Guard* editorial written by Jerry Norton. "As conservatives, then, we contradict our philosophy when we act as though one massive showing at the polls will somehow bring utopia. We must push on all fronts, from the Presidency on down, and not be disappointed if the world is not immediately dazzled by our wisdom."[438] For young conservatives, this meant that there needed to be a long-term dedication to the cause and a realization that no single event or victory would bring about the changes they desired.

It was a message well learned by most of the YAF members as they continued to pursue the promotion of principle over politics. This same message was reinforced in an article by Charles Black, YAF's chapter director, in the following issue of *New Guard*. "If we are to end the rule of liberalism in America, it will take a dedicated, comprehensive campaign, sustained over many years. Though we can right many injustices and start many trends in the next couple of years, it will take much longer to produce the emergence of the large number of American leaders that we need; leaders who will take the initiative and momentum away from the liberals in every important field; leaders who, having heard liberalism's siren song, have rejected its beckoning melody for the more rigorous strains of common sense and the discipline that produces human freedom."[439]

The emphasis on promoting new spokesmen who would go on to represent the conservative movement for many years was an important objective for Young Americans for Freedom. As one historian noted, "YAF focused on the future, using actions to attain the more important goal of capturing political power. As adults, YAF alumni and alumna were all conscious that in retrospect their time in YAF was for learning and that their actions had less important consequences than the decisions they made as adults."[440] Training young people and electing new conservative leaders to Congress ensured a continuing expansion of the conservative movement. In this way, YAF "has made its influence known in ways that proponents of other causes could only dream about."[441]

From the end of the 1972 election to the summer of 1974, the American people went through another calamitous time. First, Vice President Spiro Agnew was forced to resign in October 1973 under a cloud of corruption charges and a plea of no contest to failure to report income on his tax returns. Meanwhile, the nation was absorbed in the continuing unraveling of the Watergate affair and its attempted cover-up by the Nixon Administration. Finally, in August 1974 Richard Nixon boarded Marine One for his last helicopter ride from the White House and Gerald Ford, less than one year since being elevated to the vice presidency, was now the President of the United States.

Like most Americans in the days of 1973 and into the early months of 1974, YAF members were divided on their response to the charges against the President. Long opposed to what they viewed as his departure from conservative orthodoxy in both foreign and domestic policies, Nixon was not one of them and had been merely the lesser of two evils in the 1972 election. At the same time, his most vocal enemies were also their enemies. This led some in YAF to challenge what they saw as an attack on the presidency more than an attack on Nixon.

As Nixon departed and Ford assumed the presidency, there was some hope for change in a more conservative direction. After all, Ford had a relatively conservative voting record as a Congressman from Grand Rapids, Michigan and, while never a YAF Advisor, had supported a number of conservative positions. The honeymoon was brief. Some in the conservative movement, especially William A. Rusher, were already wondering whether there was any future for the Republican party, especially a party led by Gerald Ford. As Rusher recalled the situation, "the Republican party under Ford seemed to be going nowhere that we wanted to go, even though its relatively liberal eastern wing no longer controlled it."[442] A similar perspective was taken by YAF when the *New Guard* said of Ford, "Since his inauguration he has zealously followed the pattern of catering to the schemes of liberal-left proponents established by its predecessor."[443]

In fact, that December issue of *New Guard* had as its dramatic cover in bold letters the words: "A New Third Party: Has Its Time Come?" while inside were articles on the topic by Senator Jesse Helms, Lee Edwards, and Ron Docksai. Jesse Helms was concerned not with creating a new political party but, rather, with the realignment of the two major parties on ideological lines. As he maintained in his article in YAF's magazine, "If we are going to have honesty in government today, we must have honesty in the basic philosophies of our political parties." The challenge for Helms was "the task of realigning our existing political parties, so that the people when they go to the polls, will know what they are voting for – instead of merely whom."[444] Cautioning against the likelihood of campaign success for any new party, Lee Edwards maintained that a party seeking philosophical impact was possible but one that sought electoral impact was unlikely.[445]

With so much discussion centering on the political future of the conservative movement and whether it should attempt to pursue its goals through the existing parties or through the development of a new party, YAF brought together a group of young conservative leaders for a weekend seminar and discussion on "options for conservative political action." Thirteen YAF members met in Chicago on January 10-12, 1975 under the sponsorship of Young America's Campaign Committee. While no conclusions were sought or arrived at, the various possibilities for future political action were discussed, debated, and considered. Taking part were future YAF chairmen Jeff Kane and John Buckley, future Federal Judge Dan Manion, political consultants Bill Saracino and Ron Pearson, and future GOP leaders Charles Black and Frank Donatelli.

Six other YAF leaders made formal presentations at the seminar that were revised and published in a book issued later in 1975.[446] Ron Docksai discussed "Building a Second Major Party," and concluded that the Republican party had failed to represent its former constituency resulting in the need for a new broad-based center-right coalition to avoid one-party government. Wayne Thorburn reviewed the decline of the Republican party over the past thirty years and pointed out the "perils, pitfalls and potentialities" in forming a new party. Robert Moffit covered "Conservatism and the New Politics of Realignment," stressing that what was needed was a more cohesive vehicle than the Republican party but certainly not a purely doctrinal party. Former National YAF Vice Chairman Daniel Rea addressed the issue of "Democratic Support for a New Party" and cited a number of issues on which appeals to disaffected Democrats might be made. Jerry Norton posed some doubts as to the possibilities of a new party winning in 1976 while Ron Robinson focused on elections "Beyond Presidential Politics," emphasizing that whatever path was taken in 1976, conservatives needed to continue to work in the two existing parties to have input into congressional and state politics.

Following the seminar in Chicago, YAF, ACU, *Human Events* and *National Review* co-sponsored their second political action conference on February 13-15, 1975 in Washington, DC and the entire focus was on the correct path for conservatives to take as the presidential election approached. Some five hundred conservatives from across the country attended. Stan Evans, at the time Chairman of ACU, made evident his belief that a new party was needed at the presidential level but his position was rebutted by Karl Rove, then described as "a brilliant young orator," who emphasized the futility of a third party effort in presidential elections while Senator Helms spoke of the need for philosophical realignment of the two existing parties. As Daniel Oliver noted, "Certainly they were divided on how best to proceed, but not about their own dissatisfaction with the present Administration. There was very little outright support for President Ford.[447] Bill Rusher was there to drum up support for his idea of forming a new political party while Tom Anderson of the American Party, an offshoot of the 1968 Wallace presidential campaign, attempted to recruit supporters for his third party effort. While Rusher received a welcome audience from many in attendance, Anderson's reception was less favorable and his group ended up holding a separate meeting.[448]

The closing speaker on Saturday night, introduced by Senator James Buckley, was former California Governor Ronald Reagan. If there was unanimity on any one point among those attending the conference, it was that Ronald Reagan would be their ideal candidate for President. But Reagan was not predisposed to lead a third party challenge to the existing party system. As he asked the assembled conservatives, "is it a third party we need, or is it a new and revitalized second party, raising a banner of no pale pastels, but bold colors which make it unmistakably clear where we stand on all the issues troubling the people?"[449] Despite Reagan's remarks, those attending the conference voted the next day to establish a Committee on Conservative Alternatives (COCA). Initial members included Senator Helms, Congressmen Ashbrook and Bauman, YAF Chairman Docksai, ACU Chairman Evans, Bill Rusher and Tom Winter of *Human Events*.[450]

With Reagan out of office, Young America's Foundation initiated the "Reagan Radio Project" directed by Frank Donatelli, YAF's executive director, and Ron Docksai. As Craig Shirley, noted, "A long, warm relationship existed between the old actor and the young YAFers."[451]   The Foundation raised contributions to sponsor a five-minute daily broadcast of political commentary by Reagan. These radio broadcasts helped to gain greater name recognition and support for the former California Governor prior to his announcement of candidacy in

November 1975. After the 1976 effort, Reagan resumed his broadcasts and they continued until 1979.[452]

While an exploratory committee, Citizens for Reagan, was formed in the summer of 1975, it was not until November that Reagan officially became a candidate for the Republican presidential nomination. The members of the Reagan campaign team composed a virtual "who's who" in YAF annals. In fact, "of the 40 national staff members of Citizens for Reagan, almost half of the executive staff are now or were once active YAF members."[453] The Youth for Reagan operations in the various states were headed in most instances by YAF members. Literally thousands of YAF members volunteered for the effort to gain the Republican presidential nomination. They performed the tedious but critical chores that define a successful campaign and these YAF members were vital elements in several states, including that first losing effort in New Hampshire as well as the first victorious primary in North Carolina.[454]

The young conservatives were undertaking more than simply these tasks; they were using their experience in previous campaigns and conservative projects to get elected to the 1976 Republican National Convention in Kansas City. In the end, a total of ninety-three YAF members and alumni were represented on the convention floor with 45 as Delegates and 48 as Alternate Delegates. Reflective of its strength in all areas of the country, these YAF members could be found in twenty-seven different state delegations. YAF's efforts, through its Young America's Campaign Committee, were more substantial and direct in one crucial state as, under the leadership of Ron Robinson, it established a "Reagan California Fund" to sponsor independent expenditure radio commercials featuring Effrem Zimbalist, Jr. before the important, winner-take-all, California primary where 167 delegates were at stake.[455]

As the date for the convention in Kansas City approached, it became clear that while the two candidates each were close to obtaining a majority, neither one had been able to lock up the requisite number of votes to obtain the nomination. It was in such a situation that Reagan announced his selection of Senator Richard Schweiker of Pennsylvania as his choice for Vice President. The Reagan camp hoped to swing Schweiker-supporting delegates from Pennsylvania to their cause and perhaps influence some delegates from other Northeast states. Moreover, since Ford had been dangling the possibility of the vice presidential nomination before more than a dozen Republicans, the announcement of Schweiker would be coupled with a demand that Ford declare his own choice before the convention convened.

At first, the Schweiker selection created havoc among a number of conservatives, some of whom felt betrayed. Many YAF members were confused and uncertain. As one member told Molly Ivins, "First we hear no, it was a terrible thing for him to do, then we hear yes, he had to do it. I'll probably end up maybe. If it gets him the nomination, we'll live with it, but if it backfires on him, we'll know it was wrong."[456] While concerned over Schweiker's record, YAF's support for and long-term ties to Reagan overcame their initial uncertainty and the National Board issued a press release "reluctantly" praising the selection of Schweiker. As Craig Shirley noted, YAF "had been close to Reagan since the 1960s but it was one of the few conservative groups or individuals to praise Reagan's decision."[457]

It was in such a situation that more than two hundred YAF members descended on Kansas City to undertake a last minute blitz to help nominate their favored candidate for President. Before most of the volunteers arrived, YAF national vice chairman John Buckley was in Kansas City to testify before the Platform Committee. As he reminded the delegates, "Americans everywhere want most of all to be left alone. They are satisfied with, and accept the fairness of, keeping the fruits of their own labor."[458] Meanwhile, other YAF members and alumni were promoting the Reagan position before the Rules Committee, the critical arena for what would become the test procedural vote.

YAF had arranged for housing of its volunteers at Park College and "when housing wasn't available anywhere else, Suzanne Scholte would find one more room for a bewildered young Reaganite."[459] They met Reagan as he arrived at the Kansas City airport and both Reagan and Schweiker at a reception held at the Alameda Hotel. Volunteers distributed literature to all the various delegation hotels spread throughout both the Missouri and Kansas suburbs. On Monday morning, New York YAFers, organized by Michelle Easton, handed out copies of the special convention issue *New Guard* to those arriving for the first convention session. That afternoon, other YAFers handed out literature and held "YAF Supports Reagan" signs at the reception sponsored by the ACU.

Monday night was the time allotted for the official YAF reception for delegates and alternatives. More than two thousand attended the event at the Hilton Plaza Inn, including both Reagan and Schweiker as well as California delegates Efrem Zimbalist, Jr. and Pat Boone. "YAF Supports Reagan" signs could be seen everywhere. Meanwhile, New York YAF chairman Robert Heckman organized another literature distribution at convention hotels while Frances Owens, whose husband later served two terms as Governor of Colorado, and D. Richard Cobb were responsible for supervising a reception for YAF supporters in Overland Park, Kansas.

Wednesday night was nominating night and the time for demonstrating support for their candidate. Ron Robinson recalled, "Countless YAFers participated in the official Reagan floor demonstration on Wednesday night. National Director Cobb had worked for weeks in advance on the plans for this demonstration. Most observers agree that it was the most spirited demonstration of the convention and political year."[460]

While Ronald Reagan was not successful in obtaining the nomination, falling sixty votes short in the final roll call, he had established himself as a national conservative spokesman who would be the leading candidate in a future presidential contest. As Reagan said in his bittersweet remarks to his dedicated volunteers after the convention had closed, "The Cause goes on. Nancy and I aren't going back, to sit in a rocking chair and say that's all there is for us. We're going to stay in there and you stay in there with me – the Cause is still there. Don't give up on your ideals. Don't compromise."[461] They did not give up. In truth, literally thousands of supporters, young and older, had been identified in every state, providing a base of support for the next campaign. YAF had been there for Reagan in 1976 and it would be there for him in 1980 also.

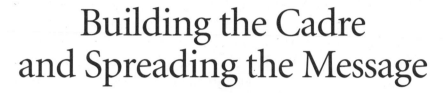

— 7 —

Building the Cadre
and Spreading the Message

W HILE THE 1970'S SAW YOUNG AMERICANS FOR FREEDOM involve itself in a wide range of campus issues and undertake even greater involvement in the political process, it was also a time of reflection, recognition, and acknowledgement of what had been achieved by the organization. After all, 1970 marked the tenth anniversary of a youth organization that had survived the traumatic prior decade and grown into a major element of the conservative movement. As testimony to its place in the movement, YAF co-sponsored a conservative awards dinner and was one of the four founding organizations responsible for the creation of the Conservative Political Action Conference in 1974, a year that also saw the young conservatives recognize the 10th anniversary of Barry Goldwater's nomination.

During the latter part of the seventies, Young Americans for Freedom launched several new projects that reflected its role in the overall conservative movement, including Zero Government Growth, opposition to the Panama Canal Treaty, and the Carter Watch as it once again transitioned to operating within the environment of a Democratic administration and Congress. To accurately tell the story of Young Americans for Freedom in this transitional decade, one must begin with the YAF10 celebration and move forward to the eve of the conservative victory that would take place as the decade ended in 1980.

Ten years after the historic meeting in Sharon, Connecticut nearly six hundred members of Young Americans for Freedom gathered at the University of Hartford to celebrate their organization's anniversary. The events were designed to not only reflect on the past and project into the future, but also to educate YAF members and train them for effective political and campus action. At the opening session on Wednesday evening, September 9th, Waggoner Carr, former Democratic Attorney General of Texas gave the keynote address. Carr "welcomed the delegates with a ringing plea for faith in the American ideal and action in accordance with that faith."[462] He urged the young conservatives to take the offensive against campus radicals and to tell those who attempted to disrupt classes to "hit the books or hit the road."[463] Following the keynote address was a panel on "Historical Perspectives on the Conservative Movement." Later that night, and each of the three nights in Hartford, YAF members could attend workshops continuing well past midnight. Each one was led by a YAF leader or outside expert.

The second day began with an address by Dr. Donald J. Devine on the topic "Conservatism: Theory and Principles." Next followed four afternoon panel discussions focusing on the Constitution, the News Media, the Academy, and Political Action. Thursday evening's program featured an address by Senator Barry Goldwater. The Arizona Senator received a raucous welcome as he was greeted with cheers of "Barry in '72" and "Barry in '76," many from students who were not even teenagers when he ran for President in 1964. After a rousing speech from Goldwater, most of the YAFers went off to late night workshops on antinew left strategy, campus issues, building an independent campus press, youth and theology, and the right to bear arms.

Dr. Philip Crane, the first YAF member to be elected to Congress, spoke on Friday night. His remarks were rather prescient, foretelling both the Reagan presidency and the Republican resurgence in Congress that was to occur in the last decade of the 20th century. Crane told those in attendance, "If YAF has not been at the center of every philosophically partisan battle in the past decade, it has been very close to all of them… It may well be that when another group of Young Americans for Freedom gathers again in 1980, they will look back upon us and upon our predecessors as the founding fathers of the new wave of conservative pre-eminence in the closing decades of this century." [464] That evening the YAF members had the opportunity to attend late night workshops on high school programming, Youth in Politics, state and local fundraising, legal action and STOP-NSA. Those less interested in direct action could take part in a discussion on "the Conservative Tradition in American Political Theory." Clearly, with all the speakers, panelists, and workshops there was something for every YAF member in attendance.

Early Saturday morning, the YAF members boarded buses to Sharon for a special luncheon at the Buckley family estate, Great Elm. It was a well-behaved group of young conservatives who were in awe and proceeded with respect as they toured the estate. As one reporter observed, "the Buckleys threw their entire house open to 600 strangers. No security guards. No credentials. No rooms closed off. No one went into the huge swimming pool, naked or otherwise."[465] The response when Buckley rose to make his remarks was overwhelmingly one of gratitude and respect. According to one recollection, "Earlier sessions of the gathering had gone wild for Barry Goldwater, Strom Thurmond, and Philip Crane, the rugged and articulate young Illinois congressman who broke into politics through YAF, but Buckley… was what they had really been waiting for."[466] He reminded those young conservatives present that "the responsibility of the conservative is altogether clear: it is to defend what is best in America. At all costs. Against any enemy, foreign or domestic."[467]

The YAF members were going back to campuses where they remained a minority, but a minority now reinvigorated for the challenge of confronting the campus left. Sometimes that challenge required one to conform to the tenor of the times in order to gain more influence and impact for one's lasting and essential beliefs. Mike Yeager, a Vietnam veteran and student at the University of Connecticut, was one who was ready for the battle on campus. "In a couple of days I'll start growing a beard, letting my hair go and dig out my torn dungarees. I'll look like a radical but talk like a conservative."[468] YAF had begun its second decade looking back and now was ready to move on to new challenges.

In August 1973, YAF members met in Washington, DC for a conference whose theme was "We Believe in America." The major event was a gala "Salute to the American Prisoners of War" banquet that was to be the capstone of the gathering. The first session included addresses by Congressmen Stanford Parris of Virginia and John Ashbrook of Ohio. In his speech, Ashbrook reminded the delegates that the conservative principles they espouse are the right ones and decried "loyalty to individuals rather than principles" in referring to the troubles then confronting President Nixon. [469]

Then came the workshops. Five state legislators from New York, Maryland, Virginia, South Carolina, and Louisiana who had been YAF members served as panelists to discuss involvement in state politics.[470] Mike Pikosky of American University and Todd Gardenhire of the University of Tennessee at Chattanooga chaired the student government session. Among the panelists discussing high school YAF activities was Kirby Wilbur, who later became director of the National Journalism Center sponsored by Young America's Foundation.

Wednesday night began with a reception for young political leaders, reached its peak with a keynote address by Bill Buckley and then concluded with delegates watching President Nixon's speech on Watergate on a special television hookup. There were mixed reactions regarding the President's involvement in the Watergate case at a time when the evidence remained murky. Clearly, while most were critical of the President on policies the verdict was still out on his involvement in the cover-up one year before his resignation.[471]

The featured speaker on Thursday morning was Senator Jesse Helms who had gained election the previous year with much support from members of Young Americans for Freedom. Helms told the delegates, "My loyalty, like your loyalty, is to the principles of American conservatism, not to any particular regime."[472] Then came three concurrent panels and presentations: "The Conservative Coalition in the Nation's Capital," "Bias in the Media," and "The Campus Left Today."

Thursday night began with a reception for the National Advisory Board, followed by an address by Senator Barry Goldwater. As Christopher Manion recalled the event, "Barry was great. We were raised on him, in our hearts he was always right. An American eagle forty feet high behind him... And what a great speech – the big issues, the recurring message – conservative principles would have kept us out of all this."[473] When he concluded his remarks, Goldwater received a resounding applause from those in attendance.

Friday's program included more speeches, panels, and workshop followed by YAF's Legal Action Committee reception honoring Clarence Manion, former Dean of the Notre Dame Law School. It was out of those who were involved in the Legal Action Committee that the first stirrings in the creation of The Federalist Society took hold some years later.

The most dramatic, emotional, and patriotic event at the convention was Saturday night's "Salute to American Prisoners of War," an event that also commemorated those missing in action. It was a major extravaganza put together by Dan Rea, who would soon become YAF National Vice Chairman. Hollywood star Pat O'Brien, who had made the famous comment "Win just one for the Gipper," in the film *Knute Rockne, All American*, served as master of ceremonies for a program that included thirteen returned prisoners, Colonel Joseph Cataldo, who participated in the Son Tay raid to free American POWs, and *USS Pueblo* Commander Lloyd Bucher. As reported in a YAF publication, "Pat O'Brien's emotional tribute to the POWs and his musical presentation in their honor brought the convention to its feet repeatedly, tears in every eye. O'Brien presented a huge birthday cake to 6 year old Jimmy Plowman. Jimmy's dad is one of several hundred Americans still listed as Missing in Action."[474]

In reporting on the events, one writer maintained, "YAF embodies an able, very dedicated group of young Americans. The time and the effort that the conservative community invested in YAF in its young years are paying off in its maturity."[475] Such a glowing picture might well be expected from an article in *National Review*, where indeed it did appear. What is more surprising was the following favorable comments that appeared in the *Washington Post* where its reporter saw the significance of the event as "the resilience of the organization, and the fact that 900 young people came to Washington to take part in an intensely political meeting during a non-election year – and at a time when public regard for the political process is at an ebb."[476] Despite the deteriorating situation in Vietnam and the depressing news from the White House, YAF members remained involved and dedicated to the principles on which their organization was founded. It was now thirteen years after that meeting in Sharon and few who participated in that original event remained active. By 1973, the torch clearly had passed to a new group of young conservatives who would take the organization through the decade of the Seventies and into the Reagan Revolution.

The year 1974 was to be an important one for Young Americans for Freedom as it became a co-sponsor of the first Conservative Political Action Conference, held a major event in San Francisco commemorating the 10th anniversary of Barry Goldwater's nomination for president, and dedicated a new national headquarters in the Virginia suburbs of the Nation's Capital. It was a year of YAF playing an essential role in the conservative movement.

YAF joined with ACU, *National Review*, and *Human Events* to co-sponsor the first Conservative Political Action Conference (CPAC). That first CPAC was held at a time when President Nixon was struggling to hold onto office and Vice President Agnew had resigned in disgrace to be replaced by Gerald Ford. Nixon did not have much support among those in attendance however. As F. Clifton White observed, "If you took a poll of this group you would find a substantial majority that wish the President would just go away, just resign." Ron Docksai maintained that Nixon should either make a thoroughgoing explanation of his part in the scandal at once or quit. The closing banquet speaker was the one individual most in attendance wished would be running for president, Governor Ronald Reagan of California who pleaded, "Let those guilty of wrongdoing accept the consequences. But for America's sake, let's get on with the business of government."[477]

YAF continued its emphasis on national political issues in 1974 with its ad hoc group, Youth for the Energy Solution (YES), attempting to show the role of the government in creating the energy shortage and opposing any policy of gasoline rationing. YAF chapters distributed over one million pieces of literature outlining how the energy crisis could be eased through a relaxing of government regulations. YAF news conferences were held in Honolulu, Boston, Los Angeles and New York.[478] Also in 1974, YAF created Students Taking Action Against Monopoly Postal Services (STAAMPS) in support of Congressman Phil Crane's proposal to eliminate the postal service's monopoly on first class mail. University of Virginia YAF leader Mary Gingell prepared a new issues paper on the post office that was used in conjunction with the STAAMPS project. YAF also opposed the United Farm Workers boycott with counter-boycotts, debates, and speakers telling the workers' side of the story. A delegation of YAF leaders including Gary Giordano, Mary Fisk and Jeff Kane made a fact-finding trip to the San Joaquin Valley in California.[479]

Goldwater 10th Anniversary in San Francisco

It was July of 1974 and Richard Nixon's hold on the White House was quickly crumbling. Amidst the gloom of Watergate, YAF brought together a phalanx of conservatives to celebrate a happier time when their efforts had contributed to the nomination of Barry Goldwater as the Republican presidential candidate of 1964. Ten years after that momentous nomination which redirected the ideological focus of the Republican party for years to come, they met at San Francisco's Sheraton Palace Hotel – ironically the site of the Rockefeller campaign headquarters during the 1964 Republican National Convention. Many of those present were only in elementary school in 1964, but there were others who had played important roles in the nomination of Barry Goldwater or the founding of YAF, including Stan Evans, author of the Sharon Statement, and Doug Caddy, the organizer of that original meeting in September 1960.

On July 18, 1974, exactly ten years after he gave his historic acceptance speech, five hundred YAF members and supporters honored Senator Barry Goldwater at a reunion conference. They were there to recognize the individual who was responsible for changing the direction and focus of American politics because, "For them, his nomination was the high point in the lives of most living American conservatives. And they have not forgotten Y.A.F.'s role in that triumph."[480] As Arnold Steinberg, former editor of *New Guard* and political aide to Senator James Buckley recalled, "For many young conservatives like me, the Goldwater campaign was the unique blend of philosophical motivation and novice political activism we craved."[481]

Senator Goldwater arrived with Congressman Sam Steiger of Arizona, who was to introduce him. Steiger maintained, "In the hearts of this country they damned sure knew he was right. He's never changed. Twenty years ago he stood for conservative principles and he's still doing it." Then came the five-minute ovation as their hero moved to the podium. Goldwater made due recognition of the role YAF played in both his nomination and the future of conservatism in America: "Today's YAF leaders are tomorrow's national leaders. You can't possibly understand the impact your organization has had and is having in the politics of the nation. I know this because I see it happening all over the nation …

It proves that what began at Sharon, Connecticut in September of 1960 is having an increasingly important impact on American politics and the battle for sound Constitutional government in a system of ordered justice."

After fondly looking back ten years, the next two days saw those in attendance focus on the future at a time when everything was uncertain. The following month would bring Gerald Ford to the presidency. Soon thereafter Nelson Rockefeller would be named Vice President and the Republicans would lose a substantial portion of their House and Senate delegations. Truly, it was a time for analysis and evaluation as to the proper path for conservatives to follow in electoral politics.[482]

Fittingly, the final event of the conference was a banquet featuring Governor Ronald Reagan who had come to national political attention in the Goldwater campaign with his televised speech, "A Time for Choosing." Reagan's welcome was "reminiscent of the Goldwater rallies of the 1960s," according to Arnie Steinberg.[483] Beginning with a retrospective on the conservative takeover of the Republican party, reviewing the various options for conservatives as the party of Richard Nixon seemed to implode, the conference ended with a message from the one who would lead them out of opposition and into the White House at the end of the decade. The symmetry was fitting.

Throughout 1975, local YAF chapters continued to carry out campus and community projects, including the addition of a new program, "Zero Government Growth," a coordinated effort of advertising, pamphlets and speakers to emphasize the need to rein in government spending. The most memorable aspect of the program was a series of advertisements run in college newspapers with a picture of a hefty government employee and the slogan, "Help Starve a Feeding Bureaucrat!"[484]

At the same time, it was a year of uncertainty and transition as the organization approached the upcoming presidential election. This was also the year when the freedom of the people of South Vietnam was finally lost and television viewers watched the ignominy of Americans and Vietnamese attempting to frantically latch on to helicopters as they left Saigon.

For the young conservatives, however, the battle continued at home. Fall 1975 saw YAF launch a project called the "Struggle for Human Rights" that new National Chairman Jeff Kane described as an effort to "alert the American people to the continued dangers Communism poses to the rights of all men."[485] Kane led a series of news conferences in more than a dozen cities to make known YAF's support for the efforts of Alexander Solzhenitsyn and opposition to IBM's plans to build a computer network for the Soviet Union's INTOURIST bureau. The project included outreach to the media, visits with members of Congress, and a request that the United Nations invite Solzhenitsyn to address the General

Assembly. As part of the overall effort, the November 1975 issue of *New Guard* included a number of articles on Soviet repression and featured a cover drawing of Solzhenitsyn as well as a reprint of the Soviet dissident's address to the AFL-CIO in New York City on July 9, 1975.[486]

The year 1976 saw Young Americans for Freedom integrally involved in a presidential campaign once again. Ronald Reagan's challenge to Gerald Ford for the Republican nomination became the focus of much attention for the first seven months of the year as has been discussed previously. But YAF continued to encourage its college chapters to take up campus issues. Community and high school chapters promoted the Zero Government Growth campaign that included a number of YAF advertisements in campus and local newspapers. YAF also took an active role in supporting efforts to recognize the American Bicentennial.

The election of November 1976 saw the election of Jimmy Carter as President of the United States. No longer did YAF confront a GOP President who, while popularly perceived as a conservative, had been undertaking policies contrary to YAF's views. Once again there would be a Democratic occupant of the White House, one who was elected with significant religious support and came from the South. Despite this background, YAF anticipated that he would be moving to the Left once in office and facing a large Democratic majority in both the House and Senate. It was in this context that YAF announced its "Carter Watch" program in late November, vowing to closely monitor the actions of the new President and committed to speaking out when his proposals, appointments and policies were perceived as counter to conservative principles. Over the next four years, the Carter White House would provide ample opportunities for YAF to take an oppositional stand.[487]

In 1977, YAF's membership became more introspective as it viewed its situation, with campuses quieter yet still as liberal dominated as ever, with no overriding foreign policy issue such as Vietnam to rally patriotic young people, with a Democrat in the White House and some of their political heroes such as Reagan and Jim Buckley having been defeated. Clifford White attempted to analyze the changed environment and the challenge to the organization in a March 1977 article where he maintained that Richard Weaver had it right when he emphasized that ideas have consequences. For White, YAF needed to emphasize issues and develop new leadership for the future, stressing quality over quantity, building a core and a cadre of philosophically sound members. YAF was trying to impact the direction of the campus as well as of the country, but at all times it should be training young conservatives for future roles in society. "A small corps of energetic and bright YAFers is more valuable than a paper organization which boasts ten times the membership."[488]

Two months later, Ron Robinson stressed the opportunities available to individual YAF members for exerting influence. From its earliest days, while the organization had promoted the development of local chapters it had also emphasized the range of "Committee of One" projects that individual members could undertake. As Robinson noted, "No YAF project has ever had sustained success until it was picked up by YAF members and carried on in their local papers, on talk shows, through film showings, and by the numerous other committee-of-one activities."[489]

New York City had been the site of YAF's first national convention and now, fifteen years later, the organization returned to Gotham. This year the theme was "Freedom – Not Socialism" and a large banner proclaiming it was placed immediately behind the podium to maximize press coverage of its message. Holding a conference in New York City had multiple benefits as all the news services, the major daily newspapers, and even *Time* magazine covered parts of the week's events.[490]

When Ronald and Nancy Reagan arrived on Friday night, those in the audience broke out into ten minutes of applause, cheers and stomping. In his speech, widely covered by the media, Reagan declared that the Senate should refuse to approve the treaties designed to turn over control of the canal to Panama. On Saturday night, it was time for the YAF members to let down their hair and attend a roast of YAF's godfather.[491] Taking part in the satirical salute to Bill Buckley was a disparate group of individuals. From the right came Congressman Henry Hyde, Bill Rusher, Stan Evans and David Keene. From the left was Allard Lowenstein. Representing the media was CBS News broadcaster Mike Wallace. And somewhere in the universe was Dr. Henry Kissinger. While most of the comments were directed at Buckley, several were focused on the other participants.[492]

With the year 1977 coming to a close, new executive director Ron Robinson looked back on the history of YAF and its continuing mission. Building new leaders for the future took precedence even over the temporary impact on present-day issues. According to Robinson, "The reason why YAF has had such a profound impact is not due to any conspiratorial reasons or coincidence. Rather, YAF has succeeded in its primary function. We have developed an excellent cadre of conservative leaders who recognized that through hard work and continued dedication they could have a profound impact on the future of their country."[493] In the end it was the efforts of individuals that produced new leaders. "YAF's challenge is ultimately a personal one. Each of us must rededicate ourselves to making our maximum contribution to continuing the "loose confederation," in building the crucial conservative cadre." Clearly, as YAF entered another challenging year its leadership was aware of the need to focus on the future and the development of those leadership traits that would help produce conservative activists for many years into the future.

During the Fall of 1977 and all of 1978, YAF emphasized a number of campus issues. Many chapters called for the abolition of mandatory student fees, or at least limits on the use of those fees for political purposes. YAF's legal affairs committee continued distribution of its newsletter, *Amicus Curiae*, and involved its law student members in projects to take legal action on various issues. John Kwapisz, a YAF activist at the University of Wisconsin Law School, was instrumental in forming a conservative law students association and led the effort to expand it nationwide. This drive eventually culminated in the formation of The Federalist Society.

Perhaps the major campus-oriented campaign during late 1977 and throughout 1978, however, was YAF's project in support of Alan Bakke's effort to strike down affirmative action and gain admission to medical school. The University of California at Davis Medical School had established an admissions policy where 16 of a total of 100 spots were set aside for disadvantaged minority applicants. Bakke, a Caucasian, applied in both 1973 and 1974 and was denied admission even though his scores on the Medical College Admission Test were higher than some admitted under the special admissions program. Bakke filed suit against the Regents of the University of California and, while the trial court declared the special program violated the Federal and State constitutions, it did not order the admission of Bakke to the medical school. On appeal, the California Supreme Court commented only on what it viewed as a violation of the equal protection clause of the 14th amendment and declared that since UC-Davis could not prove that absent the special program Bakke would not be admitted, the Court ordered his admission. This decision was appealed to the United States Supreme Court, which granted certiorari.[494]

As the controversy developed and before the Supreme Court had issued its opinion, YAF strongly supported Bakke. YAF rounded up support for the potential medical student's position on campuses across the country.[495] Local chapters made use of an issues paper, "Bakke: The Case Against Discrimination," and the organization's magazine featured a review of the main issues at hand.[496] Meanwhile, YAF retained attorney Marco DeFunis, who had brought the first significant case challenging affirmative action against the University of Washington Law School in 1971, to prepare its amicus curiae brief for submission to the Supreme Court. The brief maintained that the practice of establishing quotas and giving preference to minority groups violated the equal protection clause and that the Constitution requires neutral equality rather than race-conscious equality.[497] As Frank Donatelli, YAF's executive director and a law student, explained, "in our judgment, affirmative action attempts to guarantee equality of result, not equality of opportunity."[498]

Following the merger with Young America's Foundation, YAF chapters quickly began organizing large events on high school and college campuses that spread the conservative message to thousands of students at any given school.

YAF chapters prevailed on even the most liberal college campus including California State University – Los Angeles. The YAF chapters at this school and others were able to successfully push back against the administration after it attempted to block their activism.

YAF chapters continue to organize substantial events on college campuses such as the 9/11: Never Forget Project that attract students to get involved.

Following the unification, bonds between YAF chapters were revitalized and YAFers once again rushed to bolster other chapters' activities. Here, YAFers from across Southern California gather following a successful campus lecture.

YAFers appear often on national media outlets, including Fox News, to discuss their campus victories.

YAF continues to have a strong presence at the Conservative Political Action Conference, a conference that was in part founded by Young Americans for Freedom.

YAFers continue to rally in Washington, D.C. and elsewhere in support of conservative causes.

High school YAF chapters thrive across the country, and many high school YAFers continue their involvement into college.

YAFers at the University of Michigan tear down a mock Berlin Wall during Freedom Week to protest the Left's use of safe spaces and microaggressions to infringe on free speech.

YAFers are mentored by legendary YAF alumni including Congressman Dana Rohrabacher who is just as passionate about YAF as he was during his campus years.

YAFers, from throughout its proud history, meet for alumni luncheons during the Conservative Political Action Conference.

YAFers create a visible presence and are often the most active group on any given campus.

Developing creative ways to present conservative ideas is always a hallmark of YAF. At the University of Central Florida, YAFers held a socialism bake sale to relate the failures of socialism to their peers.

YAF chapter chairs have amazing opportunities to tour President Ronald Reagan's beloved ranch, Rancho Del Cielo, which is being protected by Young America's Foundation for future generations

Cadets at Virginia Tech sign thank you cards to veterans as part of the chapter's drive to honor America's soldiers.

YAF chapters host prominent speakers on campus that reach hundreds of students.

When the Supreme Court issued its opinion ordering the admission of Alan Bakke to the Medical School but upholding the use of race as a consideration in admissions decisions, YAF swung into action once again. As *New Guard* reported, "Minutes after the decision was announced, YAF was on the scene at the Supreme Court building telling the press that we applauded the decision to admit Bakke to medical school but were disappointed that race may still be allowed as a criteria in admissions practices."[499] Two days later, John Buckley held a news conference that received wide coverage. This media outreach was followed by a Capitol Hill seminar on affirmative action in July that was attended by 150 congressional interns and staff. YAF's task force issued a lengthy report outlining the organization's reasons for opposing affirmative action and restating its belief in individual rights. The report discussed the question of what could be done to assist minorities in attaining more equitable participation in society and possible legislation to eliminate other forms of group classification and discrimination. YAF would continue to stress the importance of the individual and oppose efforts to classify people as members of specific groups in society.

A second major concern of YAF during 1978 was the efforts of the Carter Administration to obtain Senate approval of a series of new treaties that would cede control of the Panama Canal and the Panama Canal Zone to the nation of Panama. Much of the YAF activity took place in the Nation's Capital since the critical vote would occur in the Senate. That Fall, YAF held a rally outside the Pan American Union building; Georgetown University YAF sponsored a debate on the treaty between Congressmen Philip Crane and Paul Simon, both of Illinois; and national YAF projects director Ken Boehm testified against the treaty before the Senate Foreign Relations Committee.[500]

Across the country local chapters put pressure on their senators to oppose the treaty. The University of Tennessee chapter hired a plane to fly over the UT-Memphis State football game with the banner: "Keep Our Canal – Write Sen. Baker;" and then later in the Spring a group of UT YAFers picketed outside the hall where Ellsworth Bunker was giving a speech favoring the Canal treaties.

In a related foreign policy project, YAF continued an effort against East-West trade that had brought them success and much national publicity in the 1960s. As more and more American companies began selling computers, missile guidance parts and advanced technology to the Soviet Union – all with the support of the Carter Administration – YAF once again pointed out the folly of trading with the enemy. One focal point was N. L. Industries, a company that had signed a contract for engineering and technology used in the offshore production of gas and oil. When the company held its 1978 stockholders' meeting, Kelly Kehrer, vice chairman of Texas YAF, spoke against the company's policy while other YAFers handed out flyers explaining the reasons for opposing the deal.[501]

Throughout the year, YAF continued to emphasize national policy issues. When the United States Postal Service raised first class rates to 15 cents, YAF launched a national protest on what they called "Postal Competition Day." YAF was more successful in advocating deregulation of the commercial airline industry. National directors Roger Ream and Cliff White, along with DC chairman Sally Cromwell, led the effort to contact members of Congress and push for deregulation, an effort that finally brought about greater competition and increased service in airline travel.

At the state level, YAF organizations took on projects that were traditionally associated with adult public policy organizations, filling a void in the conservative movement of the time. Thus, a number of YAF state organizations, including those in California, Georgia, Hawaii, New York, North Carolina, Tennessee, Texas, and Virginia, analyzed state legislative voting records and rated all legislators on their support for conservative positions. These legislative ratings provided needed publicity for YAF, obtained recognition for the organization among political leaders in the state, and established a means and a method for recognizing outstanding conservative legislators. In this way, YAF's role as an important political player became more recognized while it performed an essential function for the movement.

While national domestic and foreign issues and political campaigns consumed a great deal of YAF's attention in the late 1970s, there remained a strong YAF presence on several college campuses with chapters that stressed student issues, sponsored conservative speakers, trained new leaders, and published independent right-wing newspapers. Some of these YAF chapters were able to establish a continuing presence on campus, with leadership transferring from one class to another, resulting in a consistent and active YAF chapter.

In Madison, the University of Wisconsin chapter was one such continuing presence, having started in the early 1960s with leaders such as Richard Wheeler, through the late Sixties time of David Keene, and the early Seventies of Mike Kelly and Pat Korten, among others. By the latter part of the 1970s, Robert E. A. P. Ritholz was chapter chairman and John Kwapisz served as Wisconsin state chairman while the independent conservative newspaper, *Badger Herald*, was still being published with six of seven members of the Board of Directors being YAF members. At Purdue, a strong YAF presence continued through two decades and by the late 1970s the chapter was regularly sponsoring conservative speakers. In New York, Adelphi University YAF held a dinner to celebrate its 10th anniversary of continuing activity, including a regular campus newspaper column.

Georgetown University continued into the 1980s as a strong YAF chapter, as was the YAF unit at George Washington University. Both the University of Texas and the University of Tennessee at Knoxville continued to produce a number of YAF leaders who would go on to contribute to the growing conservative movement. On the West Coast, the University of Southern California and the University of Washington both carried on proud traditions of YAF involvement throughout the 1970s and served as recruiting and training grounds for conservative activists.

Yet there were new campuses also where a YAF presence was first being established in the late 1970s. At traditionally liberal Vassar College, Abram Feurstein led the YAF chapter in defeating a referendum to fund a Public Interest Research Group (PIRG) out of mandatory student fees while at Oklahoma State University, John Bryant led a chapter that produced future journalist Pat McGuigan, Janet Slaughter, and conservative activist Steve Antosh while presenting a regular column in the school newspaper. Roy Jones formed a YAF chapter at Liberty Baptist (now Liberty University), an institution founded by Jerry Falwell. Charlie Gerow was YAF chairman at Messiah College in the mid-70s and recalls "YAF was an invaluable training ground for me and helped to mold my political views and hone my leadership skills."

As the new year began, the Carter Administration invited Red China's vice premier, Teng Hsiao-ping, to visit the United States and he made stops in Seattle, Los Angeles, Houston, Atlanta, and Washington, DC. The visit was a follow-up to Carter's announcement in late 1978 that the United States would recognize Communist China and abandon its long-standing recognition of the Republic of China.[502] At each location, YAF organized protests, including fifty YAFers led by Pat Geary who "welcomed" the Communist leader when he visited Disneyland. Texas YAF, led by Steve Munisteri, sponsored an advertisement in the *Houston Chronicle* denouncing the visit while state vice chairman Greg Robertson rounded up 150 YAFers to rally against Teng's visit to Houston. In Atlanta, R. E. Phillip Linderman II and Ryan Murphy greeted Teng's arrival wearing Neville Chamberlain and Adolf Hitler costumes emphasizing what they viewed as Carter's capitulation to Communist China.[503] National YAF distributed a poster, "Welcome A Tyrant?" that pointed out mass killings, forced labor, and aggression by Red China. Given the historical record of the Communist Chinese and Teng's role in both the party and government, YAF objected strongly to the treatment being provided him by many Americans, including the Carter Administration and various academic institutions. Temple YAF's Stephen Kranz denounced the school's granting of an honorary degree to Teng.

Even in places where Teng did not appear, YAF made evident their opposition to the regime he represented. Hawaii YAF's Sam Slom devoted a commentary on the weekly YAF radio program to US-China relations while Paul Taylor, Minnesota YAF state chairman, organized sixty pickets outside the Minnesota state capitol. YAF National Chairman Jim Lacy was part of a delegation that traveled to Taiwan to show support for its freedom. As Lacy noted, "Continued friendly relations with Taiwan are essential to our status as a dependable ally. To break with a country that's always lived up to its end of a treaty can only bring us down in the eyes of the world."[504] YAF continued to be a strong supporter of the Chinese government on Taiwan even after the actions of the Carter Administration had redirected U.S. government relations.

Later that Spring, YAF shifted its focus to preventing the ratification of the second Strategic Arms Limitation Treaty (SALT-II). YAF maintained "our analysis of SALT II shows that far from reducing arms, the treaty would allow the immense Soviet buildup to continue." [505] The campaign brought together a number of local efforts to gain media attention and collect petition signatures for presenting to various Senators. In the Spring issue of its magazine, YAF devoted fourteen pages to the SALT II issue.[506] In the end, the treaty was not ratified by the Senate and withdrawn from consideration once the 1980 presidential election was concluded.[507]

When YAF members gathered again in August 1979, Frank Donatelli reflected on the fact "We've outlived Woodstock, we've outlived Students for a Democratic Society. Now we find Y.A.F. has helped set the current national agenda of issues: Tax cuts, business initiatives, maintaining military strength, regulatory reform, the whole thing."[508] This change was evident when the delegates held their third mock presidential nominating convention on Saturday. It was a landslide for Ronald Reagan with 78% of the vote while Phil Crane came in second with 18%, leaving only a few isolated votes for George H. W. Bush, Bob Dole, Howard Baker and John Connally. One year later, the American people would elect Reagan to the presidency.[509]

Fittingly, the major speaker on Saturday night was Reagan who, while not present, had prepared and taped a special message. Reagan praised YAF for its efforts in opposing the radical left on campus and in training leaders for the future. He criticized the Carter Administration on a wide range of issues from its energy policy to the Panama Canal treaty to the SALT II treaty. Citing Margaret Thatcher's recent victory in Great Britain, he maintained that much of the West was moving away from socialism. In closing, he rallied the YAF members for the upcoming presidential election: "America is better off with leadership that reflects the philosophy, the principles, and the aspirations of Young Americans for Freedom." Citing the longstanding relationship he had with YAF, Reagan reminded the delegates, "We still have very much to accomplish and after 19 years of activity I know that YAF will be up to the tasks before us and that together we will do what we must to realize that 'Shining City On a Hill.'" [510] Just as many of their predecessors had done in 1968 and 1976, most of these YAF members were ready and willing to devote their time and energies to another Reagan campaign for the presidency.[511]

As the Fall semester began, Jane Fonda and her then husband Tom Hayden launched a five week nationwide campus speaking tour. All across the country, YAF chapters turned out to protest and show opposition to the leftist pair. Ed Bender organized one hundred demonstrators with signs and distributed literature at Albright College in Pennsylvania when Fonda and Hayden appeared. John Abernethy set up a literature distribution when she spoke at Adelphi University while demonstrators held signs saying "Fonda to boat people: drop dead." The most publicized protest, which made it onto national network news, took place when fifty YAF members held a mock trial outside Fonda's Santa Monica home and hanged her in effigy. The "trial" provided a fitting end to the Fonda-Hayden national tour.[512]

November brought another situation where YAF could protest and make known their support for a strong foreign policy. As Iranian student radicals occupied the American embassy in Tehran and held Americans prisoner, the YAF Board met and passed a resolution calling for the release of all Americans and American property, advocating a freeze on Iranian assets in the United States until the crisis was ended, demanding a cessation of all American foreign aid to Iran and a blockade of the country, and the withdrawal of diplomatic recognition to the new government. On November 14th, YAF leaders attempted to meet with the Charge D'Affaires at the Iranian Embassy and present him with a copy of the resolution. While much media coverage was obtained, the embassy refused a meeting with the YAF representatives.

One week later, YAF had organized a "Youth Coalition" including the College Democrats, College Republicans, Young Republican National Federation, Young Social Democrats, and Frontlash. The coalition, led by YAF executive director Robert Heckman, met with Iran's U.S. Charge D'Affaires and press attaché at the embassy on November 23rd.[513] While YAF would continue protesting the Iranian students actions, it would not be until Inauguration Day 1981 when the American hostages would be finally released.

As the decade came to an end, more and more observers appreciated YAF's contribution to the growing conservative movement in the United States. As one writer on the development of American conservatism noted, "the generation of conservative activists that came of age in the 1970s was filled with alumni of YAF and ISI."[514] Looking back many years later, Daniel McCarthy claimed, "Campus conservatives are not just the future of the movement, they are its present as well. Alumni of the major right-wing youth organizations fill the ranks, and hold the commanding heights, of the institutions that mold conservative orthodoxy today."[515]

Perhaps no better testimony to the continued influence of YAF could be found than an article in *The Chronicle of Higher Education*, the "Bible" for college faculty and administrators published weekly to report on trends and influences on university life. Not only did the reporter conclude that "politically conservative students are increasing their influence on college campuses" but she obtained substantiation from YAF's opponents. According to the legislative director for the United States Student Association (the renamed NSA), YAF "is getting stronger on campuses" and "the conservatives work against everything we are working for. We must stop them before they stop us." Wesley McCune, who made his living researching right-wing organizations for a union-funded entity called Group Research, Inc. claimed, "The new young conservatives are a smarter bunch. They are an intelligent collection of young politicians, who learned from the 60s, who have more political savvy, and who are increasingly powerful." [516] McCune admitted that a trained cadre of right-wing student leaders who once supported the Vietnam war and countered left-wing protesters were moving into legislative and executive positions of government. He maintained that former and present YAF members were in great demand as staffers on Capitol Hill.

YAF's campaign against mandatory student fees and in opposition to Ralph Nader's PIRG's were cited as YAF projects along with its support for Alan Bakke's suit against reverse discrimination. Speaking of the mandatory fees campaign, the director of the youth caucus of Americans for Democratic Action said, "This is the type of activity which is most dangerous to campus liberals. The fees are the life-blood of student governments" and "conservatives are very quietly taking over and making inroads" in student governments. As Frank Connolly, chairman of the YAF chapter at Columbia University noted, "we have given students an alternative point of view. We fought the hippies, and now we are in place ready to fight the liberals on every issue they raise."

— 8 —

The Reagan Era

I T WAS THE BEGINNING OF A PRESIDENTIAL ELECTION YEAR and YAF had been there before, but never in quite the situation that presented itself in early 1980. While Ronald Reagan was the overwhelming favorite of YAF members and supporters, some YAF members were active in the campaigns of other candidates, including a few who were supporting the Libertarian Party and its efforts to establish itself as a third force in American politics.[517] After all, this was not YAF's first crusade for a conservative presidential candidate. Its genesis had been the Goldwater for Vice President effort at the 1960 Republican convention in Chicago and then there had been the Goldwater effort four years later, the last-minute effort for Reagan in 1968, the campaign against Gerald Ford in 1976. But this time, there was a new generation of young conservatives who were assuming leadership roles in American politics and, this time, the results would be different.

One of YAF's spinoff organizations, Fund for a Conservative Majority (FCM), launched an independent expenditure effort on Reagan's behalf. FCM came into being after the 1976 campaign as the renamed Young America's Campaign Committee. One of FCM's first projects was to round up volunteers for the New Hampshire primary effort. Some forty YAF members were bused into the state.

While the primary season was starting, YAF once again co-sponsored the annual Conservative Political Action Conference. During the CPAC events National Chairman James Lacy held a news conference to urge Congressman Phil Crane, who had received only 7% of the vote in the Iowa caucuses, to withdraw from the presidential race in favor of Reagan. A few days later, after winning the Vermont primary and coming close in Massachusetts, Reagan called Lacy to thank him for YAF's support and for encouraging Crane to withdraw. Reagan "thanked YAF for its work on his behalf throughout the country. Jim and the Governor spoke for some ten minutes about YAF and the campaign."[518] Reagan's call to Lacy was one more indication of the respect held by the former Governor for the work of the organization.

Another indication of YAF's contribution to the conservative movement could be seen at the CPAC event. Some thirty-one groups set up display tables to hand out literature and explain their purpose, a testimony to the emergence of a national movement and also to the success of YAF as most of these groups were either established or led by YAF alumni.[519] Notice of YAF's impact also came from the Left, including an article in *Rolling Stone* magazine calling Young Americans for Freedom "a movement of young conservatives that is thought by some to have generated the most influential political thinking on the right, and indeed the ideas that have framed the national political debate, in recent years."[520]

The Spring 1980 quarterly issue of *New Guard* featured a special section on "Ronald Reagan: Conservative Choice in 1980".[521] Across the country, YAF chapters became an organizing base for student support for Reagan and, as they had in 1976, several YAFers were elected as delegates or alternates to the Republican National Convention in Detroit. Still others were attracted to the campaign of Libertarian candidate Ed Clark.[522]

Meanwhile inflation and the cost of living continued on an upward spiral. In response to the economic failures of the Carter Administration, the Northwest YAF office launched "Project Free Enterprise" to inform high school and college students about laissez-faire economics. Advertisements were placed in campus newspapers, showings of the film "The Incredible Bread Machine" were scheduled, and speakers were brought to campuses and communities throughout Oregon, Idaho, and Washington. A small contingent of conservatives, led by Connie Coyne Marshner, served as delegates to the 1980 White House Conference on Families, a gathering dominated by liberals appointed by the Carter Administration.[523]

Soon it was July and time for the Republican National Convention and YAF was prepared to take part in the nomination of their candidate for President of the United States. YAF arranged to house some 120 activists at the University of Detroit where at breakfast each morning they heard from Congressman Robert Dornan, William Rusher, Charles Black, and Kathy Teague, another YAF alumnus then serving as executive director of the American Legislative Exchange Council. Volunteers engaged in literature blitzes to the various delegations, provided bodies and noise at rallies, met conservative leaders when they arrived at the Detroit airport, and distributed six thousand copies of *New Guard*. Then they reminded the delegates of the responsibilities they had in bringing about a real change in the direction of the country. "The Republican Party has this golden opportunity to show, once and for all, that it stands for something, and that what it stands for means a safer, freer and more prosperous America for all of us."[524] It was a challenge that the delegates would meet that week.

The YAF troops were omnipresent throughout the convention. The YAF volunteers not only took part in demonstrations around the city but also were able to attend sessions in the convention hall. Wyoming YAF chairman Dave Scholl and National Director George Blackman, both of whom were in their state's delegations, rounded up gallery passes for the YAF volunteers while the Michigan YAF members provided a local orientation to the out-of-staters. Special emphasis was given to rallying support for Reagan at his appearances. As *Human Events* reported, "Wherever Reagan went in Detroit, YAFers were there too. They cheered him upon his arrival at the hotel, twice when his motorcade arrived at Joe Lewis Arena, and during his addresses at the Convention Hall itself. "YAF Backs Reagan" signs, buttons and bumper stickers were everywhere. Though YAF's "Detroit '80 Youth Operation" was a serious program with set goals to accomplish, it obviously was a celebration as well." [525]

The most retrospective YAF reception, however, was held to honor Senator Barry Goldwater whose campaign sixteen years earlier was a preface to the events in Detroit. Unfortunately, due to recent surgery and a schedule mixup, Goldwater could not be present. Some five hundred did attend as he was recognized for "his heroic 1964 presidential campaign and essential support of Young Americans for Freedom as an Advisor and Friend." Accepting on his behalf was F. Clifton White.[526] Shortly after the event, Goldwater wrote and apologized for missing the reception and thanking YAF for their honor: "How sorry I was to have missed being with you and all of those wonderful members of YAF the other day as you paid tribute to me at your reception at the Pontchartrain. ... I am truly sorry it wasn't possible for me to be there and I want you to know your honoring me in this way means more to me than you will ever know."

While some YAF members were engaged in rallies, literature distribution and receptions, many other YAFers and alumni were involved with official convention responsibilities. A total of eighty-four YAF members and alumni were elected as delegates or alternates to the convention. Dick Derham presided as Chairman of the Rules Committee while Roy Brun was a key member of the Platform Committee. YAF alumni Frank Donatelli, Charles Black, Roger Stone, Loren Smith and others were Reagan campaign staffers involved with all the convention campaign details in Joe Lewis Arena.

YAF came out of Detroit with renewed media respect. The *Washington Post* said simply that "Reagan's triumph is YAF's triumph" while *Newsday* spoke of the "large throng of Young Americans for Freedom" who filled the convention aisles during the demonstrations for Reagan. Due to the many "YAF Backs Reagan" signs present, a major Reagan campaign rally was described as one where the candidate was "greeted by Young Americans for Freedom" as if YAF had organized the event.[527]   When Reagan accepted the nomination, phase one was complete. Now the YAF members had an even more important task ahead of them during the Fall – the campaign of their candidate for President of the United States. But before election day, YAF would pause to take note of another historical marker.

YAF's 20th Anniversary

Fall 1980 was more than a presidential campaign period for Young Americans for Freedom. It also marked the 20th anniversary of the organization and this milestone was commemorated in a celebration on September 27th at the Mayflower Hotel in Washington. Five distinguished members of the YAF Advisory Board agreed to serve as co-chairmen of the 20th Anniversary Committee: Barry Goldwater, Ronald Reagan, Bill Buckley, Stan Evans, and Bob Bauman. The celebration would have three elements starting with a day-long conference on "the History of the Conservative Movement" sponsored by Young America's Foundation followed by a 20th anniversary dinner.

To commemorate the anniversary YAF prepared a special issue of *New Guard* that was distributed at the dinner. In it, two of the co-chairmen who could not be present at the dinner related their experiences with YAF and its contributions to American society. Barry Goldwater recalled first hearing of the organization's formation from Bill Buckley and how he agreed to speak at its first 1961 rally in Manhattan Center with some trepidation. In the end, YAF not only filled the auditorium but left thousands standing outside disappointed. One year later, he had doubts again about YAF's ability to fill Madison Square Garden, only to be pleasantly surprised. As he noted, "With that rally at Madison Square Garden, YAF really moved into high gear. From then on, every significant conservative action throughout the country bore some trace of YAF involvement." According to Goldwater, "I feel a great measure of pride every time I encounter a leader in politics, in business, or in the newsgathering profession who cut his teeth in YAF. And their numbers are growing. I am amazed at YAF's input into the leadership ranks of this nation, and I believe this is only the beginning."[528] Goldwater concluded by saying he had a tremendous debt to the early YAF leaders who contributed much to his campaign of 1964, a campaign that laid the groundwork for future conservative success.

Reagan also praised YAF and said that it was always invigorating to be around its members. "It is when I am among young people like those in YAF that I am most forcefully reminded that what makes America different from other nations is that we're always looking forward, and never backward." He added, "a generation of young people received a priceless education in practical political action. Working in everything from campus elections to national political campaigns, YAFers have learned how to get things done in a democratic society."

The Republican presidential nominee saw YAF as providing the future leadership of not only the conservative movement but of America itself. "I've enjoyed a special relationship with Young Americans for Freedom for many years... America, and Young Americans for Freedom, are entering a new decade together. It will be a decade of fearsome challenges... But Americans, and especially Young Americans for Freedom, have always had a clear understanding of the road America was destined to travel... Americans, and especially Young Americans for Freedom, are eager to undertake the journey."[529]

These themes of survival, success, resilience, and continued challenges were echoed in the various remarks as YAF gathered to review its past and project a future that they hoped would be spent as part of a Reagan Administration in the 1980s. Stan Evans, its author, read the Sharon Statement to remind all of the principles on which YAF was founded and the foundation on which it continued to operate. Then came an address by Bill Buckley, the organization's Godfather.[530]

Writing about the event later, Stan Evans stressed the work of YAF in producing a bevy of conservative leaders for the present and future in America. Twenty years after its founding YAF had succeeded in making many of its views mainstream, much more so than the organization's founders could have thought possible. As Evans noted, "Somehow, limited government, the market economy, and defense of America's national interests overseas don't seem so laughable today as they did in 1960."[531] Less than one month later, the American people would elect a new President dedicated to those same conservative principles enumerated by Evans in the organization's credo.

On November 4, 1980 Ronald Reagan did not merely win the presidential election against President Carter and Congressman John B. Anderson. Reagan's win was nothing less than a landslide, carrying 44 states. As YAF Chairman Jim Lacy stated in the organization's annual report for 1980, "President Reagan. Those two words express the pride and optimism which all of us feel as we enter the third decade of Young Americans for Freedom."[532] The Reagan landslide also produced the first Republican control of the United States Senate since 1955. Sixteen new GOP Senators were elected to give the party a 53-47 Senate majority. With so many new Republican Senators and party control of all Senate committees, literally hundreds of new staff positions opened up in the Senate at the same time a new conservative administration was staffing the Executive Branch. If ever there were a time for young conservatives to move to Washington and seek employment, the early months of 1981 was the time.

On campuses, the Reagan victory was an opportunity to consolidate conservative support and build new YAF chapters. Even on unfriendly territory, YAF launched active organizational efforts. One week after the election, an organizational meeting for revitalizing a YAF chapter was held at Harvard University. James Higgins, YAF chapter chairman, admitted that, "I don't expect to convert a lot of people" but the organization would "let people know that there are conservatives on campus."[533]   While the Harvard chapter had only 12 members, its chairman played an active role as leader of a statewide effort against mandatory funding for Nader's PIRGs and became chairman of the Massachusetts College Republican Union.[534]

At Columbia University, Vasos Panagiotopoulis and Henry Kriegel revitalized a chapter that had become almost dormant. With Reagan's victory, a sense of pride and hope developed among campus conservatives. One year later, YAF had become such a recognized force on the Columbia campus that Kriegel's picture was featured on the cover of the *Columbia Spectator* magazine section. Kriegel noted, "the problems on campus for conservatives are fear and the effect of the "me generation.".…We are strongest where the opposition is greatest. They're stronger in YAF because they have to be. It's not numbers – it's quality."[535] Similar efforts resulted in chapters being formed at the University of Pennsylvania, Dartmouth and Cornell as well as a revitalized effort at Yale.

YAF ended 1980 with big plans for the future. It would use the election of a conservative President in appealing to students on campus as well as to supporters who could help expand the services available from the organization. With Reagan in the White House and Republicans in control of the Senate, it was no wonder that YAF looked to the decade of the 1980s with renewed optimism. As Cliff White, State & Chapter Services Director, commented, "YAF has come of age. We're ready to lead."[536]   But YAF's success in training young conservatives for leadership and in their maturing meant that they had less time and interest for building and maintaining a youth organization. More and more their focus turned from the high school and college campus to Washington, to positions in government or the growing number of conservative organizations expanding their presence in the Nation's Capitol. Having won the battle for the White House there was simply less interest and involvement in the battle for the campus. To those who had "come of age," there were bigger battles to be waged to redirect American government and society. This paradox would haunt Young Americans for Freedom throughout the decade as they tried to keep alive an organization, many of whose members were focused on other issues, environments, and battles.

January 20, 1981 was a cold and windy day in the Nation's Capital but the weather did not deter the enthusiasm of the thousands of conservatives gathered for the inauguration of a new President. For them, it was truly "a new beginning" and the opportunity to put into practice the principles and policies they had been articulating and advocating for years. To bring about those changes would require more than one individual. YAF members and alumni were ready to put aside their other occupations and careers to serve Ronald Reagan as he assumed the office of President of the United States.

The list of YAFers who joined the administration was extensive As Ken Grasso, New York YAF state chairman, observed, "Practically everyone under 40 in the Administration is an alumnus of YAF."[537] By the Summer of 1981 it was reported that some fifty YAF members or alumni had been appointed to the White House staff.[538] Outside the White House complex itself, YAF members and alumni held other key positions in the administration.

Still others obtained positions on Capitol Hill either with the new conservative members of the House and Senate or among the various Senate committees now controlled by the Republican majority. Joining YAF alumni Phil Crane, Barry Goldwater, Jr., and James Sensenbrenner in the House of Representatives were Jack Fields of Texas and John LeBoutellier of New York while Dan Quayle joined the Republican majority in the Senate.

With so many conservatives in government, the Left was in a state of apoplexy. For Molly Ivins there was little satisfaction in the fact that many were former YAFers: "The government has been taken over by YAFers. All you one time college students will remember YAFers – the Young Americans for Freedom – who used to bustle around on campus in those dorky suits, like Mormons on speed. Well, now they're in Congress. Some of the new representatives were just Young Republicans in college, rather than the YAFers, which is worse news, because at least YAF had that nice, goofy subset of libertarians who were a lot of fun. Young Republicans were never fun."[539] Little did the Left know in 1981 that Reagan would be re-elected in another landslide and Republicans would continue to be in charge of the Senate for six years before relinquishing control in 1987.

As more and more YAF members came to the Nation's Capital and became involved in the Reagan Revolution, they left fewer active young conservatives on the campuses and communities across the nation. Just as the old World War One song asked, "How you gonna keep 'em down on the farm after they've seen Paree?" the same problem was being felt by Young Americans for Freedom as a broad swath of the organization's leadership came to Washington and never left. A common comment in Washington at the time claimed "Conservatives know when they come to Washington that it's a sewer; trouble is, most of them wind up treating it like a hot tub." Apparently, for many the temperature was just right in the Nation's Capital. According to Steve Wiley, whose involvement in YAF spanned three decades, "Reagan's victory was almost the worst thing that could have happened to us. Our best guys either went home or used the Reagan connection as a stepping stone to jobs."[540]

While the new administration took much of the attention of young conservatives, YAF continued to co-sponsor the annual Conservative Political Action Conference. The 1981 event was a display of conservatism's newly won power with addresses by the President, Vice President, and numerous White House officials. CPAC played an important role in allowing YAF members to meet with conservative political leaders. In his speech that night, the President reminded those present of the seriousness of the challenge before them. "Fellow citizens, fellow conservatives, our time is now. Our moment has arrived... If we carry the day and turn the tide we can hope that as long as men speak of freedom and those who have protected it, they will remember us and they will say, 'Here were the brave and here their place of honor.'"[541]

YAF took up the challenge and launched "Youth for the Reagan Agenda" to rally support for the President's legislative program with literature and speakers as well as related efforts on campuses and in communities across America. National Chairman Jim Lacy explained, "The project is focused on generating youth support for the President's economic program which is under fire from liberals in Congress though supported by a majority of American citizens." Lacy concluded, "Only by helping ensure a stable, thriving economy now can America's young people look forward with optimism to the future." [542]

YAF also had its continuing mission to promote conservatism to fellow students. YAF campus chapters continued to hold regular meetings and sponsor a wide range of conservative speakers on economic and foreign policy concerns as well as social issues. The principles of free market economics and the Reagan program were of particular interest and comprised a number of YAF chapter programs. Foreign policy issues and the battle against Communist expansionism around the globe drew the attention of campus YAF chapters also. At Liberty University, Roy Jones and Bryan Kurtz organized Human Rights Week and circulated petitions supporting Polish freedom as well as hosted a speaker from the Committee for a Free Afghanistan.

More than economics and foreign policy caught the attention of YAF campus chapters. Southern Methodist University YAF held a forum on "Judeo-Christian Roles in American Politics," while Rutgers YAF sponsored an address by Richard Freund of the American Jewish Forum. Among a number of speakers it brought to campus, Columbia University YAF hosted Dr. Mildred Jefferson of the Right to Life Crusade. Phillip Buhler, chairman of the College of William & Mary YAF chapter, recalled those times on campus as a "tremendous experience, quite active particularly as this was during the Reagan Revolution."

Beyond hosting speakers and rallying support for the Reagan agenda, 1981 saw YAF campus chapters continue to oppose mandatory student funding of Ralph Nader's PIRGs. As YAF's campus chapters continued the battle, the national office distributed a new issues paper titled "Mandatory Fees: Wouldn't You Rather Have Control of Your Own Money?" YAF's argument was that college students were mature enough to make decisions for themselves. The paper claimed, "Apparently the college bureaucrats feel that a 18-22 year old student is not old or wise enough to make their own decisions." YAF opposed mandatory fees on both a philosophical and practical basis. "In the end, Young Americans for Freedom asks you: 'Wouldn't you rather have control over your own money?' More importantly, 'don't you think you are old enough to make your own decisions?'"[543]

When YAF members met in Boston in August 1981, William F. Buckley, Jr. gave the opening keynote address emphasizing three points for the young conservatives to keep in mind. First, supply-side economics cannot replace traditional support for budget restraint. Second, distrust of the military draft needs to be balanced with the service young Americans owe their nation in recognizing "collective responsibility as well as individual liberty." Third, YAFers were urged to devote some of their lives to caring for the elderly, an increasing part of the population.[544]

In his taped message the President thanked YAF for its support over the years and urged them to continue proselytizing and training new leaders. Reagan reminded them that they had a continuing responsibility on their high school and college campuses. "You must continue to provide the kind of philosophical and practical training which offers alternatives to today's youth in order to develop the next generation of leaders for America."[545] The President concluded his remarks by proclaiming, "As we chart the difficult course toward America's new beginning, our nation needs Young Americans for Freedom more than ever." It was the message these young conservatives wanted to hear.

Saturday evening featured a banquet billed as "A Salute to America's Forgotten Heroes" with an address by ACTION Director Tom Pauken, the administration's highest ranking Vietnam veteran, and by former POW John McCain, a frequent speaker at YAF events of the time. As one writer concluded, "The most emotional part of the convention was a tribute to veterans of the Vietnam War. John McCain, now a Senator from Arizona and a former POW, gave a stirring speech about his comrades."[546] Recognized for their sacrifices were a number of disabled veterans, former POWs, and the parents of a pilot missing in Laos.

It was a heady time for the YAFers as they met in Boston. As Deroy Murdock, a high school student from Los Angeles observed, "President Reagan has made us proud to be Americans. He's been able to focus public attention on one issue at a time." According to Michael Cross of the University of Oregon, YAF's new influence over the nation's affairs had its members in a state of euphoria.[547] YAF's success, according to University of Wisconsin graduate student Mark Huber "is because YAF is concerned with the issues that Americans are concerned with these days, taxes and the economy." California high school student John Manly claimed, "When the government is feeding you instead of stimulating you to work, the poor are still poor and the unemployed still unemployed. You get on the dole and there's no incentive to work." As Sergio Picchio observed, "We've never changed. The mood of the country changed."[548]

Working with Young America's Foundation, many YAF chapters sponsored a series of speakers on their campuses during the 1982-83 academic year. Author George Gilder toured five Ivy League campuses. Enrique Altimirano, an anti-Sandinista Nicaraguan, spoke at six campuses. Congressman Phil Crane addressed the YAFers at the University of Chicago while Dr. Richard Pipes spoke to the YAF chapter at Princeton. Harvard YAF hosted economist Alan Reynolds while Bill Buckley spoke at Ohio Wesleyan. Dr. Frank Trager provided a program on national defense policy before the University of Oregon YAF chapter and Dr. Mildred Jefferson spoke on the right to life issue at Penn State University YAF.[549] At Hillsdale College, the YAF chapter sponsored supply-side advocate Jude Wanniski while at American University chairman Jeff Michaels arranged an address by Interior Secretary James Watt. Meanwhile, Georgetown University YAF sponsored a series of lectures by White House aides Morton Blackwell, Rich Williamson, and Lyn Nofziger as well as an address by author and columnist George Will.[550] All across the country, YAF chapters were bringing to campus speakers who could describe, defend and advocate the policies of the Reagan Administration.

As an outgrowth of the speakers' tours, new chapters were formed on several campuses. By the Fall semester, YAF had chartered chapters at all eight Ivy League campuses for the first time in its history. At the same time, a number of new independent publications appeared on college campuses. Among the best known of the group formed after the Reagan election is the *Dartmouth Review*, established by Ben Hart and Greg Fossedal, a publication whose later staff included Dinesh D'Sousa and Laura Ingraham.[551]

As the national debate on nuclear arms control continued, YAF chapters distributed information on "Zero Option" and the dangers of freezing nuclear weapons at their present levels. The Zero Option project was not the only activity to occupy YAF chapters throughout 1982. At the University of Maryland the chapter organized a protest to counter the Progressive Student Alliance's mandatory fee-funded seminar on the military while Rachelle Kopperman, Columbia YAF chairman, debated the draft registration issue with representatives from the War Resisters' League. At the University of Pennsylvania,

Alan Ashkinaze sponsored a series of forums on Reagan Administration policies and helped organize a campaign for student government elections that resulted in six posts being won by YAF members.[552] When Jane Fonda appeared at the Jackson, Michigan Sheraton Hotel, 25 Hillsdale College members rallied outside and conducted "Conservative Aerobics" to respond to the radical's promotion of her aerobics program inside.[553]

Conscious of the need to remain prominent in the eyes of the national media as well as the conservative movement, YAF organized a tribute to Labor Secretary Raymond Donovan. Held at the Mayflower Hotel in Washington on October 13, 1982, it was attended by some 900 individuals, including Attorney General William French Smith, Health and Human Services Secretary Richard Schweiker, Secretary of Agriculture John Block, Chief of Staff James Baker, Director of the CIA William Casey, Counselor to the President Ed Meese, and other Reagan Administration appointees.[554] The dinner was an overwhelming success and provided needed positive publicity for YAF among the political and journalistic community in the Nation's Capital.[555]

By the Spring of 1983 Young Americans for Freedom had expanded to a number of campuses where the organization had not been active for several years or never had chartered a chapter. Some of the new chapters were on religiously affiliated campuses such as Brigham Young University, Bob Jones University, Oral Roberts University, Ohio Wesleyan University, and Loyola University of New Orleans. Still others were at state universities in traditionally conservative states. YAF outposts were established even on some less hospitable, smaller liberal arts campuses, including Swarthmore, the YAF chapter jointly organized at Haverford and Bryn Mawr colleges and at Ithaca College.[556] There was no question but that the appeal of Ronald Reagan and his association with YAF was helping to recruit new conservative leaders.

By the Fall of 1983 foreign policy issues dominated the news and occasioned a number of protests by local YAF units. When the Soviets shot down a Korean Airlines plane carrying 269 passengers and crew, including Congressman Larry McDonald of Georgia, YAF organized a rally in Lafayette Park across from the White House. The crowd carried a variety of homemade signs protesting the Soviet attack.[557] In other cities, YAF chapters organized similar protests against the Soviet regime.

Then came the crisis in Grenada where a Marxist government, aided by Cuban Communists, attempted to establish another foothold in the Caribbean. As opposition developed and order broke down, the security of American residents, including some 1,000 medical students studying there, came into question. When fellow radicals overthrew the prime minister, an appeal was made by other Caribbean nations for American assistance. In concert with other area countries, the United States sent a small contingent of troops to restore order and free the medical students.[558]

Two days later, the District of Columbia YAF organized a demonstration to support Reagan's sending of the troops. As one speaker told those assembled in Lafayette Square, the invasion of Grenada was "the first time since 1917 there's been a rollback of communism. For the first time we've taken the initiative against the Soviets instead of responding to their actions after the fact."[559] The views of the YAF members were summarized by DC YAF chairman Deroy Murdock when he concluded, "it is heartening to see a Communist country freed from its totalitarian rulers for a change. It is truly an historic event. Hopefully, Grenada will be the first of many Marxist states to regain their liberty." A Marxist regime had been rolled back, American students were safe, and young conservatives could be proud of their President's actions in thwarting a communist advance.

One year later, YAF chapters on a number of campuses celebrated the victory over communism with teach-ins, rallies, speeches, and debates. Some 75 of the rescued American medical students took part in various events. Georgetown University YAF held a rally featuring Grenada medical students Louise Batista and Jeff Geller. Geller's picture became famous when upon returning to the United States he was filmed kissing American soil. As Deroy Murdock said in a rally held to commemorate the one-year anniversary of the Grenada action, "When crisis strikes, a leader must not twittle his thumbs, pace across the floor, or bite his fingernails. Instead, he must act and act decisively. Thank God America has a President who knows what to do and gets it done."[560]

In the Fall of 1983, the ABC television network broadcast a horror film, *The Day After*, portraying a nuclear attack on Kansas City that allegedly left few people alive in Lawrence, Kansas. With ample national publicity, most conservatives viewed the program as a clear promotion of the Nuclear Freeze movement then being pushed by the left. Across the country YAF chapters responded by advocating Peace Through Strength and pointing out the fallacies of the movie. At the University of Kansas, YAF held a seminar attended by former Congressman Jim Jeffries who proclaimed, "We need more than hope, love, and wishful thinking to keep the Soviets at bay."[561] That Saturday, YAF volunteers handed out 20,000 Peace Through Strength petitions outside the Kansas-Missouri football game.

Meanwhile, in New York City some 100 YAF members picketed outside the ABC network headquarters.[562] On the west coast, YAF pickets marched outside the ABC studio in Hollywood and chanted "Better dead than red" while National Director Sergio Picchio called the film a "powerful propaganda tool" for the nuclear freeze movement.[563] In the Nation's capital, YAF leaders from George Washington, American, and Georgetown met to watch the program with a reporter from the *Washington Post*. In outlining their concerns, National

Director Richard Mathias felt that, "ABC is using passion rather than reason to convey a biased message." According to Bridget Brooker of Georgetown, after the opening scenario was set, "this is where the logic ends. The rest is pure emotion. This is so annoying. It's written to play on your emotions without giving the full story."[564] YAF took the lead in showing the American people that there was a better way of defending our country from nuclear annihilation.

Peace Through Strength was supplemented over the next several years by support for Reagan's Strategic Defense Initiative and the "High Frontier" program to develop a nuclear shield to protect against Soviet attack. YAF chapters sponsored speakers, including General Daniel Graham and other advocates of SDI, and distributed thousands of pieces of literature supporting the project. Later that summer, YAF even promoted Peace Through Strength in the Lion's Den of the Democratic National Convention in San Francisco.

Summer 1984 was the occasion for YAF's involvement in both the Republican and Democratic National Conventions. First up was the Democratic gathering in San Francisco during July. California YAFers Tim Wikle, Jeff Wright, and Curtis Helms joined DC YAF chairman Deroy Murdock as the delegation arrived early, obtained press credentials, and began spreading the conservative message in the wilderness surrounding the Moscone Center.[565] First out was a news release proclaiming "YAF Denounces Democratic Platform." Under the heading "Why is our party selling us out in Central America?" YAF noted the party's traditional support of the poor and the oppressed and asked, "Why then have the leaders of our Party turned their backs on the oppressed and the poor in Central America?" The YAF flyer concluded by declaring " THE TIME HAS COME FOR AMERICA TO STOP PROPPING UP COMMUNIST DICTATORSHIPS!"[566]

The most direct and dramatic challenge was still to come. On the third day of the convention, the four YAF members set up a table across from the Moscone Center where the plenary convention sessions were being held. The table was decorated with signs proclaiming "Democrats for Reagan" and "Democrats Defect Here" surrounded by YAF banners showing the torch of freedom logo.[567]

The following month, YAF members were in friendlier territory as they assembled in Dallas for the Republican National Convention. Some 300 activists gathered for daytime leadership conferences at the Dallas Marriott Hotel interspersed with attending official convention sessions at Reunion Arena.[568] Then came the demonstrations on the convention floor as the President was re-nominated and the young conservatives proudly displayed a 15-foot banner proclaiming "YAF Backs Reagan." Not only were the current members showing youth support for the President but dozens of YAF alumni were now delegates and alternates to the convention and still others were there as either leaders of conservative organizations or officials of the Reagan Administration.

Foreign policy and an aggressive stance against Communist inroads came to the fore in the second Reagan administration. Placing an emphasis on areas where anti-communists were taking the offensive, executive director Steve Baldwin made a trip to El Salvador a few years later and met with army officials who were battling FMLN guerrillas, much as Mike Waller had previously traveled to Nicaragua to meet with Contra rebels. Across the country, YAF chapters were rallying support against Communist advances in Latin America, Africa and Asia. William Daroff coordinated a pro-Contra rally in downtown Cleveland that included representatives from Polish and other Eastern European ethnic communities. In Albany, as pro-Sandinista elements marched, YAF members led a counter-demonstration in favor of Contra aid.[569] YAF chapters were sponsoring speakers and organizing counter-demonstrations to support the Contras in Nicaragua, anti-communist rebels in Angola, Afghanistan, and Ethiopia, and the anti-leftist forces in El Salvador.

When a Soviet peace delegation visited Minneapolis, YAF organized a protest that included representatives from the Vietnamese, Ukrainian, Jewish and Christian communities concerned about ethnic and religious freedom in Soviet controlled countries. Meanwhile, San Diego State University YAF took the initiative and erected 25 tombstones on campus to represent Communist-controlled countries. Yellow daisies were placed at the foot of each tombstone. Grossmont College YAF constructed a similar "mock graveyard". In Niagara Falls, New York, a group of YAF members demolished a Berlin Wall replica on the 25th anniversary of the wall's construction.

Throughout the 1987-88 academic year, there were more protests and counter-demonstrations on a wide range of foreign policy issues, perhaps more than at any previous time in YAF's history. One reporter commented on YAF by saying "It likes nothing better than to hold counter-demonstrations whenever liberal students protest U.S. policy." As Eugene Delgaudio noted, " We fight the left with humor. YAF takes the juggernaut of the left and flips it over. We find the weakest point on the left and penetrate it."[570] California YAF was clearly the most developed state in the late 1980s and also the most aggressive about organizing demonstrations. When leftist activists carried out a demonstration against aiding the Contras at Senator Pete Wilson's district office in Los Angeles, YAFers tried to block the elevators with their "Victory Over Communism" banners. [571]

Various YAF chapters generated so much publicity in only four months in Spring 1988 that California YAF produced a half-inch thick book of news clippings, predominantly from college newspapers.[572] By the late 1980s, the membership in YAF was smaller than in the first two decades of its history but it was still aggressively conservative and training future political and community leaders.

While California clearly had the most campus activity, other chapters throughout the country were also active. When leftists protested Contra aid at Indiana University, twenty-four YAFers counter protested chanting "Hey, Hey, Ho, Ho, Danny Ortega's Got to Go." When the left demonstrated against U.S. troop movements in Honduras, twenty Penn State YAFers counter-demonstrated. While seven thousand leftists marched in Boston Common the Boston University YAFers linked arms, blocking the march and making news on several TV stations.[573]

Upstate New York became one of the more active areas for YAF in the late 1980s and the University of Rochester was one of the more aggressive chapters. During the Spring of 1988 it held a protest for Contra aid, organized a candlelight vigil for the victims of communism, burned the Soviet flag, and created a replica of a Nicagaruan refugee camp – all of which resulted in newspaper, television and radio coverage for YAF. Under Sergio Picchio's leadership as national chairman, YAF was successful in recruiting a number of new leaders to the organization.

Throughout the 1988 primary season, YAF members had been divided in their choice of a successor to President Reagan. Many believed that Jack Kemp was the logical successor to carry on the Reagan Revolution; others backed the candidacy of television evangelist Pat Robertson or Senator Bob Dole of Kansas; to some, Reagan's Vice President, George H. W. Bush, was the best prepared to continue what Reagan had started; still others were attracted to the Libertarian party candidate Ron Paul. Regardless of their initial candidate preference, all active YAFers were committed to helping the Republican party "stay right" in terms of its rules, its platform, and its candidates for president and vice president. They were all determined to see the "Reagan Revolution" continue into the next administration.

New Orleans '88 became a major project of the organization with the theme, "The Movement at a Crossroads." Events were planned to influence the direction of the party, equip grass roots activists for what would be YAF's Fall Offensive, and develop strategy for the upcoming academic year. Beginning on Saturday August 13th, nearly 250 YAF members took part in the program and heard from both political and organizational leaders of the conservative movement. Senator Dan Quayle had accepted an invitation to address the YAF assembly but had to cancel once he had been named as Bush's choice for vice president. It was a time to learn how to be an effective activist and also to have fun and fellowship with other young conservatives. On Saturday some 75 members met in Lafayette Park in New Orleans' French Quarter to demonstrate against social security. As they shouted "No way, we won't pay!" the YAF members burned their cards in a bonfire set in a trash can. While the New Orleans police quietly stood by, the media took note of this defiant action by young people who had no faith in the future of the social security program.

For the organization, New Orleans '88 could be seen as a success. As one participant summarized the experience, "Most of us left New Orleans with new friends and a deeper commitment to YAF and her principles. Not to mention, new energy and information to be directed towards activism." Following the convention, YAF would launch another organizational drive that resulted in the formation of new chapters in areas that had not seen YAF activity for several years.

In the midst of the 1988 general election campaign and the Fall semester on campus, YAF stepped back briefly to reconsider the legacy and continuing relevance of its statement of principles. With the strong emphasis that had taken hold in the late 1980s on confrontational politics, demonstrations, and anti-leftist literature, it was especially important for Young Americans for Freedom to return to its philosophical roots and give consideration to the founding document which had unified young conservatives ever since that fateful meeting in September thirty-eight years earlier. Sponsored by the executive advisory board of YAF and under the direction of Dr. Mickey Craig of the Political Science department at Hillsdale College, "Sharon III: A Conservative Reappraisal" was held on September 22-25 on the Hillsdale campus. Thirty-five invited conservatives took part in rather weighty and highly academic discussions in a search for the conservative center. Prior to arriving at Hillsdale, each participant received an inch thick book of readings that included book chapters, journal and law review articles, op-ed columns, and even a few Supreme Court cases. Reading this was their assignment in advance of the deliberations at Sharon III.

With the Reagan Administration quickly coming to an end, the conservatives young and old who gathered to reflect on the state of conservatism and the American Republic saw the need for the revitalization of a federalism which at once precludes state interference with legitimate national powers and prevents national cooptation of legitimate state power. Looking back now from the vantage point of the 21st century and the ever-growing involvement of the Federal government in more and more areas of American life, one can see that this group of conservatives was prescient in its concern over the future of federalism and the protection of the right to self-government among the American people.

The Reagan Era Ends

In November 1988 the American people had to decide once again who would lead them from the White House. For many, the decision centered on whether to continue the policies and programs of the past eight years, albeit with the modifications that any new President would create. Ronald Reagan left office with his popularity high and that support transferred to his vice president who rather easily defeated the Democratic candidate, Governor Michael Dukakis of Massachusetts, and the Libertarian candidate, former Congressman Ron Paul. Reagan had entered politics denigrated by much of the media and the so-called establishment as merely an actor, the "great performer" who read his lines well. He left the presidency having helped to redirect much of American political thought. America now had a more positive self-image, an emphasis on entrepreneurship, and a determination that it could truly be a City on a Hill. Ronald Reagan had served the American people well and would always be a hero to his fellow conservatives. The Reagan Era was over.

— 9 —

After Reagan and Into the 21ˢᵗ Century

Young Americans for Freedom began 1989 on a high note. Reagan's Vice President had just been elected to continue a Republican administration in the White House. YAF had established itself as a positive force in American public opinion as a study by Peter D. Hart Research Associates found that 34% of a random sample had a favorable view of Young Americans for Freedom while only 6% had an unfavorable opinion.[574] And it had the backing, as honorary advisory board chairman, of the popular former President of the United States.

One YAF member of the time was honored to drive the Reagans' personal luggage from the airport to their home in Bel Air when the President returned to California on January 20, 1989. It was the experience of a lifetime for Jon Fleischman, now a political commentator in Southern California.

> *While unloading the luggage I had a chance to meet the former President (in his closet, actually). I told him that I was with Young Americans for Freedom, and thanked him for everything he had done for our country. He smiled and thanked me for bringing in his luggage. He also expressed his appreciation for everything that YAFers had done to support him throughout his time in public office and during his Presidency. It was a very short exchange, but one I will remember forever.[575]*

Reagan's ongoing commitment to YAF was reinforced a few years later for Fleischman who had become California YAF state chairman and sent out a fundraising letter to send YAFers to CPAC in Washington. Back came an envelope from Reagan's office. "I opened it to find a $400 check from Reagan, along with a handwritten note to me letting me know that the enclosed check was to help send YAFers to the CPAC conference." As Fleischman concluded, " Pretty amazing – that a former leader of the free world took the time to read my note, and respond with a generous personal contribution."[576] While he was part of the final youth generation to actually interact with President Reagan, his legacy will live on as others work hard to promote the ideals that he lived and espoused, "faith, freedom, free enterprise – and above all eternal optimism for all things."

Under Sergio Picchio's leadership as National Chairman and with strong staff support from Steve Baldwin and his successor Christopher Long, Young Americans for Freedom was more active, in more areas of the country, than it had been in several years. Just as important, YAF seemed to have regained the confidence and support of those senior conservatives who had always served as key advisors and emissaries to the wider conservative movement. Nothing symbolized this renewed faith in the organization any better than Bill Buckley's appearance at the 1987 YAF convention and the involvement of several senior conservatives in the 1988 Sharon III conference.

YAF continued to distribute its newsletter, *Dialogue on Liberty* and it served as a vehicle for spreading news to YAF members on various chapter activities across the country. One major activity during this time period was to rally support for Oliver North and for the ongoing Contra effort to overthrow the Marxist Sandinista regime in Nicaragua. YAF also called for an end to the Screen Actors Guild "blacklisting" of performers who had appeared in South Africa, taking out full-page advertisements in *Daily Variety* and the *Hollywood Reporter* to express their opposition to this move by the left.[577]

Across the country a number of local YAF chapters continued their emphasis on protests and counter demonstrations and taking stands on controversial social issues such as abortion and gay rights. Larry King was active at UCLA in the mid-1980s and then became Director of State and Chapter Services for YAF from 1987 to 1989. At the time he viewed the challenge as recreating what the left had supposedly accomplished in the 1960s. "I had this idea that we could have a 60s like demonstration from the right. We accepted as a truism in the high school class of '82 that the Hippie movement changed the world and stopped the Vietnam War. And that in the 80s we could do the same from the right."[578] One leftist writer reporting on YAF noted this change in orientation.

> *Originally shaped in the cerebral image of its wealthy, intellectual
> East Coast founder, YAF has increasingly emerged as a California-
> style populist group, hell-bent on more street action and fewer
> hallway debates over the theories of columnist Russell Kirk,
> novelist Ayn Rand, economist Ludwig von Mises and other rightist
> intellectuals who influenced Buckley's original cell.[579]*

While California YAF was perhaps the most active proponent of the demonstration and counter protest tactic, other areas also produced similar YAF efforts.

During the Spring of 1990 YAF held another series of regional conferences.[580] Looking back on that time Vince Burruano of Catholic University believes "it was a great opportunity to learn and debate topics of personal importance and to become involved in promoting and preserving those ideals. I think it is worth reminding conservatives that we need a base of young leaders who can carry the message." Jon Fleischman built on his YAF experience to develop a career in politics and journalism. He maintains that, "YAF has been perhaps the single most important contributor to my current career; the most dominant influence in my career.[581] Fleischman noted that YAF in California had developed a pervasive alumni base that helped provide useful contacts for those who wished to become more involved in politics. But those contacts were based on more than friendship or simple membership. "YAF provided a way to realize that having convictions was a good thing. In YAF, the more committed you were to your ideology, the more you rose up in the organization," according to Fleischman.

YAF continued to obtain media coverage for its various demonstrations and in April of 1990 the *Los Angeles Times Magazine* published a lengthy and somewhat favorable article on the organization, its leaders, and its activities in California. Written by a novelist and film critic who taught journalism at the University of Southern California, the article compared the YAF of 1990 with the Communist youth organizations on the UCLA campus in which he was involved in the late 1940s. It was the aggressiveness and radical approach to advancing ideological principles that was most evident to this writer.

> *They make life miserable for liberals, whether college professors,
> Democrats or Republicans like Pete Wilson. They love noise,
> argument, debate, counterdemonstrations, media attention. Blink
> an eye and they're short-haired Abbie Hoffmans or Jerry Rubins
> standing on their heads.[582]*

The article was forwarded on to Bill Buckley who, in turn, sent it to Bill

Rusher, Marvin Liebman, Stan Evans, and Tom Winter with the observation, "it does suggest signs of life in YAF greater than I supposed were there."[583]

That Fall, Orange County YAF organized a tea party to protest "King George" when President George H. W. Bush broke his pledge not to support any new taxes. Many in YAF had not supported Bush during the 1988 election, would oppose his efforts to remove Iraqi troops from Kuwait, and in 1992 would support the candidacy of Pat Buchanan in the Republican primaries.

Still other issues attracted the attention of YAF chapters around the nation. At the University of Iowa, YAFers led by Kurt Adams countered a leftist protest against ROTC recruitment on campus while across the state at Iowa State University, Greg Fetterman's YAF chapter counter protested a peace march on campus, both activities gaining significant media coverage.[584] YAF also had an active presence on a number of other campuses in Indiana, Arizona, Ohio and Louisiana.

On September 13, 1990, YAF celebrated its 30th anniversary with a banquet at the Washington Marriott Hotel. Among the speakers were several YAF alumni including Congressmen Christopher Cox and Dana Rohrabacher and Howard Phillips, chairman of the Conservative Caucus. The invocation was given by Father Vincent Rigdon, former New York YAF state chairman and currently a parish priest in the Washington area. Rohrabacher discussed the role YAF played in his political development, both philosophically and tactically, while Cox maintained that events of the time showed that individual liberty and the free enterprise system best ensure human welfare. Also addressing those at the celebration were Senator Conrad Burns of Montana and Congressman Robert K. Dornan of California.[585] Although Bill Buckley could not be present he sent a statement to be read on the occasion claiming, "the return of YAF as a force among young people seems to be assured under the present leadership, and we have no alternative than to pray that this will be so. My salute to the officers of YAF, and to its constituency…"[586]

Throughout 1991 one of the major activities of national YAF was an effort to ensure that Vice President Dan Quayle was kept on the Republican presidential ticket.[587] Quayle had been the object of critical media coverage ever since he was nominated and some in the party saw an opportunity to remove Quayle and provide an opening for others to be chosen by Bush. YAF members showed up at various gatherings throughout the year and circulated petitions pledging support for Quayle. In May, three YAF leaders met with Quayle to present him with more than 5,000 petitions of support. As Jeffrey Wright stated,

> We wanted to show the Vice President that he has a strong and enthusiastic base of support and that what the liberal media are reporting about his support is not accurate. The Vice President

was very pleased with YAF's show of support and wanted to convey his thanks to Young Americans for Freedom – its members and supporters. [588]

Quayle observed, "You and I both know the media is not friendly to conservatives. That's why it is so important that YAF is out there."[589] The effort to support the Vice President continued throughout 1992, even though many YAFers campaigned for Pat Buchanan against George H. W. Bush in the Republican primaries.[590] The *New Guard* in the Fall of 1992 featured a cover article titled "Dan Quayle and his enemies."[591]

In August 1991, Young Americans for Freedom gathered at a Best Western hotel in suburban Roslyn, Virginia outside of the Nation's Capital. Given the optimistic developments in the world, the theme was "Victory Over Communism – Finishing the Job" and the lineup of speakers was impressive.[592] Bill Buckley was back again to give a stirring keynote speech. Defense Secretary Dick Cheney represented the Bush administration while former Attorney General Edwin Meese provided a connection to the Reagan presidency. Although Congress was trying to complete work before its traditional August recess, Senator Larry Craig and Congressmen Cox and Dornan made time to address the YAF delegates. There were even taped remarks by Vice President Quayle who could not attend in person. As National Chairman Jeff Wright commented, "he made a special effort on YAF's behalf. He fit time into his busy schedule for this YAF video because he thinks YAF is that special. I'm very grateful to him"[593]

During 1992 YAF launched what they called the "Anita Hill Truth Squad" to provide background information on the University of Oklahoma law professor as she spoke on campuses across the country. As Jeff Wright observed, "many of these speaking engagements are sponsored by left-wing groups like the American Civil Liberties Union, the Communications Workers of America and others." [594] YAF also continued its efforts to keep Dan Quayle on the Republican ticket, and made a small presence at the Republican National Convention where Jeff Wright met with the Vice President.

At a YAF meeting on the evening of Lincoln's birthday during the 1994 CPAC, former National Chairman James Lacy spoke on "YAF's Historic Role in the Conservative Movement and the need for YAF in the future." By this time, however, YAF no longer had a national office nor any staff to provide direction and support to local members and chapters. Despite the lack of a coordinated national effort, there remained pockets of YAF activity throughout the country, campus chapters that organized and operated on their own.

California Young Americans for Freedom continued as a strong conservative force on campuses and in the state's political arena. It had a sizeable alumni base, including several members of the California Assembly, State Senate and congressional delegation as well as an advisory board headed by former President Reagan. In late 1994, it claimed fifteen active chapters and had adopted an aggressive plan for expansion. As Jeff Greene noted, "the rebuilding process has been done without any direct or substantial funds, and the current growth of Cal-YAF has been accomplished without any help from National YAF or any other organization."[595] In the Summer of 1994, California YAF held a conference attended by some 120 young conservatives from throughout the state.[596] During the remainder of the decade, California YAF continued to print and distribute its newsletter, *The Creative Californian*, organize demonstrations and rallies, and issue news releases. Rather than focusing its efforts on campus, however, California YAF functioned as an important advocate for conservative positions in statewide politics.[597]

During the late 1990s, Brian Park of Chapman University served as California YAF state chairman and recalled the organization's involvement in "Countless demonstrations and counter-demonstrations against various causes… First was the Academy Awards demonstration against Elia Kazan for his lifetime achievement award. The left was protesting his involvement in naming names of communists in Hollywood. We were there to support Elia Kazan and a near brawl broke out. It was covered by several publications." For Park, "being able to influence public policy at a young age through an organization like YAF," is an experience he will never forget.

Across the country, a number of campuses did have active YAF chapters. In the early 1990s, a YAF chapter was formed at Florida International University and continued to be a strong voice for conservatism on campus for several years, sponsoring addresses by a number of nationally known conservatives such as Jack Kemp and Phyllis Schlafly. The YAF chapter at Pennsylvania State University was reorganized in the early 1990s and has continued to the present day as a voice for responsible conservatism on that campus, featuring appearances by a first-class list of speakers, including William F. Buckley, Jr., Dinesh D'Souza, Star Parker, G. Gordon Liddy, and many others. Among its leaders in the mid-1990s was Patrick Coyle, now Vice President of Young America's Foundation.

Other campuses where YAF continued to have an active presence during the 1990s included the University of Minnesota, Indiana University, University of Delaware and a number of campuses in Iowa. YAF chapters operated also at Hamilton College, Catholic University, and the University of Virginia. At the University of Massachusetts, Brian Darling and Daniel Flynn were among those who kept the chapter alive for several years, including publishing an independent conservative paper, "The Minuteman." Flynn is a free-lance writer and author of several books including *A Conservative History of the American Left* and *Why The*

Left Hates America. At the University of Pennsylvania, Mark Leventhal led a small YAF chapter in the 1990s. Each year the UPenn chapter would hold a "happy birthday SDI" party on March 23rd as well as sponsor speeches by conservatives on campus.

Even with its organizational problems, YAF was continuing to develop and train that cadre of conservatives, individuals who would go on to play important roles in advancing the principles first enumerated in the Sharon Statement. As Young Americans for Freedom struggled with little or no national direction, approaches were made in 1997 and 1998 to merge the organization with its more successful offshoot, Young America's Foundation. These efforts, however, never materialized and YAF continued to function on a low level. In 2000, Erik Johnson, a graduate of Vanderbilt University, was designated national chairman and continued to hold that position for the next ten years.

Unfortunately, as the 21st century began, YAF was at the lowest point in its long history. With the absence of any national office or staff and little direction from its officers, it became easy for rogue groups to claim the YAF name. In some instances, this created problems by linking YAF to positions that were clearly outside the realm of responsible conservatism. Groups that were never officially chartered by YAF claimed its name and operated at a few Michigan college campuses promoting controversial positions and sponsoring speakers who advocated policies outside the tradition of American conservatism and even contrary to the Sharon Statement. Without an effective national organization it became difficult to protect the good name of Young Americans for Freedom and disassociate YAF from these activities. Fortunately, these rogue groups quickly died out.

Still others formed YAF chapters and carried forth programs reflective of the principles outlined in the Sharon Statement. At George Washington University, the YAF chapter became affiliated with Young America's Foundation, rather than Young Americans for Freedom. On a number of campuses, conservative clubs were organized and operated independently, although often with support from Young America's Foundation.[598] When a young high school student in Washington state expressed an interest in YAF, he was quickly named state chairman, although there is no indication of any YAF chapters in the state. Hans Zieger was an up-and-coming young conservative who later graduated from Hillsdale College and was elected as a Washington state representative at the age of 25. Shortly after being designated state chairman, with little or no assistance from national YAF, Zieger concluded, "Over time, YAF lost its influence. A few YAF chapters held on in some corners of the country, but all in all it is no more."[599]

Fortunately, Zieger's obituary for YAF was premature and merely reflective of the organization's weakness in the early 21st century. By the end of the first decade of this century, YAF was beginning to have a brief rebirth. Jordan Marks had graduated from law school at the State University of New York – Buffalo in 2009 and became executive director of YAF. Slowly but surely a national organization reasserted itself. A new generation of Americans born during and after the presidency of Ronald Reagan was beginning to carry forth that same dedication to individual liberty, free enterprise, and a strong national defense that previous generations advanced through Young Americans for Freedom.

Active YAF leaders were present on several campuses in the Nation's Capital at Howard University, University of the District of Columbia, and American University while the YAF unit at George Washington University affiliated with Young America's Foundation continued to operate at a high level. YAF chapters were also operating at Liberty University and George Mason University in Virginia while one was organized at East Tennessee State University and Tyler Trumbach reorganized the YAF chapter at Columbia University. Across the continent, Gabriella Hoffman led an active YAF chapter at the University of California-San Diego that hosted a number of speakers, including David Horowitz. After overcoming opposition from the school administration, a YAF chapter was finally recognized at the University of South Florida in 2010.

By 2010, Erik Johnson relinquished his title as YAF national chairman and was replaced by Michael Jones, a YAF chapter chairman and graduate student at East Tennessee State University. Added to the governing board were younger campus activists including Sam Settle of Penn State, Tyler Trumbach of Columbia University, and Christopher Bedford of American University. In one of its last actions, the YAF board in a clearly controversial decision voted in February 2011 to remove Congressman Ron Paul from the organization's National Advisory Board. YAF's concern centered on Dr. Paul's perceived lack of support for national security efforts. As Jordan Marks concluded, "It is a sad day in American history when a one-time conservative libertarian stalwart has fallen more out of touch with America's needs for national security than the current feeble and appeasing administration." Marks claimed that Paul had "allied himself with the radical anti-war left by laying the blame on America for the unprovoked attacks of September 11th" and "has not condemned the 9/11 'Truther' conspiracy theorists that support him."[600] By removing Paul, YAF had clearly distinguished itself on campuses from the Young Americans for Liberty that had been organized out of the youth efforts for Ron Paul's 2008 campaign.

Renewed interest in a merger with Young America's Foundation had developed in 2010 and conditions for such an action were coming together when Jones and his vice-chairman, Christopher Bedford, lined up the votes for unification. Thus, in May 2011, after lengthy discussions and negotiations, YAF ceased its existence as an independent entity and became a project of Young America's Foundation. Commenting on the unification, Young America's

Foundation President Ron Robinson said, "During this time in our country, where freedom is on the precipice, we needed to take every step to ensure the next generation understands the importance of limited government and individual freedom. Young Americans for Freedom's rich conservative legacy made it a natural partner."[601] Meanwhile, YAF chairman Michael Jones described it as "the most significant moment in the history of Young Americans for Freedom since the adoption of the 'Sharon Statement' at its founding in 1960."

Now affiliated with a non-profit educational entity, the reborn and revitalized Young Americans for Freedom serves as campus outlets for Young America's Foundation. No longer does it involve itself with internal politics, a major time-consuming activity of the old YAF which often led to "purges" of members on the losing side of convention battles. Nor is it a vehicle for direct political action and support for specific candidates, as the original YAF was with the Goldwater and Reagan campaigns. Today, Young Americans for Freedom chapters focus on bringing conservative speakers to their campuses to provide a more balanced presentation of philosophical and ideological positions. YAF chapters participate in the Foundation's action projects such as the "9/11: Never Forget" project every September, and the Freedom Week commemoration of the fall of the Berlin wall.

Young America's Foundation holds a number of weekend and week-long training sessions and conferences for high school and college students where YAF members and other young conservatives develop and expand their leadership skills and knowledge of conservative philosophy and free-market economics. YAF's activism training seminars focus on techniques for recruiting, public speaking, fundraising, public relations, graphics and design. The merger with Young America's Foundation has provided YAF chapters with promotional materials and publications, opportunities to sponsor leading conservative speakers on campus, and a full-time staff operation headed by a director of YAF chapter services for Young America's Foundation.

While the old YAF of the 20ᵗʰ century was a predominantly male organization of college students and young adults, the new YAF includes a wide range of individuals from various backgrounds. At conferences and in local chapters, one can often find more female than male participants. Some forty percent of all YAF chapters are located at private and public high schools and there appears to be a wider ethnic and racial representation among those involved in YAF activities.

Raj Kannappan, who brought Foundation speakers to his Cornell University campus, believes YAF's growth among high school students results from the absence of any other conservative groups while the left is present with various environmental and social justice organizations. Now isolated from direct political action and not tied to any political party it has been easier for YAF to gain recognition in high schools, although administrative roadblocks have been attempted in certain areas. Rick Santorum's speech at Grosse Pointe South High School was initially cancelled because the superintendent was offended by Senator Santorum's views on traditional marriage. As a result of the YAF chapter's efforts to expose the administration's intolerance, the school relented and 1,600 students and community members heard Santorum speak.

One of the most active YAF chapters developed at Canyon High School in New Braunfels, Texas. The chapter meets weekly during the academic year and in addition to carrying out traditional YAF projects has been actively involved in local charitable efforts. Kaitlyn Anderson was instrumental in the chapter's formation: "When I attended my first conference in 2013, my YAF chapter had just gotten off the ground. Attending that conference made me realize that I was only just beginning involvement in something so much larger than myself...I was fired up to promote conservative principles and mobilize members of my chapter." The next year, nine students from Canyon attended the Foundation's national high school conference in Washington, DC. As she went off to college, Anderson appreciated her involvement. "Through YAF I have formed a better understanding of what I believe and why I believe it. I have developed a renewed faith in my country and myself, and I am eager to live out my beliefs."

For some, exposure to YAF and the Foundation's conferences was the gateway to becoming a conservative. Jolie Ballantyne, a recent graduate of the Penn State law school, explained that "Before becoming involved with YAF, I never thought to question what my professors told me. I never thought to look into issues for myself and form my own opinion." Still others like Savanna Wierenga came from a politically active and conservative family and attended Hillsdale College. But it was a YAF conference that turned her into an activist, noting "I did not quite understand the power that my role as a college student could play in fighting for freedom – that is, until I actually got involved with YAF."

Apart from simply attending conferences and carrying out campus projects, becoming involved in YAF developed leadership skills for several students. As Mississippi College YAF chair Stephan Pitts noted, "Starting a YAF chapter literally changed my outlook on the future. It showed me that with a little hard work and determination you can make a difference at your school, in your state, and nationally." Nick James, YAF chairman at Clemson University noted "I have had the opportunity to learn many important attributes including how to handle the media, crisis management, and organizational skills. Leading my YAF chapter has given me a different perspective on the college experience." For Lauren McCue of Virginia Tech, her time in YAF has been "an outlet for self-discovery. I came into college as a biology major unsure of my true calling in life, but through my involvement with YAF, I discovered that the conservative cause is something I am dedicated to for the rest of my life."

After successfully leading Young Americans for Freedom in its acquisition by Young America's Foundation, Michael Jones stepped down as chairman in 2016. Jones is carrying on his academic career as a history instructor at the University of Mary Harden Baylor in Belton, Texas and remains active by heading up the YAF Alumni Board of Governors.

The current chairman of Young Americans for Freedom is Grant Strobl, a student leader at the University of Michigan. At the age of 20, Strobl became the youngest chairman in YAF's long history, having been active in the organization since his high school days. "I remember sitting in my World History class in high school, listening to a lecture on the evils of America and of Christopher Columbus...I spent that night Google-ing conservative organizations and stumbled upon Young America's Foundation which stood out from the rest. I decided to send them an email. This email changed my life and arguably launched my career in the conservative movement."

Strobl's high school chapter sponsored several speakers, including former presidential candidate Steve Forbes. After overcoming opposition from the district administration, Forbes spoke to an audience of 1,300 students, changed district policy, and impacted thousands of students. At the University of Michigan, the YAF chapter sponsored a debate between Bill Ayers and Dinesh D'Souza as well as lectures by Ben Shapiro, Congressman Tom Price, and author Jonah Goldberg. As Strobl noted, "No other organization dedicated to the conservative youth has a more successful track record than YAF. Simply put: YAF wins. If you want to make a difference on your campus and in your country, contact YAF today."

Ron Robinson, President of Young America's Foundation, was instrumental in the integration of Young Americans for Freedom into the Foundation's menu of programs. His motivation in so doing had a personal aspect to it. According to Robinson, "When I was in college, apart from my classroom studies, my involvement in YAF was a major contributor to gaining knowledge and self-confidence that led me to a lifetime of involvement in the conservative movement. YAF gave me the leadership skills and the sound philosophical foundation I needed to be effective." Noting the number of former YAF members who now occupy key positions in government, the media, and various non-profit organizations, Robinson is determined to ensure that the opportunities he had in YAF are available to young people today.

After several years of slumber, Young Americans for Freedom is once again a presence on a number of high school and college campuses, with some 220 chapters active in 2016. They continue to heed the advice of former President Ronald Reagan who once told them, "Remember your very title – you are Young Americans for Freedom. That is your mission above all others. You are most important in this particular moment of history, because so many of your peers have listened to false prophets and demagogues." Following Reagan's advice, YAF today continues to promote the principles of limited government, individual freedom, free enterprise, a strong national defense, and traditional values as outlined in the organization's 'Sharon Statement' adopted more than a half-century ago. While the issues and concerns, the individuals and the challenges may change, the principles and the philosophical foundation remain the same and serve as a lasting guide for Young Americans for Freedom in the 21st century.

— 10 —

The Rebirth of Young Americans for Freedom

THROUGHOUT ITS HISTORY, YOUNG AMERICANS FOR FREEDOM blended together an appreciation of conservative philosophy and principles with an understanding of the means to influence public opinion and public policy. Young people were exposed to a firm foundation of free market economics, strong anti-communism, and traditional American values as expressed in the organization's credo. They took this commitment into the political arena, having been trained in effective argumentation, mass communication techniques, and political organizing principles. As one historian summarized this effort, during the late 1960s and 1970s, "YAF filled in as the one group through which young people could meet, work together to achieve results, and then move on to another project, staying busy in their fight against the Left." [602]

Despite various political setbacks, those active in Young Americans for Freedom were optimistic that they could redirect American society for they believed that, down deep inside, most Americans agreed with the principles they espoused. As historian John Andrew concluded, it was YAF that provided,

> *A cadre of young men and women ideologically committed to the cause of conservatism rather than to the Republican Party or to the politics of compromise and conciliation… Unlike other grass-roots conservative or right-wing groups at the time, YAF wanted*

to do more than stir the masses; it wanted to create a political commonwealth grounded in conservative principles. YAFers believed their articulation of those principles could mobilize a mass of dormant voters and create a conservative majority.[603]

Imbued with this belief in the possibility of success, YAF both helped to create the shift in American institutions and took advantage of that shift. Contrasted with other youth of the time, most YAF members "became integrated into mainstream politics. Using the skills and resources they acquired through their activism in YAF, as adults they worked for conservative causes in mainstream institutions."[604] As one YAF founder summarized the situation, "the Left battled for the campus; the Right won politics."[605] From the experience of the Goldwater campaign of 1964 they were ready to take on the subsequent Reagan campaigns and see success come their way.

Dana Rohrabacher is a classic example of the impact and influence of YAF on American politics, rising from YAF campus activist to speechwriter in the Reagan White House, to Congressman from California. As he has noted, it was the network of friends and supporters he had made in Young Americans for Freedom that provided critical assistance in his first campaign for Congress in 1988.

By the time Reagan won the presidency in 1980, veterans of YAF were ready to assume influential positions in his administration. When I first ran for Congress, my secret weapon was the high-quality support I received from friends who had been politically active with me since the late 1960s. As far as the media was concerned, we didn't exist, but in the long run we won." [606]

Author Sandra Gurvis compared the lasting impact of Students for a Democratic Society and Young Americans for Freedom and concluded, "Washington, D.C. is where many of the original architects of the YAF found a permanent roost during the Reagan years as career conservatives, creating a dynamic network of institutions… If you were to weigh the durability of YAF versus SDS, it is obvious who tips the scale."[607]

Through YAF a community of conservative activists was created that would change the ideological orientation of the Republican Party and eventually much of the country. Speaking of those with whom he worked, David Keene, Opinion Editor for the *Washington Times*, described them as "all kids who came up together, we still are friends and still work together…We have a network of people…My closest friends were people that I met…through school and politics at that time, and then have brought each other all along since then."[608] At the start of the

Reagan Administration, David Broder observed that, "YAF has unquestionably been the primary breeding ground and training ground for the new generation of conservative leaders."[609] YAF contacts such as those described by Keene and Broder have been critical for building the network of conservative organizations in Washington.

Thirty-five years ago James Roberts wrote *The Conservative Decade* as a precursor to the coming Reagan Administration and the young conservatives poised to take a leadership role in national politics. As one reads through the names and organizations cited as having developed from the 1960s forward, the importance of Young Americans for Freedom cannot be overestimated. Name after name of those mentioned can be found on the old membership rolls of YAF, an organization that played an essential role in their leadership development. Since Roberts' book was published, these alumni of YAF have become, to employ Marvin Liebman's phrase, OAFs or Old Americans for Freedom. The early members of the organization are either retired or quickly approaching that status. Like their compatriots in the "Baby Boom" generation, many who joined YAF later have now reached the pinnacle of their careers. Time passes on. Now others would need to carry forth and prepare future generations of young Americans dedicated to conservative principle for the challenges ahead.

Today, in the 21st century, there are many more groups and resources, conferences and publications, heroes and helpers, services and mentors than any new young conservative ever dreamed about way back in 1960 when Young Americans for Freedom began its effort to create a national organization of students and young people dedicated to individual freedom. The torch must continue to be held high and, with the advice, counsel and financial support of those who were once young Americans dedicated to individual freedom, the effort to train, educate, and equip young conservatives and to nourish and expand the network must continue. Fortunately, as of 2016 Young Americans for Freedom is back as a force for conservatism and for training new leaders on a number of high school and college campuses. Now integrated as a major program of Young America's Foundation, these YAF members and chapters can take advantage of the multitude of services, conferences, materials and programs available to assist them in their efforts on campus. As it did in the past, Young Americans for Freedom will produce a new cadre for conservatism in the 21st century.

The Sharon Statement

Adopted in conference at Sharon, Connecticut
September 9-11, 1960.

IN THIS TIME of moral and political crisis, it is the responsibility of the youth of America to affirm certain eternal truths.

WE, as young conservatives, believe:

THAT foremost among the transcendent values is the individual's use of his God-given free will, whence derives his right to be free from the restrictions of arbitrary force;

THAT liberty is indivisible, and that political freedom cannot long exist without economic freedom;

THAT the purposes of government are to protect these freedoms through the preservation of internal order, the provision of national defense, and the administration of justice;

THAT when government ventures beyond these rightful functions, it accumulates power which tends to diminish order and liberty;

THAT the Constitution of the United States is the best arrangement yet devised for empowering government to fulfill its proper role, while restraining it from the concentration and abuse of power;

THAT the genius of the Constitution – the division of powers – is summed up in the clause which reserves primacy to the several states, or to the people, in those spheres not specifically delegated to the Federal Government;

THAT the market economy, allocating resources by the free play of supply and demand, is the single economic system compatible with the requirements of personal freedom and constitutional government, and that it is at the same time the most productive supplier of human needs;

THAT when government interferes with the work of the market economy, it tends to reduce the moral and physical strength of the nation; that when it takes from one man to bestow on another, it diminishes the incentive of the first, the integrity of the second, and the moral autonomy of both;

THAT we will be free only so long as the national sovereignty of the United States is secure; that history shows periods of freedom are rare, and can exist only when free citizens concertedly defend their rights against all enemies;

THAT the forces of international Communism are, at present, the greatest single threat to these liberties;

THAT the United States should stress victory over, rather than coexistence with, this menace; and

THAT American foreign policy must be judged by this criterion: does it serve the just interests of the United States?

Endnotes

1   Lionel Trilling: *The Liberal Imagination* (New York: Doubleday, 1950). See also Arthur Schlesinger, Jr.: *The Vital Center* (Boston: Houghton Mifflin Company, 1949).

2   Von Mises had emigrated to the United States in the 1930s and published two important works in the postwar period, *Bureaucracy* (New Rochelle, NY: Arlington House, 1969) and *Omnipotent Government: The Rise of the Total State and Total War* (New Haven: Yale University Press, 1944). Hayek's seminal work, *The Road to Serfdom* (Chicago: University of Chicago Press, 1976) was initially published in 1944 but became widely distributed in the postwar period. A valuable overview of the contributions of these two writers to the subsequent development of a positive conservatism can be found in George H. Nash: *The Conservative Intellectual Movement in America Since 1945* (Wilmington, DE: Intercollegiate Studies Institute, 1996), pp. 1-29.

3   This point is made by E. J. Dionne, Jr: *Why Americans Hate Politics* (New York: Simon & Schuster, 1991), p. 153.

4   See his essay "Why I Am Not a Conservative" in Frank S. Meyer, ed. *What Is Conservatism?* (New York: Holt, Rinehart and Winston, 1964), pp. 88-103.

5   See also Jeffrey Hart: *The American Dissent* (Garden City, NY: Doubleday, 1966), pp. 24-26 for a discussion of the emphasis on economics in the late 1940s opposition to the dominant liberal ideology. An additional writer whose works first appeared in the 1940s and more significantly in the 1950s is Ayn Rand. While Rand was mainly a novelist, her main characters portray a dedication to individualism, laissez-faire capitalism, and anti-collectivism. Her first important novel, *The Fountainhead* (Indianapolis: Bobbs-Merrill Company, 1943) appeared during World War II and was made into a movie by Warner Brothers in 1949. Her best-known work, however, was published in the mid-1950s and includes many of the themes she developed into a philosophical outlook known as Objectivism. *Atlas Shrugged* (New York: Random House, 1957) includes a thirty-page monologue by main character John Galt outlining the main points of her perspective on life. While many of Rand's followers became active in young conservative efforts in the 1960s and were supporters of the Goldwater presidential campaign, Rand never saw herself as a conservative and, indeed, her views were at odds with a number of essential conservative positions.

6   Nash, p. xv.

7   Lee Edwards: *The Conservative Revolution* (New York: the Free Press, 1999), p. 15 and Alfred S. Regnery: *Upstream: The Ascendance of American Conservatism* (New York: Simon & Schuster, 2008), pp. 62-63.

8   The influence and impact of the Henry Regnery Company can be seen in the number of sources referenced here that were originally produced by this company. For an informative personal overview of this period in American history and the rise of an important publishing house see Henry Regnery: *Memoirs of a Dissident Publisher* (Chicago: Regnery Books, 1985). Henry Regnery was instrumental also in starting *Human Events* as well as the quarterly journal that became *Modern Age*.

9   Nash, p. xvii. Authors John Micklethwait and Adrian Wooldridge in *The Right Nation: Conservative Power in America* (New York: The Penguin Press, 2004), p.8, maintain that over the period from 1930 to 1950, the term conservative was used only as a derogatory label by Democrats and avoided by Republicans.

10   John A. Andrew: *The Other Side of the Sixties* (New Brunswick, NJ: Rutgers University Press, 1997), p. 13.

11   (Boston: Little, Brown & Company, 1951).

12   (New York: The Viking Press, 1957).

13   M. Stanton Evans: *Revolt on the Campus* (Chicago: Henry Regnery, 1961), p. 34

14   Rebecca Klatch: *A Generation Divided* (Berkeley: University of California Press, 1999), p. 9

15   David Burner: *Making Peace With the Sixties* (Princeton: Princeton University Press, 1996). Two interesting personal histories by "Red diaper babies" active in the late 1950s and early 1960s are Ronald Radosh: *Commies* (San Francisco: Encounter Books, 2001) and David Horowitz: *Radical Son* (New York: The Free Press, 1997). Both Radosh and Horowitz later rejected their inherited Leftist perspectives.

16   For a discussion of developing trends during this period, see also Dan Wakefield: *New York in the Fifties* (Boston: Houghton Mifflin Company, 1992).

17   Ronald F. Docksai, "A Study of the Organization and Beliefs of the Young Conservative Movement," Master's thesis, New York University, 1972, pp. 26-27

18   The most valuable work published in the early 1950s was Whittaker Chambers autobiographical *Witness* (New York; Random House, 1952). Also published in 1952 and autobiographical was Herbert A. Philbrick: *I Led 3 Lives: Citizen, Communist. Counterspy* (Washington, DC: Capitol Hill Press, 1972). Philbrick's experiences were the basis for a popular television program of the same name shown from 1953 to 1956. William F. Buckley, Jr. and L. Brent Bozell provided an early defense of Senator Joseph McCarthy in *McCarthy and His Enemies* (Chicago: Henry Regnery Company, 1954). An important critique of efforts to combat Communist subversion is Eric Bentley: *Thirty Years of Treason* (New York: Viking Press, 1971) that contains very selective edited excerpts from hearings before the House Committee on Un-American Activities. But see also William F. Buckley, Jr. (ed): *The Committee and its Critics* (Chicago: Henry Regnery Company, 1962). Written by one who began believing Alger Hiss was unjustly convicted and ends convinced of Hiss's guilt, Allen Weinstein: *Perjury: The Hiss-Chambers Case* (New York: Alfred A. Knopf, 1978) complements the Chambers work with additional documentation. Subsequent investigation of Soviet archives released after the fall of Communism in Russia has produced a number of valuable works that place the extent of Communist infiltration into American life in a broader context. Among the first was Allen Weinstein and Alexander Vassiliev: *The Haunted Wood: Soviet Espionage in America -The Stalin Era* (New York: Random House, 1999). Also valuable in understanding this period and how Americans perceived the threat from Communist subversion are John Earl Haynes and Harvey Klehr: *In Denial: Historians, Communism and Espionage* (San Francisco: Encounter Books, 2003); Ronald Radosh and Allis Radosh: *Red Star Over Hollywood: The Film Colony's Long Romance with the Left* (New York: Encounter Books, 2006); and M. Stanton Evans: *Blacklisted by History: The Untold Story of Senator Joe McCarthy and his fight against America's enemies* (New York: Crown Forum, 2007).

19   Rebecca Klatch: *A Generation Divided*, p. 67

20   Douglas Caddy, "Birth of the Conservative Movement," unpublished paper in author's possession, pp. 1-2.

21   Among the many works discussing the Hungarian uprising are the personal account by a Hungarian photographer, Andor D. Heller: *No More Comrades* (Chicago: Henry Regnery Company, 1957) and the retrospective overview by Charles Gati: *Failed Illusions: Moscow, Washington, Budapest and the 1956 Hungarian Revolt* (Palo Alto: Stanford University Press, 2006). Gati was also present in Hungary during the abortive battle for independence from Moscow.

22   See Rebecca Klatch: *A Generation Divided*, pp. 87-88.

23   Kenneth Heineman: *Campus Wars* (New York: New York University Press), p. 101

24   Alfred S. Regnery: *Upstream: The Ascendance of American Conservatism* provides a valuable overview of this period by one who grew up literally in the middle of it all. See pp. 24-84 especially.

25   Some would maintain that Peter Viereck's *Conservatism Revisited: The Revolt Against Revolt* (New York: Scribner's, 1949) first introduced a serious discussion of conservatism to the postwar intellectual world. According to George Nash, "This was the book which, more than any other of the early postwar era, created the new conservatism as a self-conscious intellectual force.... it was this book which boldly used the word 'conservative' in its title – the first such book after 1945" *The Conservative Intellectual Movement in America*, p. 60. However, Viereck soon became a vocal critic of the movement that developed around the name conservative and wrote a blistering critical review of William F. Buckley, Jr.'s first book. For more on Viereck see Tom Reiss, "The First Conservative," *The New Yorker*, October 24, 2005.

26   Henry Hazlitt, "The Early History of FEE," *The Freeman*, March 1984.

27   Sam Tanenhaus, "The founder," *Yale Alumni Magazine*, May/June 2008, p. 58. In the same issue, see also David Frum, "The loyal son," pp. 50-52 and Gaddis Smith, "The ideologue," pp. 53-57.

28   Buckley's time at Yale is covered in John Judis: *William F. Buckley, Jr. – Patron Saint of the Conservatives* (New York: Simon & Schuster, 1988), pp. 52-81

29   Chicago: Henry Regnery Company, 1951. Sales totals, including the book's presence on the *New York Herald Tribune* best-seller list, are reported in Tanenhaus, p. 69. Judis indicates that the book reached number 16 on the *New York Times* list, p. 92.

30   *God and Man at Yale* (Chicago: Henry Regnery Company, 1951), foreword.

31   *Ibid.*

32   Chicago: Henry Regnery Company, 1953.

33   Henry Regnery: *Memoirs of a Dissident Publisher*, p. 146. Regnery discusses the impact of Kirk and this book, as well as some of Kirk's other works, on pp. 146-166.

34   Kirk's background and his groundbreaking book are discussed in George H. Nash: *The Conservative Intellectual Movement in America Since 1945*, pp. 61-73 especially.

35   Docksai, p. 17.

36   Lee Edwards, "The Other Sixties," *Policy* Review 46 (Fall 1988), p. 60.

37   As quoted in Godfrey Hodgson: *The World Turned Right Side Up* (Boston: Houghton Mifflin Company, 1996), p. 78.

38   *Why Americans Hate Politics*, p. 159.

39   *The Conservative Intellectual Movement in America*, p. 140.

40   *A Time for Choosing: The Rise of Modern American Conservatism* (New York: Oxford University Press, 2001), p.38.

41   William F. Buckley, Jr.: *Up From Liberalism*, p. 219.

42   J. David Hoeveler, Jr.: *Watch on the Right: Conservative Intellectuals in the Reagan Era* (Madison: University of Wisconsin Press, 1991), p. 23.

43   Tom Reiss, "The First Conservative," *The New Yorker*, October 24, 2005.

44   *Human Events*, February 28, 2008.

45   Buckley presents some interesting stories from this period in his chapter "Early Days at National Review" in *Flying High: Remembering Barry Goldwater* (New York: Basic Books, 2008), pp. 27-34.

46   *A Generation Divided*, p. 68.

47   The fascinating story about Dean Manion's efforts to get the Goldwater book written, published and distributed is told in Nicole Hoplin and Ron Robinson: *Funding Fathers* (Washington: Regnery Publishing, 2008), pp. 87-117.

48   Barry Goldwater: *The Conscience of a Conservative* (Shepherdsville, KY: Victor Publishing Company, Inc., 1960).

49   *The Conscience of a Conservative*, p. 14.

50   *The Conscience of a Conservative*, p. 23.

51   *The Other Side of the Sixties*, p. 19

52   Docksai, p. 56

53   John Kolbe, "Arizona legend talks politics," *Phoenix Gazette*, December 3, 1986.

54   Lee Edwards, "The Other Sixties," p. 59.

55   See Nash *The Conservative Intellectual Movement in America*, pp. 30-73 for a discussion of some of these libertarian and individualist contributors to the conservative movement.

56   E. J. Dionne: *Why Americans Hate Politics*, p. 162

57   Meyer's attempted synthesis is explained in his book *In Defense of Freedom: A Conservative Credo* (Chicago: Henry Regnery Company, 1962) and also in the opening and closing chapters of his edited work *What Is Conservatism?* (New York: Holt Rinehart and Winston, 1964).

58   Lee Edwards, "The Conservative Consensus: Frank Meyer, Barry Goldwater, and the Politics of Fusionism," Heritage Foundation "First Principles" series, number 8 (January 22, 2007).

59   *Why Americans Hate Politics*, p. 161

60   The National Defense Education Act of 1958 (PL 85-864)

61   M. Stanton Evans: *Revolt on the Campus* covers the student loyalty oath campaign on pages 74-86. The oath and the affidavit can be found on p. 75.

62   Greg Schneider: *Cadres for Conservatism* (New York: New York University Press, 1999), p.21-23.

63   This section relies especially on an interview with Caddy in Houston, Texas on December 10, 2007 as well as his "Birth of the Conservative Movement."

64   *The Road Ahead: America's Coming Revolution* (New York: Devin-Adair Company, 1949).

65   Schulz would later go on to become executive editor of *Reader's Digest*, which along with the *Saturday Evening Post*, tended to provide a vehicle for some conservative writers in the 1950s.

66   Douglas Caddy, "The Birth of the Conservative Movement," p. 5.

67   Richard A. Viguerie and David Franke: *America's Right Turn* (Chicago: Bonus Books, 2004), p. 65.

68   Rick Perlstein: *Before the Storm: Barry Goldwater and the Unmaking of the American Consensus* (New York: Hill and Wang, 2001), p. 69.

69   "The Birth of the Conservative Movement," p. 7

70   Interview with Douglas Caddy, Houston, Texas, December 10, 2007.

71   Perlstein: *Before The Storm*, p. 75.

72   Caddy, "Birth of the Conservative Movement," p.7

73   *The Other Side of the Sixties*, p. 30.

74   Lee Edwards: *Missionary for Freedom: The Life and Times of Walter Judd* (New York: Paragon House, 1990).

75   Marvin Liebman: *Coming Out Conservative* (San Francisco: Chronicle Books, 1992), p. 147.

76   Shadegg/Goldwater collection, Box 3H506. Center for American History, University of Texas, Austin, TX.

77   Caddy, "Birth of the Conservative Movement," p. 14.

78   Letter of Marvin Liebman to William A. Rusher dated April 22, 1983, Personal Papers of William A. Rusher, Box 174, Manuscript Division, Library of Congress, Washington, DC.

79   Liebman: *Coming Out Conservative*, pp. 149-151 and Evans: *Revolt on the Campus*, pp. 107-108.

80   *Flying High*, p. 20

81   Niels Bjerre-Paulsen, "Organizing the American Right, 1945-64," doctoral dissertation, University of California – Santa Barbara, 1993, p. 284.

82   Seth Offenbach, "Power of Portrayal: the Media and the Young Americans for Freedom: 1960-1968," unpublished paper presented at the Journal of Policy History Conference, Charlottesville, VA, June 4, 2006, p. 9.

83   For a first hand account of the events in Sharon, see M. Stanton Evans: *Revolt on the Campus*, pp. 108-124 and Lee and Anne Edwards: *You Can Make The Difference* (New Rochelle, NY: Arlington House, 1968), pp. 283-288. Another valuable source for this founding conference is John A. Andrew: *The Other Side of the Sixties*, pp. 53-74.

84   Matthew Dallek, "Young Americans for Freedom: The Rise of Modern Conservatism, 1960-1964," Master's thesis, Columbia University, 1993, pp. 6-7.

85   Lee Edwards: *You Can Make The Difference*, p. 286.

86   Rick Perlstein: *Before The Storm*, p. 106.

87   The complete "Sharon Statement" is reprinted later in the present work. The Sharon Statement has been reprinted in numerous works on 20th century conservatism As testimony to the continued importance of the document, it has been credited with helping launch and define the conservative movement in America.

88   *Flying High*, p. 25.

89   Schneider: *Cadres for Conservatism*, pp. 33-34 discusses the vote on including reference to God in the Sharon Statement. According to Perlstein, the vote was 44-40; *Before The Storm*, p. 106.

90   M. Stanton Evans, "Reflections of the Sharon Statement," *New Guard*, September 1970, p.9.

91   Matthew Dallek, "Young Americans for Freedom: The Rise of Modern Conservatism, 1960-1964," p. 8.

92   William A. Rusher: *The Rise of the Right* (New York: National Review Books, 1993), p. 63.

93   See: "Robert Schuchman – As His Friends Remember Him," *New Guard*, April 1966, pp. 7-9.

94   *The Other Side of the Sixties*, p. 6.

95   *National Review*, September 24, 1960. The editorial also is reprinted in Gregory L. Schneider, editor: *Conservatism in America Since 1930* (New York: New York University Press, 2003), pp. 226-228.

96   Rebecca Klatch: *A Generation Divided*, p. 20.

97   Perlstein: *Before the Storm*, p. 105.

98   Dallek, "Young Americans for Freedom: The Rise of Modern Conservatism, 1960-1964," p. 38.

99   Roberts: *The Conservative Decade* (Westport, CT: Arlington House, 1980), p. 25.

100   "Birth of the Conservative Movement," p. 9.

101   Charles G. Mills, e-mail to the author dated January 14, 2009.

102   The author retains a formal invitation card from the Tufts University Young Republican Club to a "Sherry Hour" at the Theta Chi fraternity house on March 22, 1963.

103   "Campus Conservatives," *Time*, February 10, 1961, p. 37.

104   Based on her interviews with a number of YAF activists from the early 1960s, Rebecca Klatch lists these as core values that motivated the young conservatives. *A Generation Divided*, pp. 44-46.

105   "Birth of the Conservative Movement," p. 15.

106   Schoenwald, "The Other Counterculture: Young Americans for Freedom, 1960-1969," unpublished paper, Towards a History of the 1960s, State Historical Society of Wisconsin, Madison, WI, April 28, 1993, p. 9.

107   Offenbach, "Power of Portrayal", p. 23. A rather humorous description by a left-wing author of YAF's methods was presented in Mike Newberry: *The Fascist Revival* (New York: New Century Publishers, 1961). In his section titled "Young Americans for Fascism," on page 36 Newberry claims: "Its members are trained not only in ringing doorbells, but in breaking up progressive and union meetings. Its hecklers, picketlines, and hoodlums – white collar hoodlums to be sure – have begun to descend like a plague of gnats on peace rallies and civil liberties gatherings." The Far Left clearly saw the emerging organization as a serious threat.

108   Minutes of the Board of Directors Meeting, New York, November 26, 1960, Personal Papers of William A. Rusher, Box 174, Manuscript Division, Library of Congress, Washington, DC.

109   Bjerre-Poulsen, "Organizing the American Right, 1945-1964," p. 281 and M. Stanton Evans: *Revolt on the Campus*, pp. 114-116.

110   Alan C. Elms, "The Conservative Ripple," *The Nation*, May 27, 1961, p. 458; Murray Kempton, "On Growing Up Absurd," *The Progressive*, May 1961, p. 12; See also Ed Cain: *They'd Rather Be Right* (New York: MacMillan Company, 1963) p. 171.

111   *Revolt on the Campus*, p.115.

112   *Cadres for Conservatism*, p. 40.

113   David Franke, "Breaking The Liberal Barrier," *New Guard*, March 1961, p. 10.

114   Marvin Kitman, "The Button Down Revolution," *Nugget*, October 1961, p. 46.

115   *New Guard*, March 1961, p.3.

116   "Pickets Busy as Goldwater Packs House," *New York Daily News*, March 4, 1961.

117   Robert Conley, "3,200 Here Cheer Goldwater Talk," *New York Times*, March 4, 1961.

118   *Ibid.*

119   *Revolt on the Campus*, p. 122.

120   *New Guard*, May 1961, p. 10

121   George J. Marlin: *Fighting The Good Fight* (New York: St. Augustine's Press, 2002) provides a general overview of the party's history in the 20th century.

122   J. Daniel Mahoney: *Actions Speak Louder* (New Rochelle, NY: Arlington House, 1963), p. 33.

123   *New York Post*, May 22, 1961 as quoted in Andrew: *The Other Side of the Sixties*, pp. 91-92.

124   *Ibid.*

125   Andrew: *The Other Side of the Sixties*, p. 93. Much of the following relies on Andrew, pp. 91-101.

126   Edward Cain: *They'd Rather Be Right*, p. 172. See also, Austin C. Wehrwein, "Rightists Divide Student Congress," *New York Times*, August 21, 1961.

127   Robert M. Schuchman, "Charge of the Right Brigade," *National Review*, September 9, 1961.

128   Schneider: *Cadres for Conservatism*, p. 62.

129   The founding of Associated Student Governments is recalled in Tom Charles Huston, "Student Leaders Form New Alliance," *New Guard*, June 1964, pp. 10-12.

130   Schneider: *Cadres for Conservatism*, pp. 63-64.

131   "We Like Nike," *New Guard*, December 1961, pp. 3-4.

132   Gordon L. Durnil, "Communist Cars and Polish Hams," *New Guard*, October 1961, p. 13.

133   Mary Perot Nichols, "Beat, and Conservative, Too," *Village Voice*, June 8, 1961.

134   Dan Wakefield: *New York in the Fifties*, p. 267.

135   Directory of College Conservative Clubs, Personal Papers of Henry Regnery, Box 80, Hoover Institution, Stanford University. See also *New Guard*, July 1961, p. 12.

136   Dan Wakefield, "The Campus Conservatives: Where Are They Now?" *Mademoiselle*, August 1963, p. 330.

137   For the early years see: Lawrence F. Schiff, "The Conservative Movement on American College Campuses," unpublished doctoral dissertation, Harvard University, 1964, pp. 116-119.

138   Edward Cain: *They'd Rather Be Right*, p. 174.

139   *New Guard*, May 1961, p. 6.

140   Offenbach, "Power of Portrayal," pp. 12-13.

141   *Ibid.*, p. 12.

142   Thomas Hayden, "Who Are the Student Boat-Rockers?" *Mademoiselle*, August 1961.

143   Kitman, "The Button Down Revolution."

144   Alan C. Elms, "The Conservative Ripple," *The Nation*, May 27, 1961; Murray Kempton, "On Growing Up Absurd," *The Progressive*, May 1961; Marvin Kitman, "New Wave from the Right," *The New Leader*, September 18, 1961.

145   Joanne Grant, "Right Wing Youth Groups Look to Elders for Advice," *National Guardian*, May 15, 1961, p. 7.

146   Arnold Forster and Benjamin Epstein: *Danger on the Right*, p. 224.

147   Quoted in Kenneth Heineman: *Put Your Bodies Upon The Wheels* (Chicago: Ivan R. Dee, 2001), p. 58.

148   *Danger on the Right*, p. 222.

149   Robert Martinson, "State of the Campus: 1962," *The Nation*, May 19, 1962, p. 435.

150   Cabell Phillips, "Pickets Parade at White House," *New York Times*, October 28, 1962.

151   "Notes from the YAF Rally," *National Review*, March 27, 1962, pp. 190-191.

152   The remarks of most rally speakers and award recipients were printed in the March 1962 issue of *New Guard* that was distributed to all who attended the rally.

153   "And Why Not?" *National Review*, March 27, 1962, p. 190.

154   Dallek, "Young Americans for Freedom: The Rise of Modern Conservatism, 1960-1964," p. 42.

155   Richard A. Viguerie and David Franke: *America's Right Turn*, p. 66.

156   Interview with Richard A. Viguerie, August 13, 2008, Manassas, VA.

157   Sara Diamond: *Roads to Dominion* (New York: The Guilford Press, 1995), p. 61.

158   Viguerie & Franke: *America's Right Turn*, pp. 96-97.

159   *Ibid.*

160   Tom Huston, "Revolt Ahead in NSA?" *New Guard*, August 1962, p. 9.

161   Quoted in "NSA: Leftists Still in Control," *New Guard*, October 1966, pp.4-5.

162   Neil Sheehan, "A Student Group Concedes It Took Funds from CIA," *New York Times*, February 14, 1967.

163   Gary Russell, "YAF Charts Far-Ranging Program for Victory," *New Guard*, November 1962, pp. 8-9.

164   Robert Martinson, "State of the Campus 1962," p. 436.

165   Murray Kempton, "On Growing Up Absurd," *The Progressive*, May 1961, p. 14.

166   Irving Howe, "Notebook: Journey to the End of the Right," *Dissent*, Winter 1962, p. 79.

167   Lisa McGirr: *Suburban Warriors* (Princeton: Princeton University Press, 2001), p. 148.

168   Lee Edwards, "Needed: A Conservative Establishment," *New Guard*, June 1962, p. 2.

169   Barry M. Goldwater: *Why Not Victory?* (New York: McGraw-Hill, 1962).

170   Indicative of the ever-present interest in the 1964 presidential contest, the cover article in the December 1962/January 1963 issue of *New Guard* was "Can Goldwater Win?" and it featured a photo of the Arizona Senator.

171   *New Guard*, April 1963, p. 15. The poster "tear down the wall" virtually mirrored one of Ronald Reagan's most memorable phrases delivered some twenty-five years later outside the Berlin wall.

172   "YAF Highlights: 1960-1965," Personal Papers of Herbert A. Philbrick, Box 218, Folder 3, Manuscript Division, Library of Congress, Washington, DC.

173   R. J. Bocklet, "Trading With the Enemy: An Indictment," *New Guard*, May 1963, pp. 7-8.

174   *New Guard*, September 1963, p. 5.

175   Telegram of January 30, 1964 from Robert E. Bauman, White House Central File, Name File: Alfreda Young, Box 26, Lyndon Baines Johnson Presidential Library, Austin, TX.

176   Richard Derham, "Should Freedom Take the Offensive?" *New Guard*, September 1964, pp. 13-14, 19.

177   *The Republican Establishment* (New York: Harper & Row, 1967), p. 76.

178   *New Guard*, March 1963, p. 15.

179   "3,000 Cheer Goldwater," *New Guard*, May 1963, p. 12.

180   F. Clifton White: *Suite 3505: The Story of the Draft Goldwater Movement* (New Rochelle, NY: Arlington House, 1967), pp. 127-135.

181   *Ibid*, p. 182.

182   "Over 9,000 attend Draft Goldwater Rally," *Human Events*, July 20, 1963.

183   White: *Suite 3505*, pp. 181-189.

184   *New Guard*, May 1964, p. 16; June 1964, p. 16; July 1964, p. 20.

185   *New Guard*, September 1964, p. 23.

186   *Ibid.*

187   Heineman: *Campus Wars*, p. 148.

188   *New Guard*, September 1964, p. 23.

189   Brian Doherty: *Radicals for Capitalism* (New York: Public Affairs, 2007), pp. 389-392.

190   Dallek, "Young Americans for Freedom: The Rise of Modern Conservatism, 1960-1964," p.32.

191   *New Guard*, June 1963, p. 12.

192   Noel E. Parmentel, Jr. and Marshall J. Dodge, III: *Folk Songs for Conservatives by Noel X and his Unbleached Muslims* (New York: Unicorn Press, 1964).

193   John Kolbe, "Arizona legend talks politics," *Phoenix Gazette*, December 3, 1986.

194   Theodore H. White: *The Making of the President, 1964* (New York: Atheneum Publishers, 1965), p. 111, 120-122.

195   Quoted in Roberts: *The Conservative Decade*, p. 26.

196   *New Guard*, March 1964, pp. 7-8.

197   Marilyn Manion, "What You Can Do in '64," *New Guard*, February 1964, pp. 13-15.

198   Stephen Hess and David S. Broder: *The Republican Establishment* (New York: Harper & Row, 1967), p. 77.

199   Perlstein: *Before the Storm*, p. 455.

200   For a more detailed discussion of YAF's role in the nominating campaign, see Andrew: *The Other Side of the Sixties*, pp. 187-204.

201   Buckley interview with Matthew Dallek, May 12, 1993, quoted in "Young Americans for Freedom: The Rise of Modern Conservatism: 1960-1964," p. 52.

202   An overview of YAF activities in San Francisco can be found in "A Generation Arrives," *New Guard*, August 1964, pp. 13-18 from which much of this section is drawn.

203   *New Guard*, September 1964, p. 25.

204   *Ibid.*

205   *New Guard*, August 1964, p. 13.

206   Judis: *William F. Buckley, Jr: Patron Saint of the Conservatives*, p. 229.

207   Buckley: *Flying High*, p. 141. The rally is discussed in more detail on pages 139-142.

208   Charles Mohr, "Goldwater Sees A Trend to Right," *New York Times*, July 15, 1964.

209   Schneider: *Cadres for Conservatism*, p. 82; *New Guard*, August 1964, p. 17.

210   *New Guard*, August 1964, p.6.

211   Quoted in Klatch: *A Generation Divided*, p. 83.

212   Perlstein: *Before the Storm*, p. 471.

213   Klatch: *A Generation Divided*, p. 81.

214   Kessel: *The Goldwater Coalition* (Indianapolis: The Bobbs-Merrill Company, 1968), pp. 130-131.

215   *New Guard*, November 1964, pp. 19, 21-22.

216   Linda Bridges and John R. Coyne, Jr.: *Strictly Right: William F. Buckley, Jr. and the American Conservative Movement* (Hoboken, NJ: John Wiley & Sons, 2007), pp. 85-87.

217   Judis: *William F. Buckley, Jr.: Patron Saint of the Conservatives*, p. 231.

218   Buckley, "We, Too, Will Continue," *New Guard*, December 1964, pp. 11-12, 14.

219   John Kolbe, "Arizona legend talks politics," *Phoenix Gazette*, December 3, 1986.

220   Gillion Peele: *Revival and Reaction: The Right in Contemporary America* (London: Clarendon Press, 1984), p. 131.

221   Klatch: *A Generation Divided*, pp. 83-84.

222   Lee Edwards, "The Other Sixties: A Flag-Waver's Memoir," *Policy Review*, Fall 1988, p 61.

223   This point is made especially by Niels Bjerre-Poulsen, "Organizing the American Right: 1945-1964," p.323.

224   Quoted in Roberts: *The Conservative Decade*, p. 34.

225   Lee Edwards: *Reagan-A Political Biography* (San Diego: Viewpoint Books, 1967), p. 79. For the story of the three contributors who funded the national television broadcast of Reagan's speech, see: Hoplin and Robinson: *Funding Fathers*, pp. 131-138.

226   Ronald Reagan: *An American Life* (New York: Pocket Books, 1990), p. 143.

227   Schoenwald: *A Time for Choosing*, p. 249

228   Liebman: *Coming Out Conservative*, pp. 159-160.

229   Judis: *William F. Buckley, Jr: Patron Saint of the Conservatives*, p. 233.

230   Liebman: *Coming Out Conservative*, p. 160.

231   Schoenwald: *A Time for Choosing*, p. 250; Rusher: *The Rise of the Right*, pp. 132-134.

232   Bjerre-Poulsen, "Organizing the American Right: 1945-1964," pp. 269-270.

233   William F. Buckley, Jr.: *The Unmaking of a Mayor* (New York: The Viking Press, 1966), pp. 169-238. There is no better history of the campaign than this first-hand recollection by Buckley.

234   "Lindsay Is Greeted With Buckley Signs," *New York Times*, July 2, 1965.

235   McCandlish Phillips, "Bright, Young Aides of Buckley Are Spirited, Stylish and Witty," *New York Times*, October 16, 1965.

236   Paul Hope, "Back Conservative of Either Party, Goldwater Urges," *Washington Evening Star*, May 10, 1966. Personal Papers of Henry Regnery, Box 80, Hoover Institution, Stanford University, Palo Alto, CA.

237   James J. Kilpatrick, "Goldwater at His Best Before Young Americans," Washington Evening Star, May 17, 1966. Personal Papers of Henry Regnery, Box 80, Hoover Institution, Stanford University, Palo Alto, CA.

238   Hope, "Back Conservative of Either Party, Goldwater Urges."

239   Hess and Broder: *The Republican Establishment*, p. 74.

240   Hope, "Back Conservative of Either Party, Goldwater Urges."

241   Dana Rohrabacher, "Us Young Americans for Freedom," *The American Enterprise*, May/June 1997, pp. 37-39.

242   Rusher: *The Rise of the Right*, pp. 158-159.

243   Bruce Weinrod, "The Conservative Case for Ronald Reagan," pp. 8-9 and David A. Keene, "The Conservative Case for Richard Nixon," pp. 10-11, *New Guard*, Summer 1968.

244   *New Guard*, June 1970, pp. 21-22.

245   Robert M. Schuettinger, "Wallace and Grenier: The Old and New South," *New Guard*, September 1966, pp. 24-25.

246   Alan MacKay, "Prospects for '68," *New Guard*, January 1968, p. 6.

247   *New Guard*, January 1970, p. 22.

248   *Ibid.*

249   Mary Brennan: *Turning Right in the Sixties* (Chapel Hill: University of North Carolina Press, 1995), p. 128.

250   Email to the author from Michael Thompson, April 20, 2009.

251   "Johnson's Address at VMI," *New York Times*, May 24, 1964.

252   "Firestone Calls Off Deal With Reds," *New Guard*, June 1965.

253   Gwertzman, *Washington Evening Star*, May 8, 1965.

254   *Washington Post*, May 12, 1965.

255   As quoted in "Firestone Calls Off Deal with Reds," *New Guard*, June 1965.

256   YAF Press Release of January 24, 1967, inserted by Representative James Utt in *Congressional Record*, January 26, 1967, pp. H699-700. Group Research Archives, Box 340, Columbia University, New York, NY.

257   "Soviet Union: Leadership at the Crossroads," *Time*, May 4, 1970.

258   "YAF Has a Better Idea," *Human Events*, May 2, 1970.

259   Richard Witkin, "Accord is Signed for Soviet Plant by Mack Trucks," *New York Times*, June 18, 1971.

260   "Mack Truck Drops Plans to Build a Russian Plant," *New York Times*, September 16, 1971.

261   Robert G. Harley, "South Viet Nam: Asian Battleground," *New Guard*, January 1962, pp. 14-15.

262   Richard Derham, "Should Freedom Take the Offensive?" *New Guard*, June 1964, pp. 13-14.

263   Heineman: *Campus Wars*, p.133.

264   Several other similar letters and petitions are also on file in White House Central Files, Name File: Alfreda Young, Box 26, Lyndon B. Johnson Presidential Library, University of Texas, Austin, TX.

265   "President Receives Strong YAF Support on Vietnam, Dominican Republic Intervention," *New Guard*, June 1965, p. 20.

266   Thomas W. Pauken: *The Thirty Years War* (Ottawa, IL: Jameson Books, 1995), p. 55.

267   Schneider: *Cadres for Conservatism*, p. 109.

268   See: Richard E. Peterson, "The Student Left in American Higher Education," *Daedalus*, Winter 1968, pp. 293-294 as well as the Andrew and Heineman works cited in this chapter.

269   "No More Koreas!" *New Guard*, January 1966, pp. 4-5.

270   *New Guard*, October 1966, p. 7. See also: "Victory in Vietnam Students Escalate Campus Activities," *New Guard*, February 1967, p.4.

271   Andrew H. Malcolm, "Nationwide Strike Planned by Students to Protest the War," *New York Times*, July 10, 1969.

272   Robert M. Smith, "Leaders of Moratorium Now Look to November," *New York Times*, October 17, 1969.

273   Heineman: *Put Your Bodies Upon The Wheels*, p. 160.

274   *New Guard*, November 1969, pp. 3-4.

275   "Campus Communique," *Time*, December 19, 1969.

276   "2,500 back Nixon's Vietnam policy at 'Tell it to Hanoi' rally in Boston," *Boston Globe*, December 8, 1969.

277   David Brudnoy, "This Time, *Our* Side in Boston Common," *National Review*, December 30, 1969, p. 1315.

278   "Three Arrested in Scuffle," *Baltimore News American*, December 14, 1969.

279   Andrew, "Pro-war and Anti-Draft," p. 16.

280   Dana Rohrabacher, "Young Czechoslovakians for Freedom," *New Guard*, October 1968, pp. 9-10.

281   John Herbers, "McGovern Charges U.S. is Partly to Blame for the Crisis in Czechoslovakia," *New York Times*, August 24, 1968.

282   Frederick Obear, "Student Activism in the Sixties," in Julian Foster and Durward Long, editors, *Protest! Student Activism in America* (New York: William Morrow & Company, Inc., 1970), p. 18.

283 E. Joseph Shoben, Jr., "The Climate of Protest," in *Protest!*, p. 576.

284 Phillip Abbott Luce, "Yes, S.C., There Really is an SDS," *New Guard*, December 1967, p. 12.

285 Heineman: *Put Your Bodies*, p. 118-119.

286 Heineman: *Put Your Bodies*, pp. 120, 123.

287 Heineman: *Put Your Bodies*, p. 125.

288 David A, Keene, "Freedom, Force and the University," *New Guard*, March 1968, p. 10.

289 John C. Meyer, "What Happened at Columbia (and why)," *New Guard*, September 1968, p. 14.

290 Meyer, p. 15.

291 Sophy Burnham, "Twelve Rebels of the Student Right, *New York Times Magazine,* March 9, 1969, p.32.

292 Quoted in Burnham, p. 119 from an article in the *Boston Globe*, October 1, 1968.

293 Burnham, p. 32.

294 Meyer, p. 16.

295 *Ibid.*

296 Heineman: *Put Your Bodies*, p. 141.

297 Burnham, p. 32.

298 Heineman: *Campus Wars*, pp. 198, 201.

299 "Disorder at PSU? YAF Will Sue," *New Guard*, December 1968, p. 26.

300 Heineman: *Campus Wars*, pp. 204-205.

301 "Suits Threatened in Campus Rioting," *New York Times*, October 4, 1969.

302 "Legal Responses to Campus Disorder," Young Americans for Freedom, September 1969.

303 Heineman: *Put Your Bodies*, pp. 153-154.

304 Kenneth Reich, "Conservatives Strike Back on U.S. Campuses," *Los Angeles Times*, March 2, 1969.

305 George Fox, "Counter Revolution," *Playboy*, March 1970, p. 178.

306 Reich, "Conservatives Strike Back."

307 Bernard Weinraub, "Unrest Spurs Growth of Conservative Student Groups, *New York Times*, October 12, 1969.

308 "SDS vs. YAF," *Texas Ranger*, December 1969, p. 12.

309 Michael E. Kinsley, "Conservatives Open Harvard Unit of Young Americans for Freedom," *The Harvard Crimson*, October 3, 1969.

310 Weinraub, "Unrest," *New York Times*, October 12, 1969.

311 Ibid.

312 Randal C. Teague, "YAF: A Presence in the Room," *New Guard*, January/February 1971, p. 19.

313 Philip Manger, "Conservative Youths Are Alive on Campus," *Baltimore News American*, May 27, 1970.

314 This count is reported in Heineman: *Put Your Bodies*, p. 170.

315 *Ibid*, p.171. These are only a few of the radical events during Spring 1970 covered in Heineman: *Put Your Bodies* on pp. 170-180.

316   Douglas Robinson, "Townhouse Razed by Blast & Fire," *New York Times*, May 7, 1970. It was only days later when the bodies found in the destruction could be identified. Wilkerson and Kathy Boudin fled the scene with minor injuries and were underground for the next ten years.

317   Flyer, "Leftist 'Young Idealists' Cause Student Death," Harvard-Radcliffe Young Americans for Freedom, HUD 3890-7000, Harvard University Archives, Pusey Library, Harvard University, Cambridge, MA.

318   Robert B. Semple, Jr., "Nixon Sends Combat Forces to Cambodia," *New York Times*, May 1, 1970.

319   Linda Charlton, "Big Rallies Are Planned, Students Protest Nixon Troop Move," *New York Times*, May 2, 1970.

320   Heineman: *Put Your Bodies*, p. 176.

321   Frank J. Prial, "Students Step Up Protests on War," *New York Times*, May 6, 1970. J. W. Stillman, "Strike Hits 166 Colleges, Administrators Close B.U.," *The Harvard Crimson*, May 6, 1970.

322   Robert D. McFadden, "College Strife Spreads, Over 100 Schools Closed and Up to 350 Struck," *New York Times*, May 8, 1970.

323   Marion E. McCollom, "324 Universities Strike Nationally; Protests expand," *The Harvard Crimson*, May 7, 1970.

324   Heineman: *Put Your Bodies*, p. 176.

325   Andrew H. Malcolm, "Some Colleges In Area to Reopen Today; Lawsuits Threatened," *New York Times*, May 11, 1970.

326   Schneider: *Cadres for Conservatism*, p. 124.

327   Malcolm, "Some Colleges in Area to Reopen Today; Lawsuits Threatened."

328   "Colleges Reopen; Protests Continue All Over Nation," *The Harvard Crimson*, May 12, 1970.

329   Manger, "Conservative Youths are Alive on Campus."

330   Heineman: *Put Your Bodies*, pp. 178-179.

331   Robert Reinhold, "Harvard Bomb Blast Damages Center for International Affairs," *New York Times*, October 15, 1970.

332   Joyce Heard, "200 Attend Rally Against Bombing," *The Harvard Crimson*, October 16, 1970.

333   Roger Rosenblatt: *Coming Apart: A Memoir of the Harvard Wars of 1969* (Boston: Little, Brown & Co, 1997), p. 173.

334   "Pro-War Teach-In Dissolves in Turmoil; Administration Warns of Full Discipline," *The Harvard Crimson*, March 27, 1971.

335   "Rads Rate Teach-In Socko; Cite SRO House: Tremendous," *The Harvard Crimson*, April 1, 1971.

336   "Putnam Cheered at Free Speech Forum," *The Harvard Crimson*, April 15, 1971.

337   "Clash at teach-In Upsets Harvard," *New York Times*, April 4, 1971.

338   Phillip Abbott Luce, "Whatever Happened to the New Left?," *New Guard*, May 1972, pp. 5-7.

339   Schneider, *The Other Sixties*, p. 7.

340   Schneider, *The Other Sixties*, p. 8.

341   Schoenwald: *The Other Counterculture*, p. 9.

342   James L. Buckley, quoted in "What They're Saying About Young Americans for Freedom," brochure, April 1973.

343   Alan Rinzler, editor: *Manifesto – Addressed to the President of the United States from the Youth of America* (New York: Collier Books, 1970).

344   Wayne Thorburn, "Unrepresentative Youth," *New Guard*, Summer 1971, pp. 18-20.

345   Stephen Kurkjian, "YAF: Wake Up America," *Boston Globe*, April 26, 1970.

346   Similar ads appeared in *Washington Star* on May 4, 1970 and in the *Washington Post* on May 10, 1970 as well as other newspapers across the country.

347   Michael Coates, "All's quiet on the right wing," *Daily Trojan*, February 22, 1971, p. 15.

348   "The Fourth: Showing the Flag," *Newsweek*, July 13, 1970. Martin Flusser, Jr., "Rally Round Trip: Anticipation to Anger," *Newsday*, July 6, 1970.

349   Andrew, "Pro-War and Anti-Draft," p. 12.

350   "YAF Plans Rally to Support POWs," *Topeka Capital*, April 30, 1970.

351   "Prisoner of War Action Kit," Young Americans for Freedom, June 1970.

352   *New Guard*, January/February 1971, p. 40.

353   David Brudnoy, "Free Them Now!," *National Review*, December 29, 1970, p. 1404.

354   *New Guard*, Summer 1971, p. 29.

355   *New Guard*, November 1971, p. 30.

356   *New Guard*, February 1969, pp. 24, 26.

357   "YAF Visits Veterans," *Brooklyn Home Reporter*, April 21, 1972.

358   *New Guard*, June 1972, p. 20.

359   Jerry Norton, "No Amnesty," YAF Issues Paper, 1973.

360   Don Nordheimer, "60% of Deserters Leave Amnesty Service," *New York Times*, September 15, 1975.

361   C. S. Horn, "Reunion in Sharon," *National Review*, October 6, 1970, p. 1057.

362   Ronald B. Dear, "Young America's Freedom Offensive, a 1969 report," *New Guard*, January 1970, pp. 12-15.

363   *New Guard*, October 1970, pp. 32-33.

364   Mark Deardorff and Pat Nolan, "The Siege of USC," *New Guard*, July/August 1975, pp. 10-11.

365   "Resistance at State University of New York," *New Guard*, September 1969, p. 7.

366   *New Guard*, July/August 1972, p. 23.

367   *New Guard*, October 1974, p. 33.

368   *New Guard*, June 1972, p. 21.

369   Stephen Karganovic, "Is There An Alternative to Mandatory Fees?" *New Guard*, July/August 1975, pp. 14-16.

370   Deardorff and Nolan, "The Siege of USC," p.10.

371   College 'Activities Fees' Fund Liberalism," *Dialogue on Liberty*, December 1976, p. 1.

372   Letter from William F. Buckley, Jr. to Ron Robinson, May 13, 1996.

373   While several could be cited, the best example is Howard Phillips, a Sharon attendee who served on YAF's initial Board of Directors while serving as president of student government at Harvard University.

374   Rich Wiseman, "Left Throttled on Campus – Nolan," *Daily Trojan*, February 23, 1971, p. 3.

375   Quoted in Robert McDonald: *YAF in the Arena*, unpublished paper, p. 24.

376   Carol Dawson Bauman, "A Conservative View of Women's Liberation," *New Guard*, April 1972, pp. 4-8.

377   Kathy Teague, "The Most Admired Woman," *New Guard*, June 1972, pp. 12-13.

378   "You'd Better Get Straight," *New Guard*, October 1973, pp. 7-9.

379   "Marijuana – the Continuing Debate," *New Guard*, March 1974, pp. 12-13, 25.

380   Paul Healy, "Kid Power and the New Politics," *New York Daily News*, September 11, 1970.

381   *You & Politics* (Washington, DC: Young Americans for Freedom, 1970).

382   Kemp obtained 82,939 votes on the Republican line while his opponent had 86,142 votes on the Democratic line. It was only with the additional 14,050 votes Kemp received on the Conservative Party line that he became the winner.

383   Interview with William E. Saracino, October 11, 2008, Newport Beach, CA.

384   The Reagan 1970 re-election campaign is discussed in Lou Cannon: *Governor Reagan – His Rise to Power* (New York: Public Affairs, 2003), pp. 336-347.

385   Letter from William F. Buckley, Jr. to James L. Buckley, quoted in Judis: *William F. Buckley, Jr.: Patron Saint of the Conservatives*, p. 311.

386   *New Guard*, Summer 1968, p. 28.

387   *New Guard*, October 1968, p. 22. Nixon had both the Republican and Conservative Party endorsements in 1968 so technically it was a "Nixon-Buckley" ticket on the Conservative Party row on the ballot.

388   E-mail to the author, February 29, 2008. Steinberg was editor of *New Guard* at the time and would become press secretary to Buckley in the 1970 campaign.

389   Frank Lynn, "Charles E. Goodell, Former Senator, Is Dead At 60," *New York Times*, January 22, 1987.

390   Maurice Carroll, "O'Dwyer Finishes Second on Strong City Showing; Ottinger Beats Three Senate Rivals," *New York Times*, June 24, 1970.

391   Samuel G. Freedman: *The Inheritance: How Three Families and America Moved from Roosevelt to Reagan and Beyond* (New York: Simon & Schuster, 1996) presents an interesting overview of the 1970 Senate campaign.

392   Email to the author, March 18, 2009.

393   Freedman: *The Inheritance*, p. 253.

394   White: *Politics*, p. 193.

395   Freedman: *The Inheritance*, p. 258.

396   "Youth for Buckley: A Success," *New Guard*, December 1970, p. 30.

397   Rick Perlstein: *Nixonland* (New York: Scribner, 2008), p. 530.

398   Steven R. Weisman, "Buckley's Drive Mobilized the Youth of the New Right," *New York Times*, November 7, 1970.

399   Steinberg, "It Happened in New York," p. 29.

400   Weisman, "Buckley's Drive," *New York Times*, November 7, 1970.

401   "Youth for Buckley: A Success," *New Guard*, December 1970, pp. 29-30.

402   Email to the author, March 18, 2009.

403   Herbert Stupp, "We Have A Senator!" *New Guard*, September 1975, pp. 15-16.

404   Steinberg, "It Happened in New York," *New Guard*, December 1970, p. 30.

405 "Firing Line," Box 59 (218), Folder 228, Hoover Institution Archives, Stanford University, Palo Alto, CA.

406 David R. Jones memo to William A. Rusher, January 7, 1969. Personal Papers of William A Rusher, Box 46, Manuscript Division, Library of Congress, Washington, DC.

407 David R. Jones to William F. Buckley, Jr., February 17, 1969. Personal Papers of William F. Buckley, Jr., Box 67, Yale University, New Haven, CT.

408 The Ripon Society and Clifford W. Brown, Jr.: *Jaws of Victory* (Boston: Little Brown & Company, 1974), p. 302.

409 Kiron K. Skinner, Annelise Anderson, and Martin Anderson, editors: *Reagan: A Life in Letters* (New York: Free Press, 2003), pp. 174-175.

410 Jeffrey Bell, "The Ordeal of the President," *New Guard*, May 1971, pp. 5-9.

411 "YAF Regionals Attract 1000," *yaf letter*, June 1971, p. 4. Newsletter published by Young Americans for Freedom.

412 Jerry Norton, "The Ashbrook Campaign: The Making of a Conservative Candidate," *New Guard*, March 1972, p.7.

413 Lee Edwards: *The Conservative Revolution*, pp. 169-172.

414 The estimate of 1,500 attendees is from Diamond: *Roads to Dominion*, p. 116.

415 Wayne Thorburn, "Agenda for the New Politics," *New Guard*, October 1971, p. 13.

416 Comments from a spokesman for Byrd quoted in Broder, "Conservative Youth Meet on '72 Strategy," *Washington Post*, September 3, 1971. A few months later an article by Byrd, "In Defense of Conservatism," was published in *New Guard*, March 1972, pp. 11, 14-15.

417 Broder, "Conservative Youth Meet on '72 Strategy," *Washington Post*, September 3, 1971.

418 Jared C. Lobdell, "Scenes from Houston," *National Review*, October 8, 1971, p. 1131.

419 David S. Broder, "YAF Condemns Nixon, Backs Agnew for '72," *Washington Post*, September 5, 1971. Warren Weaver, Jr., "YAF Suspends Support of Nixon," *New York Times*, September 5, 1971.

420 Broder, "YAF Condemns Nixon, Backs Agnew for '72."

421 Diamond: *Roads to Dominion*, p. 116.

422 "Houston: Making it Perfectly Clear," p. 3

423 Broder, "YAF Votes Fund to Oppose Nixon," *Washington Post*, September 6, 1971.

424 Kiron K. Skinner, Annelise Anderson, and Martin Anderson, editors: *Reagan In His Own Hand* (New York: Simon & Schuster, 2001), pp.449-453.

425 *Ibid.*

426 Jerry Norton, "The Right Wing Heals," *New Guard*, March 1972, p. 8.

427 "Ashbrook Weighs Race in Primary," *New York Times*, December 8, 1971. Ken Clawson, "News of Ashbrook Challenge Perils Nixon Bid to Pacify Conservatives," *Washington Post*, December 8, 1971.

428 Frank Lynn, "Nixon Scored by State Conservatives," *New York Times*, December 11, 1971.

429 Edwards: *The Conservative Revolution*, p. 173.

430 Schneider: *Cadres for Conservatism*, p. 153.

431 Edwards: *The Conservative Revolution*, p. 174.

432 Larry Mongillo, "Conservatives and 1972: A Rebuttal," *New Guard*, March 1972, p. 9.

433 Jerry Norton, "The Meaning of Miami," *New Guard*, November 1972, pp. 9-11.

434   Theodore H. White: *The Making of the President 1972* (New York: Atheneum Publishers, 1973), p. 320. This is the same author who in 1969 wrote that YAF had faded from the scene.

435   "YAF Blasts McGovern, Plans Truth Squads," *YAF in the News*, Summer 1972.

436   Alfred E. Neuman was a dunce-like character popularized by MAD magazine. McGovern had selected Senator Tom Eagleton of Missouri as his vice presidential candidate and then dropped him after it became known he had received electro-shock treatment for mental illness. He was replaced on the ticket by R. Sargent Shriver, brother-in-law of the late President John F. Kennedy and father of Maria Shriver Schwarzenegger. White: *The Making of the President 1972*, pp. 256-289.

437   Thorburn, "Agenda for the New Politics," pp. 12-13.

438   Editorial, *New Guard*, December 1971, p. 3.

439   Charles Black, "A Presence in History," *New Guard*, January/February 1972, p. 20.

440   Schoenwald, "The Other Counterculture," p. 10.

441   *Ibid*, p. 11.

442   Rusher: *The Rise of the Right*, p. 196.

443   *New Guard*, December 1974, p. 4.

444   Jesse Helms, "American Parties: A Time for Choosing," *New Guard*, December 1974, pp. 6-9.

445   Lee Edwards, "A Conservative Party: Has Its Time Come?" *New Guard*, December 1974, pp. 9-12.

446   Wayne Thorburn, editor: *Which Way for Conservatives?* (Baltimore: Publications Press, 1975).

447   Daniel Oliver, "Taking the Initiative," *National Review*, March 14, 1975, pp. 276-278.

448   Diamond: *Road to Dominion*, p. 146.

449   Steven Hayward: *The Age of Reagan: The Fall of the Old Liberal Order- 1964-1980* (Roseville, CA: Prima Publishing, 2001), p. 449.

450   R. W. Apple, Jr., "Study of 3d Party for '76 Approved by Conservatives," *New York Times*, February 17, 1975. The conference speeches of Congressmen Bauman and Ashbrook, Senators Helms and Buckley, Governor Reagan, M. Stanton Evans, Kevin Phillips, and Ron Docksai are reprinted in *New Guard*, April 1975 along with all the resolutions passed at CPAC. Also included is the motion creating the Committee on Conservative Alternatives with a list of committee members.

451   Craig Shirley: *Reagan's Revolution* (Nashville: Nelson Current, 2005), p. 67.

452   Skinner, Anderson, and Anderson, editors: *Reagan in His Own Hand*, pp. 503-525.

453   Pam Dutton, "The YAF Voice in the Reagan Campaign," *New Guard*, April 1976, pp. 16-17.

454   Jeffrey Kane, "The Liberation of the Conservative Movement," *New Guard*, January/February 1977, p. 14.

455   Shirley: *Reagan's Revolution*, p. 229.

456   Molly Ivins, "Young Conservatives Convention Abuzz With Talk of Schweiker," *New York Times*, July 31, 1976.

457   Shirley: *Reagan's Revolution*, p. 278.

458   Ron Robinson, "YAFers Storm Kansas City," *New Guard*, September-October 1976, p. 16.

459   Ron Robinson, "The Cause and YAF's Crescendo," *New Guard*, January/February 1977, p. 16.

460   Robinson, "YAFers Storm Kansas City," p. 17.

461   Robinson, "The Cause and YAF's Crescendo," p. 14.

462   C. S. Horn, "Reunion in Sharon," *National Review*, October 6, 1970, p. 1056.

463   William Keifer, "YAF Urged to Ask Demands on SDS," *Hartford Courant*, September 10, 1970.

464   Philip M. Crane, "In Ten Short Years," *New Guard*, September 1970, pp. 11-13.

465   Barbara Long, "A Day at the Buckleys: Big Blight at Great Elm," *Village Voice*, September 17, 1970.

466   Michael Kenney, "Buckley and YAF Wind Up a Decade," *Boston Globe*, September 13, 1970.

467   William F. Buckley, Jr., "Conservatism Revisted," *New Guard*, September 1970, pp. 14-18.

468   Joseph B. Treaster, "500 Youths Plan Antiradical Crusade," *New York Times*, September 14, 1970.

469   Linda Charlton, "Conservative Unit Seems in Doubt on Nixon's Role," *New York Times*, August 16, 1973.

470   They were Senator Owen Johnson, Delegate C. A. Porter Hopkins, Delegate George Mason Green, Representative Sherry Shealy, and Representative Woody Jenkins.

471   Charlton, "Conservative Unit Seems in Doubt on Nixon's Role," *New York Times*, August 16, 1973.

472   *Ibid*, p. 999.

473   Christopher Manion, "Remember," *National Review*, September 14, 1973, p.999.

474   "We Believe in America," *Dialogue on Liberty*, Fall 1973.

475   Manion, "Remember," p. 999.

476   Ted Frederickson, "YAF: Resilient and Resolute," *Washington Post*, August 20, 1973.

477   R. W. Apple, Jr., "Dismay and Outrage Over Nixon Erupt at Conservatives' Parlay," *New York Times*, January 27, 1974.

478   Ron Robinson, "From the States Director," *New Guard*, January/February 1975, pp. 17-18.

479   "Chavez Charges Investigated," *Dialogue on Liberty*, September 1974, pp. 6-7.

480   Douglas E. Kneeland, "Young Americans for Freedom Pay Tribute to Sen. Goldwater at Conference," *New York Times*, July 20, 1974.

481   Arnold Steinberg, "Where Were You in '64?" *National Review*, August 16, 1974, p. 917.

482   "YAF Honors Barry," *Dialogue on Liberty*, September 1974, p. 1, 4-5.

483   Steinberg, "Where Were You in '64?"

484   Zero Government Growth was the cover topic discussed in a series of articles in *New Guard*, June 1975.

485   *New Guard*, November 1975, p. 33.

486   Alexander Solzhenitsyn, "From Under the Dragon's Belly," *New Guard*, November 1975, pp. 6-13.

487   "YAF Begins Carter Watch," *Dialogue on Liberty*, December 1976, p. 1.

488   Clifford White, "A Time for Reassessment," *New Guard*, March 1977, pp. 16-17.

489   Ron Robinson, "A Program for the Individual," *New Guard*, May 1977, pp. 18-20.

490   See especially "Carter's Dog-Day Afternoons," *Time*, September 5, 1977, p. 12.

491   "Buckley, Kissinger are 'roasted' at convention," *Houston Chronicle*, August 29, 1977.

492   Marc Rosenwasser, "Conservative cohorts liberally 'roast' Buckley," *Portland Oregonian*, August 29, 1977.

493   Ron Robinson, "YAF and the Movement," *New Guard*, February 1978, p. 14.

494   *Regents of the University of California* v. *Bakke*, 438 U.S. 265 (1978).

495   "Students Back Bakke," *Dialogue on Liberty*, Winter 1977, p. 6.

496   John F. Zink, "The Legal Issues of Reverse Discrimination," *New Guard*, November/December 1977, pp. 6-8.

497   "Bakke Reverse Bias Case Backed by Young Americans for Freedom," *New York Times*, August 28, 1977.

498   Steven V. Roberts, "Longtime Allies On Rights Split By Bakke Case," *New York Times*, September 25, 1977.

499   "YAF Begins Post-Bakke Effort," *New Guard*, September 1978, p.22.

500   *New Guard*, January 1978, p. 20.

501   Ken Boehm, "YAF Launches Project to Halt Technology Sales to the Soviet Union," *Dialogue on Liberty*, June 1978, pp. 1,8.

502   Hedrick Smith, "China Move Reflects Carter's Aim to Protect Arms Pact and Taiwan," *New York Times*, December 16, 1978.

503   "Carter Shanghais Taiwan," *New Guard Bulletin*, volume XIX, number 1, pp. 1, 5.

504   *Ibid*, pp. 1.

505   "YAF Launches Campaign to Stop SALT II," *New Guard Bulletin*, volume XIX, number 2, p. 1.

506   "Senator Jake Garn on SALT II," pp. 20-24 and Greg Gegenheimer, "The Soviets: Preparing for a First Strike?" pp. 28-31, *New Guard*, Spring 1979.

507   Carl Marcy, "A SALT Opportunity," *New York Times*, December 6, 1980.

508   *Ibid*.

509   "Reagan's Candidacy is Endorsed by Young Americans for Freedom," *New York Times*, August 19, 1979.

510   "Reagan: 'America Better Off With YAF,'" *New Guard*, volume XIX, number 8 (1979), pp. 1, 6.

511   Not all YAF leaders were for Reagan, however. David Keene was a political director for the campaign of George H. W. Bush while Roger Ream was part of the Phil Crane presidential effort.

512   Ken Boehm, "YAF Rains on Fonda/Hayden Parade," *Dialogue on Liberty*, Fall 1979, pp. 4-5.

513   Young Americans for Freedom News Release: "Youth Coalition Meets With High Iranian Officials," November 23, 1979.

514   Jerome L. Himmelstein: *To the Right: The Transformation of American Conservatism* (Berkeley: University of California Press, 1990), p. 88.

515   Daniel McCarthy, "GOP and Man at Yale," *The American Conservative*, November 6, 2006.

516   Noreen McGrath, "Right-Wing Students Exert Growing Influence on Campus," *The Chronicle of Higher Education*, January 8, 1979.

517   Among those backing candidates other than Reagan, David Keene was Political Director for the George Bush campaign; Roger Ream was a regional director for the Crane for President effort while David Boaz was a supporter of Libertarian candidate Ed Clark.

518   Memo from the executive director to the Board of Directors, March 6, 1980, p. 2.

519   Roberts: *The Conservative Decade*, p. 39.

520   "Profile on George Bush," *Rolling Stone*, March 20, 1980, p. 60.

521   *New Guard*, Spring 1980, pp. 11-26.

522   E. J. Dionne, Jr., "Libertarian Party Bids for Conservative and Liberal Votes," *New York Times*, July 10, 1980.

523   William Martin: *With God on Our Side* (New York: Broadway Books, 1996) discusses Marshner's efforts on pp. 174-177.

524   James Lacy and Robert Heckman, "An Open Letter to our Friends at the Republican National Convention in Detroit," *New Guard*, Summer 1980, p. 2.

525   "YAF's Detroit '80 Youth Operation,'" *Human Events*, August 2, 1980, p. 694.

526   "YAF's Detroit '80 Youth Operation," *Dialogue on Liberty*, Summer 1980, p.1.

527   Howell Raines, "Reagan Voices Optimism on Unity for Convention," *New York Times*, July 15, 1980.

528   Barry Goldwater, "YAF and the Early Years," *New Guard*, Fall 1980, pp. 14-15.

529   Ronald Reagan, "YAF: Twenty Years of Conservative Leadership," *New Guard*, Fall 1980, p. 13.

530   "YAF Celebrates 20th Anniversary," *New Guard*, volume XX, number 10, pp. 1, 4-6. Personal Papers of William F. Buckley, Jr., Box 189, Folder: YAF, Yale University, New Haven. CT.

531   M. Stanton Evans, "The Conservative Mainstream," *National Review*, October 31, 1980, p. 1326.

532   James Lacy, "YAF's Principles Triumph in 1980," *New Guard*, Winter, 1980-81, p. 8.

533   Jacob M. Schlesinger, "YAF Meeting," *The Harvard Crimson*, November 14, 1980.

534   "Purging PIRG," *The Harvard Crimson*, March 16, 1983.

535   Rifka Rosenwein, "Fighting the liberals at CU," *Broadway: Columbia Spectator's Bi-weekly Magazine of Issues and the Arts*, October 29, 1981, pp. 5-6.

536   *New Guard*, Winter 1980-81, p. 14.

537   Rosenwein, "Fighting the liberals at CU," p. 5

538   Dudley Clendinen, "After 20 Years, Young Conservatives Enjoy a Long-Awaited Rise to Power," *New York Times*, August 22, 1981.

539   Molly Ivins: *You Got to Dance with Them What Brung You* (New York: Random House, 1998), p. 142.

540   Quoted in Clancy Sigal, "Doing the Right Thing," *Los Angeles Times Magazine*, April 29, 1990, p. 28.

541   "Conservative Political Action Conference Features President, Administration Officials," *Dialogue on Liberty*, Spring 1981, p. 1.

542   "YAF Project Mobilizes Conservative Youth," *Dialogue on Liberty*, Spring 1981, p. 6.

543   "Mandatory Fees" issues paper, Young Americans for Freedom, 1981.

544   David Pietrusza, "Coming of Age," *National Review*, September 18, 1981, p. 1081.

545   Clendinen, "After 20 Years."

546   Schneider: *Cadres for Conservatism*, p. 171.

547   Clendinen, "After 20 Years."

548   Gloria Negri, "Young conservatives – with jeans," *Boston Globe*, August 20, 1981.

549   "YAF Sponsored Speakers Continue to Spread the Conservative Message," *Dialogue on Liberty*, Fall 1982, p. 1.

550   *New Guard*, Winter 1982-83, p. 56.

551   *New Guard*, Winter 1982-83, p. 56.

552   *New Guard*, Summer 1982, pp. 48-49.

553   David M. Les Strong, "YAF-1, Fonda-0," *New Guard*, Winter 1982-83, pp. 44-45.

554   Seth S. King, "Donovan Dinner Dais: No Reagan, No Bush," *New York Times*, October 13, 1982.

555   "Donovan Honored by 1,000 Friends," *New York Times*, October 14, 1982.

556   *New Guard*, Spring 1983, p. 48; *New Guard*, Summer 1983, p. 57; *New Guard*, Winter 1983-84, pp. 50-51.

557   John A. Barnes and Dwight Cunningham, "More than 400 protest near Soviet Embassy," *Washington Times*, September 2, 1983.

558   Michael T. Kaufman, "1,900 US troops, with Caribbean allies, invade Grenada and fight Leftist units; Moscow protests; British are critical," *New York Times*, October 26, 1983.

559   "Rally Supports Reagan Policy in Caribbean," *Washington Post*. October 29, 1983.

560   "Grenada Liberation celebrated by YAF Across The Nation," *Dialogue on Liberty*, November/ Fall 1984, pp. 1-2.

561   "Project America the Free, Not the Freeze, Awakens America," *Dialogue on Liberty*, January/ Winter 1984, p. 1.

562   "It's 'Day' time for millions," *New York Post*, November 21, 1983.

563   "'Day After' sparks new arms debate," *Los Angeles Daily News*, November 21, 1983.

564   Carol Krunoff, "The Right & the Wrong of It," *Washington Post*, November 21, 1983.

565   Deroy Murdock, "Fear and Loathing in San Francisco," *New Guard*, August 1984, pp. 20+.

566   Flyer distributed by Young Americans for Freedom under the title National Coalition for America's Survival, July 1984, Democratic National Convention, San Francisco, CA.

567   Murdock, "Fear and Loathing in San Francisco," p. 47.

568   "YAF Dominates Dallas," *Dialogue on Liberty*, September/Summer 1984, p. 1.

569   "The Right Scene," *Dialogue on Liberty*, Spring 1986, p. 4.

570   Charlotte Hays, "The right stunts –YAF's Young Conservatives Dare to be Outrageous," *Washington Times*, March 9, 1988.

571   Jim Bieber, "Contra Vote Sparks Protest," *The Creative Californian*, Spring 1988.

572   California YAF Press Coverage, Post CPAC, Spring 1988.

573   "The Right Scene," *Dialogue on Liberty*, June/September 1988, p. 2.

574   E. J. Dionne, Jr., "A.C.L.U. Studies Its Image and Finds It Intact," *New York Times*, May 14, 1989. The study found the liberal group with a 47% favorable rating and 18% negative. Hart conducted a telephone survey of 1,000 adults with a margin of error of plus or minus 3%.

575   Interview with Jon Fleischman, Newport Beach, CA, October 11, 2008.

576   From a column by Jon Fleischman on June 7, 2004, forwarded to the author by Sergio Picchio on June 7, 2009, the fifth anniversary of Reagan's passing.

577   "YAF Calls for End to Blacklist," *Dialogue on Liberty*, April/June 1989, p. 1.

578   Interview with Lawrence King, Washington, DC, October 4, 2008.

579   Clancy Sigal, "Doing the Right Thing," *Los Angeles Times Magazine*, April 29, 1990, p. 26.

580   "Regionals 1990," *Leadership Bulletin – Young Americans for Freedom*, April-May 1990.

581   Interview with Jon Fleischman, Newport Beach, CA, October 11, 2008.

582   Sigal, "Doing the Right Thing," p. 24.

583   Memorandum from William F. Buckley, Jr., July 10, 1990, Personal Papers of William F. Buckley, Jr., Box 190, Folder: YAF 1990, Sterling Library, Yale Unversity, New Haven, CT.

584 Sonja West, "Protesters diverge on ROTC issue, *Daily Iowan*, October 14, 1990; "2 ISU groups get into fracas at peace rally," *Des Moines Register*, November 10, 1990.

585 Program, "Thirtieth Anniversary Reception and Dinner," The Washington Marriott Hotel, Washington DC, Thursday, September 13, 1990. "YAF Celebrates 30th Anniversary," *Leadership Bulletin – Young Americans for Freedom*, October 1990, pp. 1-2.

586 Statement for YAF 30th Anniversary Dinner, Personal Papers of William F. Buckley, Jr., Box 190, Folder: YAF 1990, Sterling Library, Yale University, New Haven. CT.

587 Interview with David Ray, Washington, DC, August 14, 2008.

588 "YAF Chairman Presents Over 5000 Petitions of Support to Vice President Dan Quayle," *Leadership Bulletin – Young Americans for Freedom*, June 1991, p. 1.

589 *Ibid.*

590 According to columnist John Elvin, writing just prior to the 1992 CPAC, Buchanan "has been their hero for years now, and YAFers are among those working as volunteers in the 'Buchanan Brigade.'" John Elvin, "Inside The Beltway," *Washington Times*, February 20, 1992.

591 Richard A. Delgaudio with Jeff Wright, "Dan Quayle and his enemies – The War on Reagan Continues," *New Guard*, Fall 1992, pp. 5-7, 11, 17. The issue also included a laudatory article titled "What Buchanan Accomplished for Conservatives."

592 "Yikes, It's YAF," *Washington Times*, August 2, 1991.

593 "YAF Quayle Campaign Continues in High Gear," *Leadership Bulletin – Young Americans for Freedom*, October 1991, p. 1.

594 "Young Americans for Freedom Leads Movement to Fight Radical Anita Hill," *New Guard*, Fall 1992, p. 11.

595 Letter from Matt Zandi, Cal-YAF Executive Director to James V. Lacy, November 15, 1994. "A Business Plan for Cal YAF," 1994.

596 Ted Balaker, "YAF Convention Oozes Conservatism," *The Creative Californian*, Fall 1994, pp. 4-5.

597 For further information on California YAF activities during the 1990s, see Hieu Tran Phan, "The Life of the Party," *Orange County Register*, October 22, 1996; Jean O. Pasco, "Young Americans for Freedom Say the Time is Right for a Resurgence," *Los Angeles Times*, July 5, 1998.

598 For a lengthy review of conservative youth in the early 21st century as reflected in the independent Bucknell University Conservative Club see John Colapinto, "Armies of the Right: The Young Hipublicans," *New York Times*, May 25, 2003.

599 Hans Zieger: *Reagan's Children – Taking Back the City on the Hill* (Nashville: Broadman & Holman Publishers, 2006), pp. 157-158.

600 Kerry Picket, "YAF national board expels Ron Paul from advisory board," *Washington Times*, February 12, 2011. For criticism of this action see David Franke, "Young Americans for Foolishness," *The American Conservative*, February 15, 2011.

601 Young America's Foundation Unites with Young Americans for Freedom," *Human Events*, May 24, 2011.

602 Schoenwald: *A Time for Choosing*, p. 249.

603 Andrew: *The Other Side of the Sixties*, p. 216.

604 Klatch: *A Generation Divided*, pp. 260-261.

605 Unnamed YAF alumni quoted in Margaret M. Braungart and Richard G. Braungart, "The Effects of the 1960s Political Generation on Former Left- and Right-Wing Youth Activist Leaders," *Social Problems*, 38:3 (August 1991), p. 309.

606   Dana Rohrabacher, "Us Young Americans for Freedom," *The American Enterprise*, 8 (May/June 1997), p. 38.

607   Sandra Gurvis: *Where Have All The Flower Children Gone?* (Jackson: The University Press of Mississippi, 2006), p. 93.

608   Quoted in Klatch: *A Generation Divided*, p. 284.

609   Quoted in Roberts: *The Conservative Decade*, p.34.

Also by Wayne Thorburn

A Generation Awakes: Young Americans for Freedom and the Creation of the Conservative Movement
(Jameson Books, 2010)

"If anyone—conservative, liberal or whatever—wants to understand how the conservative movement grew and flourished, Wayne Thorburn's encyclopedic history of Young Americans for Freedom is a perfect place to start."

> – Adam Clymer, former chief Washington Correspondent
> *The New York Times*

"Few imagined when Young Americans for Freedom was founded in 1960 that it would have a profound and deep effect on American politics and political thinking over a span of almost half a century. But it did. Wayne Thorburn tells the story in fascinating detail in *A Generation Awakes*. It's essential reading for anyone who wants to understand the rising influence of conservatism in American life."

> – Michael Barone, Senior political analyst
> *The Washington Examiner*

Red State: An Insider's Story of How the GOP Came to Dominate Texas Politics
(University of Texas Press, 2014)

"*Red State* is critical reading for anyone looking to understand Texas's dramatic political changes of the last fifty years. Thorburn takes a deep dive into the state's politics from 1960 to 2010, presenting an insightful look at our state's demographic, economic, and political changes. If you want to know the Lone Star State's future, read this book about its recent past first."

> – Karl Rove

"*Red State* is not only a history of the Republican Party; it is necessarily also a history of the Texas Democratic Party. Everyone with an interest in Texas politics and the shift from Democratic to Republican dominance since the 1950s needs to read this book. This history continues to inform Texas politics today."

> – Paul Burka, Senior Executive Editor
> *Texas Monthly*

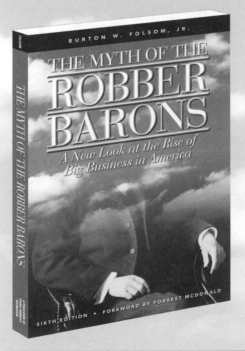

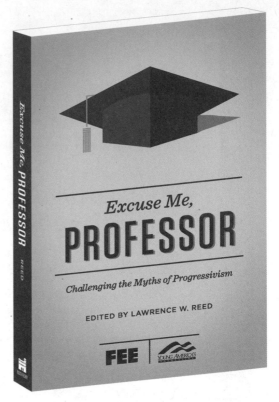